Tips for Teaching with

CALL

Practical Approaches to Computer-Assisted Language Learning

Carol A. Chapelle
Iowa State University

Joan Jamieson
Northern Arizona University

Series Editor: **H. Douglas Brown**
San Francisco State University

PEARSON
Longman

Tips for Teaching with CALL: Practical Approaches to Computer-Assisted Language Learning

Copyright © 2008 by Pearson Education, Inc.

Pearson Education, 10 Bank Street, White Plains, NY 10606

Staff credits: The people who made up the *Tips for Teaching with CALL* team, representing editorial, production, design, and manufacturing, include Elizabeth Carlson, Pam Fishman, Nancy Flaggman, Maja Grgurovic, Lester Holmes, Katherine Keyes, Melissa Leyva, Jaime Lieber, Lise Minovitz, Sherry Preiss, Elise Pritchard, Mary Perrotta Rich, Barbara Sabella, and Ken Volcjak.

Cover design: Barbara Sabella
Text design: Elizabeth Carlson
Text composition: Integra
Text font: 10.5/12.5 Garamond Book

Library of Congress Cataloging–in–Publication Data
Chapelle, Carol.
    Tips for teaching with CALL : practical approaches to
computer-assisted language learning / by Carol A. Chapelle and Joan
Jamieson.
        p. cm. — (Tips on teaching)
    Includes bibliographical references and index.
    ISBN-13: 978-0-13-240428-0
    ISBN-10: 0-13-240428-1
    1.   English language—Study and teaching—Foreign speakers.   2. English
language—Computer-assisted instruction for foreign speakers. I.
Jamieson, Joan. II. Title. III. Title: Practical approaches to
computer-assisted language learning.
    PE1128. A2C445 2008
    428.6′40785—dc22
                                                                2007039893

ISBN-13: 978-0-13-240428-0
ISBN-10: 0-13-240428-1

Printed in the United States of America
1 2 3 4 5 6 7 8 9 10—CRK—13 12 11 10 09 08

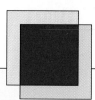

Contents

About the Series v

Preface vii

INTRODUCTION: What Is CALL? 1

CHAPTER 1: Vocabulary ~~Dr. P   post~~ 11

CHAPTER 2: Grammar ~~Me + Annne lead~~ 39

CHAPTER 3: Reading ~~post~~ 63

CHAPTER 4: Writing 95

CHAPTER 5: Listening ~~post~~ 125

CHAPTER 6: Speaking 151

CHAPTER 7: Communication Skills ~~post~~ 171

CHAPTER 8: Content-based Language 195

CONCLUSION: After Class 211

Bibliography 215

Name Index 223

Subject Index 225

Credits 237

About the Series

English language teachers always appreciate and enjoy professional reference books with practical classroom approaches that are firmly grounded in current pedagogical research. *Tips for Teaching* is a response to this demand in the form of a series of books on a variety of topics of practical classroom-centered interest.

Designed for teachers of ESL in native English-speaking countries as well as teachers of EFL in non-native English-speaking countries, *Tips for Teaching* addresses audiences in secondary schools, colleges, and adult education courses with students at varying levels of proficiency. Each book in the series is a practical manual that provides teachers with clearly conceived methodological ideas, approaches, tasks, activities, and/or techniques to better accomplish their pedagogical goals. Users may be novice teachers seeking practical guidelines for instruction in a specified area, or experienced teachers in need of refreshing new ideas.

Each book in the series is committed to offering soundly conceived, realistic approaches to classroom instruction. There is some treatment of underlying pedagogical principles of language learning and teaching in clearly comprehensible terms. These treatments are brief and concise but not trivial. The methodology of *Tips for Teaching* is based on communicative and/or task-based language teaching foundations. Student-centered, interactive classroom activities receive primary focus, but not at the expense of appropriate teacher-centered approaches or tasks for individual in-class or homework activity.

In this first book in the series, I'm delighted to see one of the most popular "hot topics" treated so well by my colleagues Carol Chapelle and Joan Jamieson. *Tips for Teaching with CALL* provides just the right mix of practicality and theoretical soundness that teachers everywhere will appreciate. Some of us can be easily intimidated by technology, but in this volume the authors have offered a reader-friendly approach that will be appreciated by all.

Teachers who use this volume not only gain access to a multitude of practical "hands-on" techniques for using CALL in their classrooms, but also acquire awareness of the rationale behind such techniques. This underlying knowledge enables teachers to adapt techniques to their own contexts. Teachers also will find *Tips for Teaching with CALL* to be an invaluable handbook of information that is easily accessed through chapter headings, an index, and a useful bibliography of electronic and paper-based references.

Best wishes as you use the tips in this book to help your learners achieve their linguistic goals.

H. Douglas Brown
Professor Emeritus, San Francisco State University
Series Editor

Preface

Tips for Teaching with CALL is the result of our over twenty-five years of teaching English language classes and graduate courses on computer-assisted language learning (CALL) for prospective second/foreign language teachers. The tips come from research and practice with new technologies as they have evolved over the past twenty-five years. Our experience suggests that most teachers are interested in connecting their students with technology to help them learn English. They simply need guidance through the maze of possibilities.

The teachers with whom we work always want to know not only *how* but also *why*. For example, *how* CALL can be used for teaching vocabulary and *why* CALL is useful for learning vocabulary. We have therefore attempted to capture as concisely as possible our perspectives on how and why to use CALL—in keeping with the aims of this series. We explain the many opportunities technology offers students for exposure to English as well as for interaction using English. This is useful not only during their formal study of English, but throughout the rest of their lives as their English language needs further develop and expand.

In order to present these tips in the most concrete terms possible, we have included examples from CD–ROMs and Web sites. We intentionally chose materials that are easily accessible rather than those that exist only in research labs. Over time, some examples may disappear as CD–ROMs go out of print and Web links change. If a recommended site is no longer available, we suggest searching for the name of the specific activity on the Internet, or simply looking for similar CALL materials. There are many more CALL activities available than we could include in our examples.

Software readily available today can provide powerful opportunities for language learners—if teachers help them get started. We hope this volume will prompt many teachers to introduce their students to learning English through CALL.

ACKNOWLEDGMENTS

We would like to express our appreciation to the many people who contributed insight and assistance throughout the completion of this project. We would like to thank Sherry Preiss and Laura Le Dréan for their vision in conceptualizing the book and their clear understanding of the need for such an introduction to the range of CALL activities from which students can learn English. We are grateful for the enormous amount of work Maja Grgurovic, Reiko Komiyama, Lester Holmes, and Ken Volcjak contributed to the development of materials for the CD-ROM. We thank Elise Pritchard and Doug Brown for their thoughtful comments on the many drafts of the manuscript. We are very grateful to Lise Minovitz for her diligence and meticulous attention to detail in seeing the project through to its completion.

We would like to thank the following reviewers who offered invaluable insights at various stages of development: **Christine Bauer-Ramazani**, Saint Michael's College, Colchester, Vermont; **Ivonne del Pino**, Escuela de Idiomas del Ejercito de Chile, Santiago, Chile; **Joy Lynn Egbert**, Washington State University, Pullman, Washington; **Robert Fischer**, Texas State University, San Marcos, Texas; **Peiya Gu**, Suzhou University, Suzhou, People's Republic of China; **Deborah Healey**, Oregon State University, Corvallis, Oregon; **Dr. Trude Heift**, Simon Fraser University, Burnaby, Canada; **Phil Hubbard**, Stanford University, Stanford, California; **Renée Jourdenais**, Monterey Institute of International Studies, Monterey, California; **Greg Kessler**, Ohio University, Athens, Ohio; **Thomas Leverett**, CESL, Southern Illinois University, Carbondale, Illinois; **Susanne McLaughlin**, Roosevelt University, Chicago, Illinois; **Miriam Salazar**, Universidad Andrés Bello, Santiago, Chile; **Claire Bradin Siskin**, University of Pittsburgh, Pittsburgh, Pennsylvania; and **Vance Stevens**, Petroleum Institute, Abu Dhabi, United Arab Emirates.

We dedicate this book to our former professor, Robert Hart, who encouraged and developed our interest in and knowledge of computer-assisted language learning many years ago.

Carol A. Chapelle
Professor, Iowa State University

Joan Jamieson
Professor, Northern Arizona University

WHAT IS CALL?

CALL is the acronym for "computer-assisted language learning," the area of applied linguistics concerned with the use of computers for teaching and learning a second language. Some CALL professionals develop CALL materials, that is, software specifically designed for second-language learning. Others investigate how learners work with CALL software and other online learning materials, as well as how effective particular CALL activities are. CALL as an academic area includes learning any of the world languages in many different situations. Research on learning French as a second language or Japanese as a second language, for example, is relevant to basic questions that English teachers have about CALL. This book draws on this range of research to make recommendations about English language teaching and learning in the classroom, and all examples demonstrate English learning through CALL. Throughout the book, English language or English as a second language (ESL) is used to refer to both ESL and EFL (English as a foreign language), unless the setting is explicitly described otherwise.

The purpose of this book is to provide English language teachers with a practical introduction to the use of CALL. It links rationales based on theory, research, and experience with specific techniques intended to help learners develop their English language abilities. In other words, it explains in concrete terms how learners can benefit from CALL and what teachers can do to help learners benefit. The intended audience is English language teachers at any level who are new to using CALL or wish to learn more about how their students might benefit from CALL. In particular, this book answers the question: *Why do English language teachers use CALL?*

Answering this question requires looking at how the computer fits into English language pedagogy.

ENGLISH LANGUAGE PEDAGOGY

English language pedagogy in the classroom includes the three main components shown in Figure 1 on page 2: the teacher, the learner, and the English language itself. Since pedagogy must address the question of how the teacher can help the learner acquire English, pedagogy includes the teaching strategies, the materials, and the activities that

1

teachers provide in the classroom. As Brown (2000) points out, a teacher has many responsibilities, including guiding and facilitating learning, setting the conditions for learning, and evaluating learning. He advises teachers as follows: "Your understanding of how the learner learns will determine your philosophy of education, your teaching style, your approach, your methods, and classroom techniques" (2000, p. 7). But where does the computer come in?

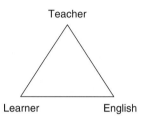

Figure 1 Three components of English language pedagogy

Many teachers find that the computer makes them expand, and sometimes even revise, their understanding of how learners learn and what learners need to become successful English users. Researchers who study advanced ESL learners have made the following important observation: "In today's complex world, literacy means far more than learning to read and write in order to accomplish particular, discrete tasks. Continual changes in technology and society mean that literacy tasks are themselves always changing" (Colombi & Schleppegrell, 2002, p. 1). The fact that many English language learners are computer users is prompting ESL teachers to think about using computers in their classes. How can a computer help students learn English? As Figure 2 shows, many teachers find that the computer is an important part of the pedagogy when it serves as a tool in the classrooms.

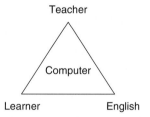

Figure 2 Three parts in English language pedagogy and the computer as a tool

However, if the computer is to play a central role in pedagogy, does this mean that the computer has a philosophy of learning? Is the computer's philosophy of learning—rather than the teacher's—going to make decisions about classroom strategies? No. Teachers can use the computer as a part of their pedagogy without letting it take over their lesson plans.

This book is intended for English language teachers who want to maintain control of their pedagogy but update and strengthen it by learning more about how to use the computer as a tool in their classrooms. It is for teachers who have experience in teaching but have not yet fully explored how computer technology can help their learners.

THE COMPUTER'S TEACHING PHILOSOPHY

The computer itself does not have a philosophy of teaching and learning. However, the professionals who develop CALL and conduct research on learners' use of CALL do. Therefore, teachers can find many different types of CALL activities to choose from. The ones that are selected in this book include the following three assumptions about language, the learner, and the teacher:

- Learners need guidance in learning English.
- There are many styles of English used for many different purposes.
- Teachers should provide guidance by selecting appropriate language and by structuring learning activities.

In order to become autonomous learners, students need guidance in choosing what to learn and how to learn it. It is frustrating for teachers and learners when learners are exposed to language that is too difficult or boring for them to engage in. Language that is too easy or simplified does not help push learners to develop their language knowledge. Krashen (1982) described the issue clearly when he wrote that the language input for learners should make them stretch their language knowledge just the right amount. This idea has important implications for selecting materials for learners.

Research on second-language acquisition suggests that learners are likely to benefit from guidance that helps them focus on specific language that they need to learn. Further, almost anything that draws learners' attention to the language that they need to learn may be beneficial (Doughty & Williams, 1998). Research also suggests that it is good to provide learners with opportunities for interaction because interaction often entails getting clarification about the meaning of language that learners do not initially understand (Pica, 1994). In CALL activities, beneficial interaction can occur between the learner and the computer or between the learner and another person (Chapelle, 2003). The interactions that learners have in class position them to develop strategies for future communication and learning so that they can take advantage of CALL materials on the Internet after they leave their English classes.

English language on the Internet reflects some of the many styles of English that are used on different occasions to accomplish a variety of purposes. The grammar and vocabulary that a student chooses to ask a friend for a favor, for example, is different from language that a student might use to request an extension on a paper from a professor. It can be confusing for students to choose the appropriate language to accomplish their goals. Examples of English should be carefully selected to provide learners with useful models. These models must include the target language that the learners need to learn, and they must also have a level of difficulty that is appropriate for the learners' level of development. In addition, learners must develop strategies for distinguishing among the different registers of language that they are exposed to. In other words, like the corpus linguists who study samples of real language used in different situations (e.g., Biber, Johansson, Leech, Conrad, & Finegan, 1999), English learners need analytic skills for interpreting the styles of English on the Internet.

Teachers provide the guidance that learners need by selecting materials, structuring activities for learning, evaluating performance, and offering their expertise and encouragement in many ways. Most students do not know how to learn English when they arrive in class, but when they complete a course they should have acquired knowledge of the language, the ability to use their knowledge, and strategies for continuing to expand their knowledge of English. Teachers juggle ideas about English, learning, and teaching and quickly make decisions each day within specific school contexts to try to use their resources to the best advantage of their students. We know that learners count on teachers to provide them with explicit instruction and evaluation of their performance through specific feedback on responses in class, as well as on quizzes and tests. Research has shown what teachers know: Testing helps to push students to get organized, to study, and to learn. This important purpose of classroom assessment, called washback, is a part of the language learning process (Cheng & Watanabe, 2004).

DIVIDING UP THE WORK

Students count on teachers to divide up the job of language learning into manageable pieces. The tips in this book have been grouped into the types of units that teachers typically think about when they are planning a unit of study or writing learning outcomes. Figure 3 shows the pieces within three concentric circles, with the most discrete and concrete building blocks at the center and the most holistic, integrated abilities in the outer layer. Each piece in the circle is discussed in one chapter of this book.

The English vocabulary and grammar that teachers help learners with throughout their language studies are the building blocks of language knowledge at the core of the circle. The use of CALL for helping students develop knowledge and strategies for learning English vocabulary and grammar beyond the classroom is discussed in Chapters 1 and 2. These chapters present CALL activities that are consistent with the current perspectives of experts on learning second-language vocabulary (Nation, 2002) and grammar (Hinkel & Fotos, 2002); and these experts advocate teaching these components of language. As building blocks, these components of knowledge are revisited in other chapters because they are integral to the

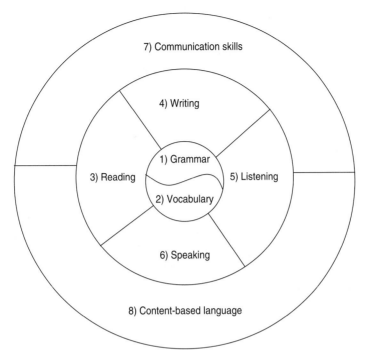

Figure 3 Divisions of language learning from the teacher's perspective

development of all of the skills, as well as for overall communication and use of content-based language.

Moving outward, the next layer contains the four skills of reading, writing, listening, and speaking. These skills require knowledge of vocabulary and grammar, but learners do not finish learning vocabulary and grammar before they begin to read or write. Instead, vocabulary and grammar learning is strengthened through practice in the four skills. CALL activities are used for helping learners develop in all of these skill areas. Chapters 3, 4, 5, and 6 discuss CALL's dual role in teaching these skills while helping students develop greater language proficiency through practice with the skills. This reflects current research on how language is learned (Lightbown & Spada, 2006).

In the outer circle are the large areas of communication skills and content-based language, both of which draw upon grammar and vocabulary knowledge, as well as combinations of the four skills. Chapter 7 describes how communication software such as e-mail, chat, and bulletin boards can provide learners with practice communicating in English. The underlying idea is that the interaction that learners engage in during communication is valuable for their language development (Ellis, 1999). Chapter 8 illustrates CALL activities that provide practice with content-based language pertaining to students' individual needs. This chapter reflects research on

English learning in content classrooms as well as language for specific purposes (Schleppegrell, 2004).

The "After Class" section at the end of the book paints a picture of the autonomous learner, who, after studying in a class where the teacher has introduced CALL, is able to take advantage of electronic resources outside the classroom. This section also summarizes the key points of the book, reemphasizes the teacher's role, and provides some additional resources that teachers might consult to learn more about CALL.

Throughout the book, we have attempted to highlight the best of CALL through explanations and examples. Of course, not all CALL reflects these qualities, and therefore, teachers must view potential software with a critical eye. In addition, teachers must be prepared to supplement CALL activities with classroom activities such as preteaching vocabulary, assessing learning, and assigning group projects based on what was learned in the CALL activity. There are suggestions for such activities throughout this book. The examples and rationales can help to focus the critical eyes of teachers as they choose and adapt CALL activities that are valuable for learners. To help with this selection of activities, we have included a set of questions at the end of each chapter that teachers can use to examine the quality of CALL activities in each area.

IS CALL SPECIAL?

If CALL is used for teaching primarily the same knowledge and skills that teachers teach in the classroom, what is special about CALL? The answer is that CALL provides opportunities to supplement familiar teaching strategies in important ways. Each chapter of this book discusses the specific advantages of computer technology for each area of language development, but generally speaking, two types of CALL activities are described. One type presents information, guides the learner, provides practice, and assesses learning, which in CALL terminology includes interactive activities such as drills, tutorials, and tests (Allessi & Trollip, 2001). The second type incorporates technology tools such as electronic dictionaries and e-mail into English language teaching.

Technology performs functions similar to what many teachers do in class and through textbooks, but the important difference is that CALL provides individualized interactive instruction unmatched by what can be provided in the classroom. CALL programs, like textbooks, contain carefully selected linguistic input that is intended to interest learners while providing language at the appropriate level. Reading software, for example, might contain expository and narrative texts selected for and adapted to learners. Similarly, by selecting and adapting appropriate video and multimedia software for listening and speaking, teachers can target practice for learners at a particular level. The vocabulary and grammar help provided in such programs also allows learners to comprehend and stretch their knowledge.

Like researchers who recognize that learners are ready for particular aspects of language at a particular time (e.g., Lightbown & Spada, 2006), teachers recognize the value of linguistic input that is selected for learners at a particular level. Unlike textbooks, CALL materials also allow learners to vary the amount of time they spend, the help they request, or the path they take through a learning activity. Because CALL can tailor instruction specifically to individual learners, CALL has a greater potential for good *learner fit* than do other materials (Chapelle, 2001).

A second important function that technology provides is individualized interaction. For example, learners interact with the computer when they work on CALL for reading or writing. A learner might click on a word, or call up an online dictionary to find the definition of *candidate* during reading, for example. There is no limit to the number of times that the learner can consult a dictionary or use other interactive help options while engaging in an activity. No other students are waiting for a turn; the lesson is not held up; and the teacher is not anxious to move on. The amount of interaction is determined by the learner. These interactions, in addition to those that take place in most computer-mediated communication, often occur through writing. Written interaction helps to direct learners' attention to important linguistic features in a way that fast-paced and temporary oral language cannot (Warschauer, 1997). It represents a significant extension to the interaction that typically occurs in the classroom.

CALL materials offer learners explicit instruction to help them with specific knowledge and skills. Particularly, tutorial CALL is designed for instruction and includes explanations and controlled practice. There are presentations of grammatical points similar to how they might be found on the grammar page of a textbook, but they are dynamic. They might include animation to make a point and practice exercises with feedback that allow students to test their understanding of the point. Perhaps because of their regular use of the Internet, students feel more engaged by interactive materials that provide feedback than they do with exercises in a workbook. Some of these materials also include assessments—an important part of instruction—to help learners know how well they have performed so that they can decide if they want to review or go on.

Because many types of CALL activities are designed for learners to study individually, one might argue that CALL helps learners develop learning strategies that will benefit them beyond the language classroom. In particular, it is important for students to view the computer as a means for finding examples of language that they can analyze and to use the computer as a database where texts are stored and language can be explored. This book describes many of the strategies that learners should use to select instructional materials, use online help, and respond to online evaluation.

The examples in the book include many CALL programs designed specifically for language teaching, but the book also explains how teachers and learners can work with computer technology that is designed to serve as a tool for a variety of purposes. Such software tools (like dictionaries) serve as references for learners in the classroom and beyond. Communication tools such as e-mail, instant messaging, and blogs expand learners' opportunities to communicate in English. Some people try to make a distinction between the first type of computer technology, which includes explicit presentation and teaching, and the second, which involves the development of pedagogical activities through software used both in and outside the classroom. They wish to reserve the term *CALL* for the first type of technology.

In fact, such a distinction is difficult to maintain because of the ever-changing technologies and their potential implications for language learning. For example, years ago a word processing program would simply allow learners to type text. It was perhaps simply a tool for getting the words onto a page. Today, when learners type they can receive instant feedback about spelling and grammar. If students learn to use such feedback, it can provide a source of learning. Have word processing programs become part of CALL? Or can they be considered part of CALL only if the learners are using the grammar and spelling feedback?

In recent years, new acronyms to replace *CALL* have been created, such as *WELL* ("Web-enhanced language learning") and *MALL* ("mobile-assisted language learning"). What unifies these new terms is that they denote the use of computer technology for language learning. The examples depicted in this book are intended to engage learners while helping them learn English. We would distinguish these activities, having clear pedagogical aims, from activities such as recreational Web surfing, which may provide learning opportunities but is not connected to the teacher's plans in the same way as activities with clear pedagogical aims. In this sense, we focus on those activities that fit into the pedagogical goals of developing the core language knowledge, the four skills, and language use for communication and content learning. The examples throughout this book, a variety of free and commercial programs, show that computer technology, whether or not it is referred to as CALL, provides new and unique opportunities for teachers and learners.

HOW DOES CALL FIT?

Teachers must decide how CALL fits into their pedagogy. Teachers in different secondary schools, institutes, colleges, and universities vary in the types of classes they teach and the amount and type of access they and their students have to technology. In most countries today, teachers and learners can find computers to use, if not in the school then at an Internet café, a public library, or a friend's house. Many English learners are using computers for many purposes.

In considering CALL, teachers should recognize that the classroom is likely to be the place where learners are exposed to the options, approaches, and strategies for learning English. As a consequence, teachers play an important role in introducing their students to learning practices that they can engage in outside the classroom. Even if students are avid computer users, they probably do not know how to use the computer for language learning. Introduction of CALL in the classroom will hopefully result in learners being guided toward constructive, individualized, and collaborative CALL activities outside of the classroom.

USING THE CD-ROM ⊙

This book and the enclosed CD-ROM are intended to help teachers see the options afforded by CALL so that they can guide their students to productive learning through technology. The chapters in the book offer a number of tips that teachers can use together with their rationales and examples. The CD-ROM at the back of the book has video clips showing how these tips work with various kinds of software. There are two video clips for each of the Chapters 1 through 8. The first clip is a real-time video demonstration that shows how a learner might perform an activity. The second clip is a simulation that guides teachers through an activity as if they were students. These interactive video clips should help teachers to see how and why CALL might fit in at various points in their pedagogy. After reading about CALL in this book and trying it out on the CD-ROM, teachers should have plenty of new ideas about how they might use computer technology to help their students learn English.

CHAPTER 1

VOCABULARY

In the introduction, vocabulary and grammar were called the building blocks of language. More precisely, vocabulary words and phrases are the building blocks and grammar is the glue that holds them together. Grammar lets you know who chased whom when you hear, "The dog chased the cat." Your knowledge of English grammar tells you that the first animal mentioned in the sentence did the action. But your knowledge of English vocabulary allows you to interpret what the dog is, what the cat is, and what they did. In fact, vocabulary is the most important aspect of language for students to learn.

Some people think that learners acquire vocabulary by guessing the meanings of words from context. However, Folse (2004) disputes the ideas that students are able to learn a lot of new words by guessing their meanings from context and that vocabulary is less important than other aspects of language. He explains the importance of learning vocabulary, the need for explicit learning and teaching, the utility of L1 (first-language) translations for learning, and the need to expand the methods that most teachers use. He cites some of the studies of CALL that we will discuss in the chapter on reading, but in this chapter we will examine the ways in which CALL can be used to help students learn vocabulary.

Regardless of teachers' beliefs about vocabulary acquisition, most students believe that they need to study vocabulary—and they are right. Most researchers today agree that English language learners need to spend time and effort studying vocabulary. They point out that learners do not have sufficient exposure to words in the English that they hear and read. Moreover, when learners encounter unfamiliar words, those words often remain unknown unless students get help from a teacher, a dictionary, or a computer. Even when learners guess the meanings of new words in context, they often guess them incorrectly, and therefore do not learn the correct meanings from such guesses. Learners need an explicit introduction to vocabulary, accurate and effective support in interpreting new vocabulary, and practice for remembering vocabulary. The tips in this chapter will help teachers use CALL to work toward these goals for vocabulary teaching.

TIPS FOR TEACHING VOCABULARY WITH CALL

The six tips described in this chapter are listed below. They provide some specific advice about how CALL can be used to teach vocabulary. The tips are based on the ideas about second-language (L2) acquisition described in the Introduction.

TIPS

1. Select CALL materials that teach appropriate vocabulary.
2. Choose CALL materials that explicitly teach English vocabulary.
3. Provide learners with opportunities for interaction with the computer.
4. Let the vocabulary tasks spark interaction among learners. ⊙
5. Include regular evaluations of answers and summaries of performance.
6. Help learners develop strategies for explicit online vocabulary learning through the use of online dictionaries and concordancers. ⊙

Throughout the rest of the chapter, we explain each of these six tips with

- a description of *what it means* for the teacher who is using CALL for vocabulary,
- a summary of *what the research says* about the tip, and
- a suggestion of *what teachers can do* in the classroom.

Along with each tip, illustrations of CALL activities from published CALL software and Web sites are provided. The Web addresses are given so that readers can visit them to try out the activities.

FEATURE: Examples of how to use two types of vocabulary software are on the CD-ROM at the back of this book. The examples include a demonstration of Tip 4 and a simulation of Tip 6.

Select CALL materials that teach appropriate vocabulary.

Appropriate vocabulary refers to the words students need and are prepared to learn. The words that students need are those that fit within the topics or subject areas that are useful and of interest to them. Words that students are able to learn are words with an appropriate level of difficulty. Defining word difficulty is a challenge, so vocabulary researchers use word frequency to estimate the level of difficulty. This means that vocabulary that appears most frequently in the English language is appropriate to teach to beginning students, whereas words that appear less frequently would be appropriate for more advanced students.

What the research says

For general vocabulary, particularly through the intermediate level, researchers use word lists arranged by frequency to identify words that appear most frequently and words that appear less frequently (Nation, 2001). It is thought that students can make the best use of their time studying vocabulary if they begin by learning the words that are used most frequently. These are the words that they are most likely to run across in everyday conversation and reading. For more advanced levels, researchers attempt to identify how many words learners need for particular contexts, such as academic work (Hazenberg & Hulstijn, 1996), and which words are most frequent in those contexts (Coxhead, 2000). Some CALL materials have drawn upon these principles for selecting words, and they are available for teachers and students to try.

What the teacher can do

Teachers can start by determining the vocabulary levels of their students. Figure 1.1 on page 14 shows a Web site that offers vocabulary tests at the lower frequency bands. These tests would be good for less proficient students. A similar type of program, shown in Figure 1.2 on page 15, is intended for students across a range of proficiency levels. Teachers can choose CALL activities that direct students to find an appropriate level of vocabulary. Teachers can help students interpret the results of such tests and guide their choices for vocabulary study.

Material	*The Compleat Lexical Tutor*
Level	Beginning to Advanced
Description	This free Web site contains a series of tests that students can use to determine their vocabulary knowledge and monitor its growth. Tests are available at the 1,000–5,000 levels, the university word list level, and the 10,000 level. The 1,000-level test is shown in Figure 1.1. Students answer thirty-nine multiple-choice questions based on the 1,000 most frequent words in English. Their scores appear in the left-hand column when they complete the test. If a student's score is below a specified level (83 percent), activities are suggested.
Web site	http://www.lextutor.ca/tests/
Notes	Students may need guidance on how to use this Canadian site because of the large variety of links. The site uses the frequency of words as well as common academic words as its basis.

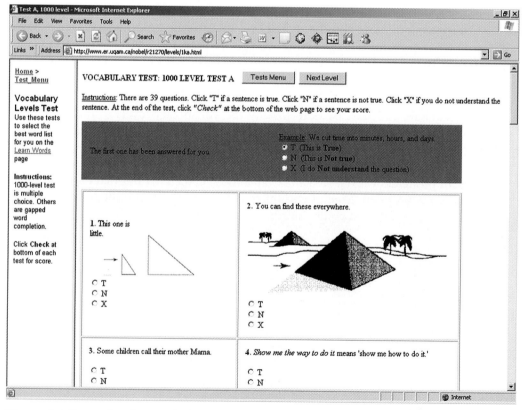

Figure 1.1 Example of a vocabulary test of the 1,000 most frequent words in English.

Material	*WordSmart*
Level	High Intermediate to Advanced
Description	This program has an online placement test to determine the appropriate level for students, as shown in Figures 1.2 through 1.4. Students can register for free and then take placement tests. As illustrated in Figure 1.3, a key word appears at the top of the screen, with five choices below it. A student's level is derived from the number correct and the time spent. Figure 1.4 shows the recommended level. Four levels (C–F) are advertised as suitable for TOEFL® test preparation. For less proficient learners, there is also an ESL level including the most frequent English words.
Web site	http://www.wordsmart.com/wsc_b/index2.php
Notes	The vocabulary level software must be purchased. Each of ten levels has 200 core words with five types of exercises: multiple-choice with explanation (explanations provide synonyms, antonyms, derivations, and percentage of incorrect usage by adult native speakers); flash cards; matching; sentence completion; and an arcade-like game review.

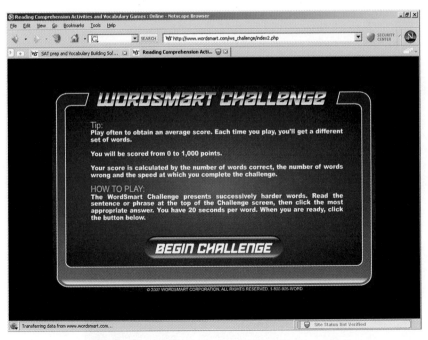

Figure 1.2 Example of the title page from *WordSmart's* online vocabulary placement test.

Figure 1.3 Example of *WordSmart*'s multiple-choice placement test.

Figure 1.4 Example of *WordSmart*'s level recommendation.

Choose CALL materials that explicitly teach English vocabulary.

CALL programs can teach vocabulary explicitly by presenting new words and then providing learners with practice for learning their meanings. Many techniques—including presentation of images, first-language translations, synonyms, and contexts in which the words appear—are used to draw learners' attention to the new words and to ensure their understanding. Other teaching approaches are used for creating exercises that allow students to test themselves and to practice using the new words.

What the research says

Research indicates that vocabulary must be taught. Learners must be provided with clear definitions, and they must be instructed on the various forms of related words. Explicit instruction may direct students to engage in a variety of cognitive strategies, including directing their attention to words and their precise meanings, repetition, and memorization. Researchers who have studied the processes that successful students use for vocabulary learning have found that strategies for directing attention and memorizing words are among those that help most (Gu, 2003). Other researchers, such as Folse (2004), have claimed that guessing words from context is not the best strategy for learning second-language vocabulary. Nassaji (2003) concluded that learners often guess incorrectly when they are left on their own to infer word meanings, and that guessing can result in imprecise or incorrect word knowledge, or no learning at all. Others have suggested that explicit instruction should include vocabulary production. Schmitt and Zimmerman (2002) found that learners may comprehend the general meaning for a single token within a word family but cannot produce the specific forms required in different contexts.

Research on CALL has shown that CALL programs can be effective for explicit vocabulary teaching. Atkinson (1972) found procedures in computer-assisted vocabulary instruction for optimizing learning through systematic presentation and practice of vocabulary. Tozcu and Coady's (2004) research showed that computer-assisted vocabulary instruction increased vocabulary learning as well as reading comprehension more than extensive reading alone. These studies demonstrate the promise of systematic vocabulary instruction through technology that can be carried out by future CALL developers and researchers.

What the teacher can do

Teachers can use CALL programs and Web sites that include vocabulary illustration, explanation, and practice. One benefit of multimedia CALL is that pictures, words, and sounds are all available to learners. Teachers can introduce students to dictionaries, as shown in Figure 1.5 on page 18. Another way that students can interact with a program for vocabulary study is by creating their own word lists, shown in Figure 1.6 on page 19. Still another approach to teaching vocabulary is to introduce and practice it in a meaningful context, as shown in Figure 1.7 on page 20. These examples show some of the many ways that CALL can help to teach vocabulary explicitly.

Material	*8 in 1 English Dictionary* from English Computerized Learning, Inc.
Level	Adult Literacy/Beginner
Description	The English dictionary program in Figure 1.5 provides learners with definitions, pictures, and translations in twelve languages. Learners can search for words by letter (as shown in the figure), themes, or sounds. The plurals of nouns are given and verbs are conjugated. Learners can also listen to the pronunciations, and record and playback their own pronunciations.
Web site	http://www.englishelearning.com/en/8in1.html
Notes	Translations are in Arabic, Chinese, French, German, Japanese, Korean, Polish, Portuguese, Russian, Spanish, and Vietnamese. Demonstrations of this commercial program from English Computerized Learning, Inc., are available at the Web site above.

Figure 1.5 Example of vocabulary practice with Arabic translations in *8 in 1 English Dictionary.*

Has free 3 levels of vocabulary tests – MC
Nav Bar

Material	*Vocaboly*
Level	Intermediate to Advanced
Description	This vocabulary program lets the user select a pool of vocabulary to study. Words can be added to the study cards seen at the bottom of the screen so students can work on just those words. In Figure 1.6, TOEFL® vocabulary has been selected. The "free study" mode has also been selected. On this screen, the student can click on the phonetic transcription to hear each word pronounced. Students can assign a difficulty level from 0 to 5 to each word, and can study only words at a certain level. As illustrated in the left-hand column, this program provides students with seven types of interactive vocabulary exercises in three areas—study, test, and game. In the exercises, students work with sound, spelling, and meaning.
Web site	http://www.vocaboly.com/
Notes	Three hundred words each are targeted from TOEFL®, SAT®, GMAT®, GRE®, and VOA Special English. There are three levels of vocabulary tests online. The sound in the downloadable version is computerized, but if you purchase the program you will get a human voice with an American accent.

Figure 1.6 Example of vocabulary exercises in *Vocaboly*.

Very stilted dialogue + acting

Material	*EASY – English Academic Success for You* from *EASY*, the ESL Series
Level	Adult Literacy/Beginner
Description	This integrated skills CD-ROM includes vocabulary instruction in each unit, using audio, video, and text displayed on the screen. Figure 1.7 is from a unit on health care. In this example, the student clicks on the "play" icon to view a movie that presents key vocabulary; the word *medicine* is introduced on this screen. Every unit begins with an introduction of key vocabulary. Then more vocabulary is introduced throughout the different segments of the unit.
Web site	http://www.easyesol.com/
Notes	This screen is from the CD-ROM for *EASY*, Part 2 Community Essentials, Unit 8 Health Care. Different demos are available online at the address above. This series is also available on VHS video and DVD. Detailed lesson plans, worksheets, and quizzes (on paper) accompany each unit.

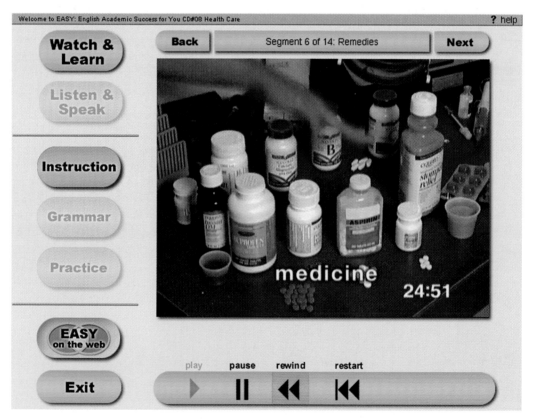

Figure 1.7 Example of the vocabulary introduction in *EASY* health care unit.

3 Provide learners with opportunities for interaction with the computer.

Interaction with the computer for vocabulary learning occurs when learners request a definition of a word in context, and when they engage in practice exercises for vocabulary learning. In both types of interactions, students have the opportunity to see where gaps exist in their vocabulary knowledge. By raising awareness of gaps in knowledge and providing students with help as needed, interactions with the computer can provide an efficient means of teaching vocabulary.

What the research says

CALL programs for vocabulary development help learners improve their vocabulary through interaction with the computer in at least two ways. First, the interactive programs mentioned earlier explicitly present and provide *interactive* practice. Research has shown that such interactions can help students learn second-language vocabulary (Atkinson, 1972; Tozcu & Coady, 2004). Second, a number of studies have found that learners who have access to word definitions while they are reading or listening on the computer are able to remember word meanings. Such activities provide an ideal means of teaching vocabulary in context, rather than having students guess meanings from context. Research suggests that the more types of help that students use (e.g., verbal help and imagery rather than verbal help alone) the better for their vocabulary acquisition (Yoshii & Flaitz, 2002). In short, more interaction is better for learning words, and CALL provides some useful types of interactions by offering learners a variety of help.

What the teacher can do

Teachers can choose CALL activities that engage students in vocabulary practice. One type of program uses vocabulary as the foundation on which to build phrases and then sentences, as illustrated in Figure 1.8 on page 22. Other CALL multimedia programs provide online vocabulary support and include a section that reinforces the vocabulary that was incorporated into a story that learners watched. Figure 1.9 on page 23 illustrates one such program. One major benefit of programs like this is that vocabulary that has been presented in context is reinforced with synonym practice. In both types of programs, students practice vocabulary by linking sounds, spellings, and meanings. They make choices and are told by the computer program whether their answers are correct. Teachers can recycle the words that students practice in their CALL material in the classroom, providing opportunities for repeated exposure to the input.

Material	*Rosetta Stone*
Level	Beginner to High Intermediate
Description	This program uses pictures to establish relationships with spoken and written words rather than relying on translations. Figure 1.8 is an example of a screen that students see in Level 1, Unit 1. In this segment, students can practice new vocabulary that they see, and they can also click on the words to hear them pronounced.
Web site	http://www2.rosettastone.com/en/
Notes	The commercial software is available in thirty different languages and it contains a variety of activities, including listening, speaking, reading, and writing. The Web site for *Rosetta Stone* has two downloadable demos: a brief online version and a fully functional version in all thirty languages.

Figure 1.8 Example of the initial vocabulary instruction in *Rosetta Stone.*

Material	*Longman English Interactive 3* from Pearson Education, Inc.
Level	High Intermediate
Description	In this vocabulary exercise, students work with vocabulary that they first heard in an accompanying video. As shown in Figure 1.9, students are given two choices and are instructed to click on a synonym of the key word. Then, students check the accuracy of their answers. Students can click on "Vocabulary Help" to see definitions of the vocabulary as well as example sentences.
Web site	http://www.pearsonlongman.com/ae/multimedia/
Notes	This screen shot was taken from American English, Lesson 2 of the software. You can take a "demo tour" of this commercial program or download complete sample units of the CD-ROM from the address above.

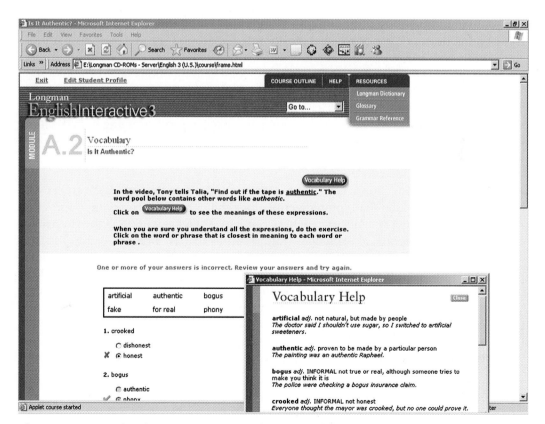

Figure 1.9 Example of a practice activity for vocabulary learning in *LEI 3*.

Let the vocabulary tasks spark interaction among learners.

Most CALL programs that introduce new vocabulary can be extended into discussions between pairs of learners to provide additional practice with the new words as well as opportunities for interaction. In particular, vocabulary games on the computer are useful for helping stimulate conversation about vocabulary. In such conversations, learners help each other, thereby stretching each other's competence. The computer keeps the conversation moving by providing learners with immediate feedback on the accuracy of their answers.

What the research says

Research on collaborative tasks in the classroom has shown that learners can help each other with vocabulary that appears in the reading materials when they work together (Klingner & Vaughn, 2000). Collaborations can also be developed around CALL activities. In some studies, the focus of an activity is a set of vocabulary words (e.g., items on a shopping list), but as long as the students are targeting a goal or product as an outcome to their collaboration, they are likely to encounter and focus their attention on new vocabulary. Research on collaborations in CALL has shown that students can learn new vocabulary through computer-mediated communication if tasks are specifically focused around the targeted lexical items (Smith, 2004). However, if students are to learn vocabulary from reading or listening input through collaboration, computer-provided help functions will be more important than collaboration among the learners (Jones, 2006). In other words, the types of interactions described in Tip 3 are the most important for vocabulary learning even if collaborations are useful for practicing speaking and engaging with the input in a way that increases comprehension.

What the teacher can do

Teachers can choose vocabulary activities and games that provide learners with vocabulary practice that complements other things they are working on in class. When preteaching vocabulary, teachers can have students work together in pairs at the computer, looking at sentences from a corpus that contain key words. Teachers may then ask students to guess the meanings and check their guesses against dictionary meanings. This type of activity is illustrated in Figures 1.10 and 1.11. Students can be asked to print the final page or note their score so teachers can check on the outcomes. Teachers can also pair students to complete vocabulary games such as those shown in Figures 1.12 and 1.13 on pages 27 and 28. Vocabulary practiced in games or online activities should be recycled in future classroom activities. Interaction during the games is only one part of the process of learning vocabulary.

didn't visit

Material   *Gerry's Vocabulary Teacher* from CPR4ESL

Level   Intermediate to Advanced

Description This program provides lists of key words that are each used in at least ten sample sentences. In the Help section, Gerry suggests grouping students in twos or threes and giving them a set of key words in context. Students can make their own definitions, or be given additional sentences with the words blanked out so that they have to deduce the meanings to fill in the blanks correctly in the other sentences. In Figure 1.10, sentences containing forms of *accelerate* were selected and moved to the output window. The sentences in the output window were automatically format- ted into the exercise in Figure 1.11 by clicking "RTF" and opening the file in Microsoft Word.

Web site   http://www.cpr4esl.com/gvthomepage.htm

Notes   A demo version of this British English commercial software program can be downloaded from the Web site above. It includes the first half of the alphabet, and it allows users to create exercises of up to five sentences. A complete version of the software is available for purchase on the Web site.

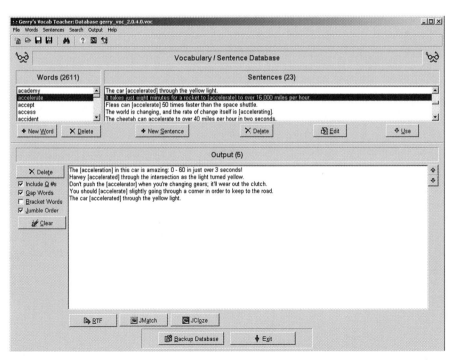

Figure 1.10 Example of a vocabulary in context selection from *Gerry's Vocabulary Teacher.*

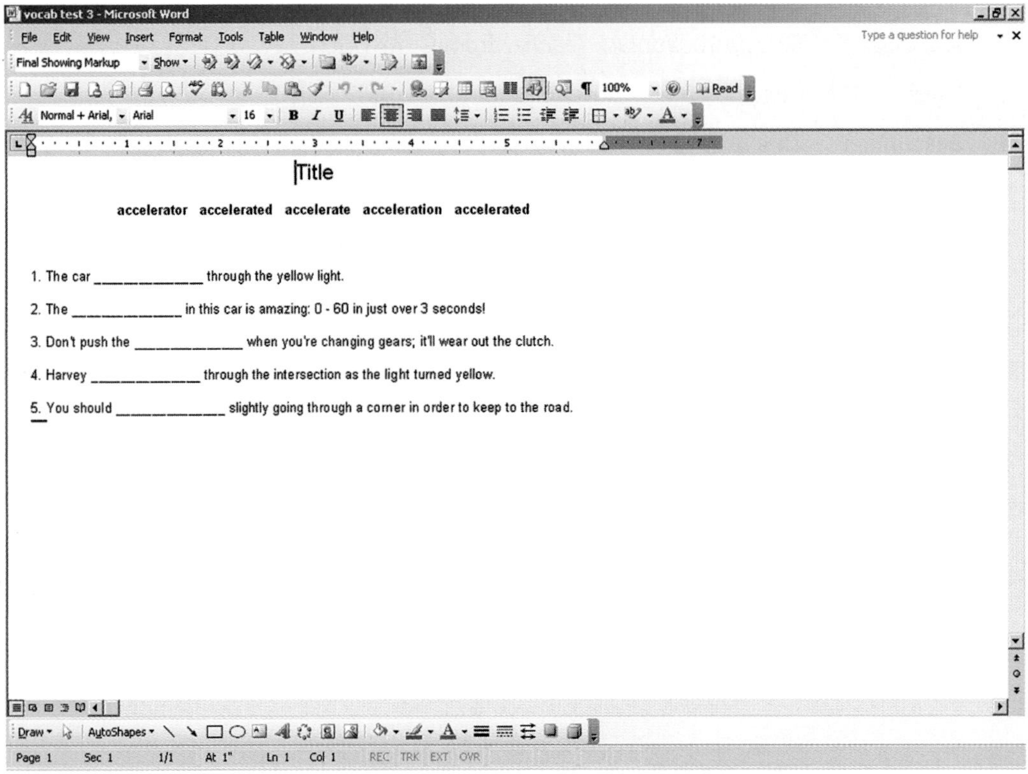
vocab test 3 - Microsoft Word
File Edit View Insert Format Tools Table Window Help
Type a question for help
Final Showing Markup Show
100% Read
Normal + Arial, Arial 16
Title
accelerator accelerated accelerate acceleration accelerated
1. The car ____________ through the yellow light.
2. The ____________ in this car is amazing: 0 - 60 in just over 3 seconds!
3. Don't push the ____________ when you're changing gears; it'll wear out the clutch.
4. Harvey ____________ through the intersection as the light turned yellow.
5. You should ____________ slightly going through a corner in order to keep to the road.
Draw AutoShapes
Page 1 Sec 1 1/1 At 1" Ln 1 Col 1 REC TRK EXT OVR

Figure 1.11 Example of a cloze exercise created from output in *Gerry's Vocabulary Teacher.*

Fun + easy

Material	*Crossword Puzzles for ESL Students* from *The Internet TESL Journal*
Level	Beginning to High Intermediate
Description	The *Internet TESL Journal* offers a variety of crossword puzzles that students can work on in pairs to spark interaction between learners. Teams can work on the same puzzle and compete to try to finish it first. In Figure 1.12, two screen shots are displayed. On the left, the easy puzzles are listed. On the right, students click on a number to get the clue. Then they type the word in the box and press "Enter." Four words of puzzle 1 have been entered.
Web site	http://iteslj.org/cw/
Notes	This free Web site has crossword puzzles that range in level from easy to difficult. It also links to Activities for ESL/EFL Students (http://a4esl.org/), which has vocabulary quizzes that students can complete in pairs.

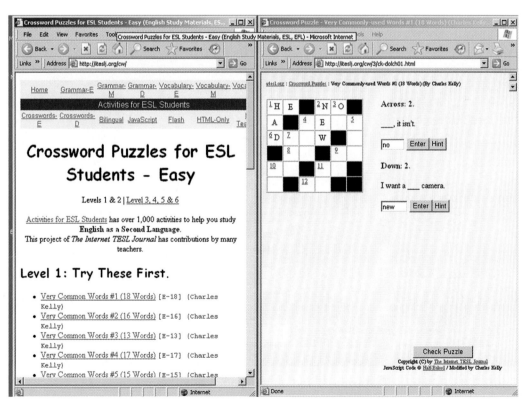

Figure 1.12 Example of crossword puzzles from *The Internet TESL Journal.*

Material	*Lingonet*
Level	High Intermediate to Advanced
Description	In the puzzle shown in Figure 1.13, students work together to brain-storm words about actions, people, places, or things in a hotel room in order to fill in the blanks. The learners can get clues about the correct answer by clicking on the red banks at the bottom of the screen.
Web site	http://www.lingonet.com
Notes	This free set of British English word puzzles is based on the idea that words are learned by association with a common setting or situation. From the *Lingonet* home page, send an e-mail to get a password. Once you receive your password, download the *Lingonet* demo (taster.exe) and any other puzzles. There are fifty downloadable *Lingonet* puzzles on topics such as business, hobbies, places, and technology.

For a demonstration of students using this program, see the CD-ROM at the back of this book.

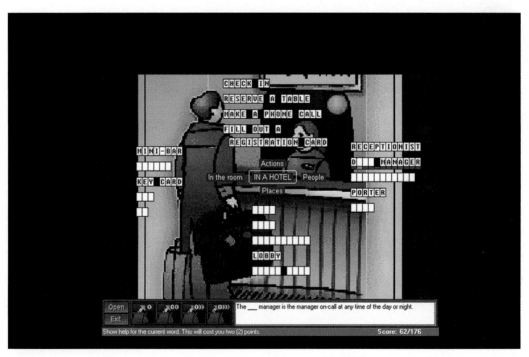

Figure 1.13 Example of a puzzle based on things in a hotel from *Lingonet.*

Include regular evaluations of answers and summaries of performance.

Many CALL programs include assessment of students' vocabulary achievement on words that were taught in the program. Students take these quizzes and tests and the programs record their scores so they can see how successful they have been. If assessment is not provided for the vocabulary that has been taught, teachers should make vocabulary quizzes, and inform learners about the dates of the quizzes so that they can study.

What the research says

Research is needed to demonstrate how evaluation affects vocabulary learning, but based on the experience of most teachers, we know that assessments help to focus students' attention on explicit study of vocabulary, and this is an important use of classroom evaluation. Read (2000) points out the need to use vocabulary assessment in a way that supports program objectives; the explicit assessment of vocabulary can help students see the importance of vocabulary study. Vocabulary assessments are included as part of many CALL activities.

What the teacher can do

Teachers can select CALL programs that include vocabulary assessment at the end of practice exercises (such as the program shown in Figure 1.14 on page 30) and at the end of units (as shown in Figure 1.15 on page 31). One benefit of end-of-study assessments is that they provide both the student and the teacher with a score that represents how well the student remembered the meanings of words they spent time practicing. Another benefit is that its inclusion in assessment and score reporting highlights the importance of vocabulary to both teacher and student.

Material   *Vocabster* from Edulang

Level   Beginning to Intermediate

Description   In this vocabulary program, when a student works on an exercise, he or she can check each answer. The program determines the accuracy of an answer, and gives the correct answer. At the end of the exercise, the student can ask to have it "graded." A connected program for the teacher keeps track of student performance. These last two features of evaluation and summary of performance are displayed in Figure 1.14. Here we can see the actual items a student worked on (correct answers in green and incorrect answers in red) and the summary of the results.

Web site   http://www.vocabster.com/

Notes   Teachers might consider both topic and level in order to decide what to use in class. It might take students fifteen to twenty-five minutes to work through one topic. This program also permits teachers to add their own vocabulary words, exercises, pictures, and audio by using an authoring tool. Demos of this commercial software can be downloaded after filling out a form at the Web site above.

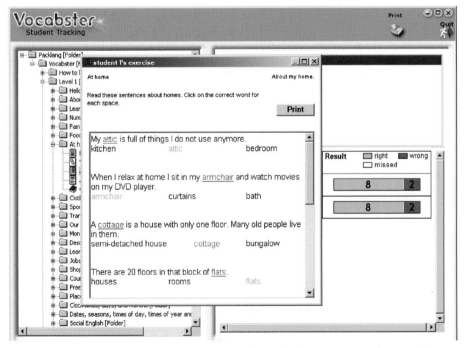

Figure 1.14 Example of an evaluation at the end of an exercise in *Vocabster.*

Material	*ELLIS Academic-Basic* from Pearson Digital Learning
Level	Beginning
Description	Evaluation of summary performance on vocabulary is illustrated in the *ELLIS Academic-Basic* software shown in Figure 1.15. Students work through nine lessons that focus on vocabulary. At the end, they take this vocabulary test in which they hear words or phrases and then click on the printed words or pictures. After the test, they are given scores for the percentage of correct answers and can then review each word. If a mistake was made, the student's selection appears in blue and the correct answer is outlined in green.
Web site	http://www.pearsondigital.com/ellis/
Notes	This commercial program was purchased by Pearson Digital Learning in 2006. The Web site above offers no demonstrations or downloads.

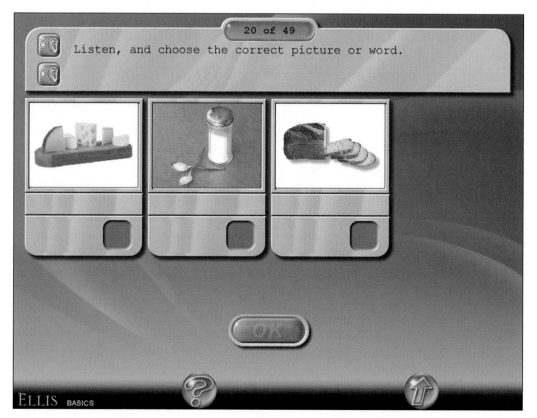

Figure 1.15 Example of a vocabulary test in *ELLIS Academic-Basic.*

Help learners develop strategies for explicit online vocabulary learning through the use of online dictionaries and concordancers.

Despite teachers' best efforts, they cannot teach all of the vocabulary that learners will need for their future lives as English users. Therefore, learners must leave the class not only with new words, but also with strategies for using Internet resources as a means of expanding their vocabularies. In particular, learners should become accustomed to looking up words in online dictionaries and checking vocabulary use in online concordancers. Learning these strategies, along with new vocabulary, will help students become more confident in their abilities.

What the research says

Vocabulary learning must continue beyond the ESL classroom, and therefore, research on vocabulary strategies is useful for identifying strategies that learners should be taught in class. Several studies have explored the combination of learner strategies and computer software for storing students' vocabulary in databases, offering help with word meaning and use, and creating practice exercises (Goodfellow & Laurillard, 1994; Lamy & Goodfellow, 1999). Horst, Cobb, and Nicolae (2005) investigated the use of a range of software tools including a concordancer, a dictionary, a cloze exercise builder, hypertext, and a database with an interactive self-quizzing feature to help students learn vocabulary strategies in class. Results indicate that the learners were able to use the tactics required for learning vocabulary through these tools. Because the tools are available on the Web, students may continue to use them in the future.

What the teacher can do

The teacher could choose a concordancing program that is free on the Web, such as *Compleat Lexical Tutor*, to introduce learners to the idea of using Internet resources for English language learning. The teacher should turn to the concordancer regularly in class to show learners examples of lexical phrases that have been used incorrectly in students' writing or that are being taught in class. The first set of examples in Figures 1.16 and 1.17 demonstrate how teachers can use *Compleat Lexical Tutor* to show students a key word in context and then access an online dictionary to see its definition. The second set of examples, Figures 1.18 and 1.19 on pages 35 and 36, demonstrate that teachers can show students how to analyze the vocabulary levels of sentences they wrote or read on the Web. By modeling these programs with regular classroom activities, teachers familiarize students with tools they can continue to use, even after they have completed the class.

Material	*Compleat Lexical Tutor*
Level	Beginning to Advanced
Description	One of the activities a student can perform after taking a vocabulary level test (described in Figure 1.1) is illustrated in Figures 1.16 and 1.17. In Figure 1.16, the student first clicks on the word level (such as 001–1000) in the upper left portion of the screen. Then, a list of words appears in the lower left portion of the screen, as shown in Figure 1.17. The student clicks on a word to hear it pronounced. The student can double-click on a word and a concordancer will show the selected word—*ability*, in this case—in context in the top portion of the screen. If the student types the word into "Quick Look-Up" on the home page, its dictionary definition will be shown.
Web site	http://www.lextutor.ca/lists_learn/
Notes	This Web site offers a free program. To hear words pronounced, you will need to download a specific speech plug-in. The link to the plug-in is at the top of the screen.

For a simulation that guides you through this program, see the CD-ROM at the back of this book.

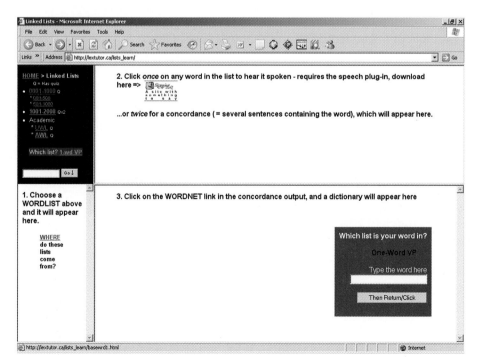

Figure 1.16 The first page of linked word lists in *Compleat Lexical Tutor.*

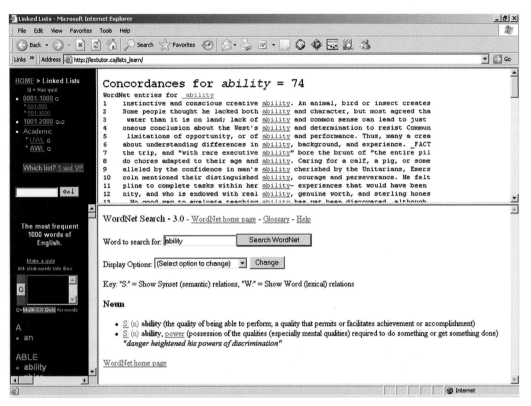

Figure 1.17 Example of linked word lists in *Compleat Lexical Tutor.*

Material	*Vocabulary Profiler*, from *The Compleat Lexical Tutor*
Level	Beginning to Advanced
Description	In another of Tom Cobb's vocabulary tools, a student can paste text into the window of the program shown in Figure 1.18 and then click on "Submit." The frequency of the vocabulary will be displayed in a few seconds. Figure 1.19 illustrates the type of information a student would get: the first 1,000 words in blue, the second 1,000 words in green, an academic word list in yellow, and the off-list words in red. The distribution percentages might also be informative for students.
Web site	http://www.er.uqam.ca/nobel/r21270/cgi-bin/webfreqs/web_vp.html
Notes	This Web site offers a free program. Additional free programs at this Canadian Web site can be found on the home page http://www.lextutor.ca.

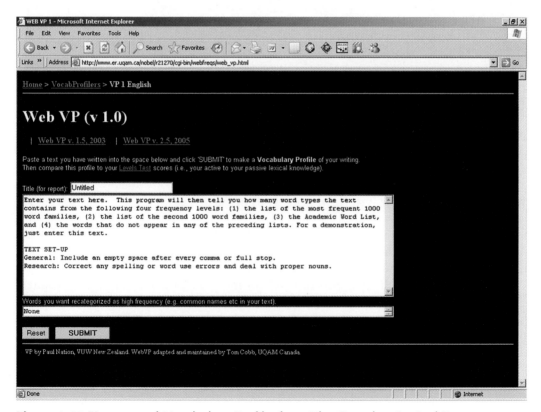

Figure 1.18 First page of *Vocabulary Profiler* from *The Compleat Lexical Tutor.*

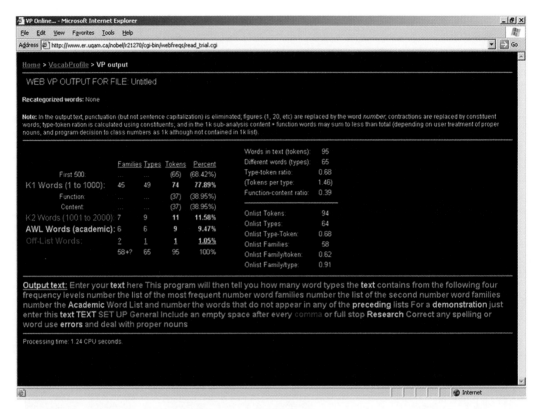

Figure 1.19 Output file for *Vocabulary Profiler* that shows the frequency of words.

FINDING GOOD VOCABULARY ACTIVITIES

Activities presented in this chapter illustrate some of the potential for using CALL for vocabulary learning, but not all vocabulary materials offer the language learning opportunities that have been described. If learners are expected to enjoy the language learning benefits of CALL for increasing their vocabularies, teachers might select vocabulary software that incorporates the points outlined in this chapter. The specific questions that one might ask are summarized in the table on page 37.

What to look for	Focus questions
Learner fit	Do the vocabulary words fit the learners in terms of the topics that are covered?
	Will the students be able to see the need for learning the vocabulary words? Are vocabulary words chosen to match the students' levels of language?
Explicit vocabulary teaching	Do the activities provide explicit instruction to teach vocabulary?
Interaction with the computer	Do the activities provide opportunities for interaction with the computer in a way that focuses students' attention on unfamiliar vocabulary?
	Does the computer provide students with help understanding the vocabulary that they do not know?
Interaction with other learners	Do the activities guide learners to work with classmates and contribute to online discussions?
	Can you think of other collaborative activities you could develop that are based on the vocabulary?
Two types of evaluation	Do the activities provide *feedback* to learners about their responses?
	Does the program provide evaluation of learning outcomes through *quizzes* that give learners information about their performance?
Strategy development	Do the activities promote good vocabulary learning strategies?
	Do the activities promote good reading strategies?
	Do the activities provide guidance for students to develop strategies that will help them continue to learn vocabulary on the Internet?

CONCLUSION

Research and practice suggest that vocabulary is an area of English language learning that can be developed through the use of CALL programs. However, much remains for teachers, learners, and researchers to discover about the best types of CALL activities for learners. A particularly important area of vocabulary teaching is one that helps learners move beyond individual word learning to learning lexical phrases and collocations. Currently, most CALL programs for vocabulary do not teach lexical phrases extensively. However, with the help of concordancers and corpora, teachers can construct their own materials and help students understand how to learn the lexical phrases that they will need beyond the English class. The glue of grammar is not so strong that it can hold any combination of words together on its own. Extensive learning of lexical phrases must occur as well.

CHAPTER 2

GRAMMAR

In the eyes of most language teachers and students, grammar is the core of language teaching. While many teachers agree that learning grammar is essential for second-language (L2) acquisition, they might disagree about the best grammar learning activities. Some experts would advise not to plan a syllabus around grammatical topics, such as adverbs or relative clauses. Instead, they would focus on teaching learners how to accomplish particular goals in English, such as buying plane tickets, asking for directions, or taking a phone message for a co-worker. The grammar lesson would come from whatever language it takes to accomplish the particular goal (e.g., *be* + negative in "She is not here now"). Ellis (1998) points out that regardless of how grammar topics are chosen, grammar learning requires that learners receive a combination of structured input, explicit instruction, production practice, and feedback about correctness. CALL can help provide students with opportunities for learning grammar in all of these ways (Doughty, 1987).

Research has increased our understanding of how students learn grammar. Hinkel and Fotos (2002) summarize some important ideas that demonstrate ways in which CALL can be used for teaching grammar, including discourse-based grammar, form-focused instruction, and interaction. Discourse-based grammar prompts teachers to select grammar on the basis of its importance in particular situations and to present grammar examples within their relevant contexts, which provides a type of structured input. Form-focused instruction refers to opportunities for learners to direct their attention to grammar. These opportunities include activities that require learners to produce language, receive explicit instruction and feedback, analyze grammatical patterns, or comprehend language that demands an understanding of grammatical relations. Interaction refers to the alternate turn-taking between the student and the computer, or between the student and other people. Interaction can provide opportunities for form-focused instruction within the discourse of a conversation, and such conversations can even be about grammar.

The tips for using CALL to teach grammar offer a variety of approaches and activities to direct students' attention to grammar in discourse contexts. Some draw learners' attention to grammatical structures and provide students with practice in recognizing and producing those structures. Others offer explicit rules, followed by practice and assessment. In all cases, the activities are intended to help students increase their strategies for continuing to learn grammar beyond the classroom.

TIPS FOR TEACHING GRAMMAR WITH CALL

Each of the five tips listed below is explained and illustrated with several CALL activities. Some of the activities were designed specifically for grammar teaching, but this chapter also shows how teachers can use authentic texts found on the Web to construct grammar lessons. Accessible, authentic electronic texts offer very useful opportunities for English learners to study grammar beyond the classroom.

TIPS

1. Select CALL materials that teach carefully chosen grammar in a manner that is appropriate for learners.
2. Provide learners with opportunities for interaction with the computer that include explicit teaching, discovery, analysis, and production of grammar.
3. Let grammar tasks spark interaction among learners.
4. Include evaluation of learners' responses and regular summaries of their performance. ⊙
5. Help learners develop strategies for learning grammar from texts on the Web through explicit practice and inductive learning. ⊙

Throughout the rest of the chapter, we explain each of these five tips with

- a description of *what it means* for the teacher who is using CALL for grammar instruction,
- a summary of *what the research says* about the tip, and
- a suggestion of *what teachers can do* in the classroom.

Along with each tip, illustrations of CALL activities from published CALL software and Web sites are provided. The Web addresses are given so that readers can visit the sites to try out the activities.

FEATURE: Examples of how to use one type of grammar software and one grammar Web site are on the CD-ROM at the back of this book. They include a demonstration of Tip 4 and a simulation of Tip 5.

Select CALL materials that teach carefully chosen grammar in a manner that is appropriate for learners.

This tip directs teachers to consider three factors when selecting CALL for grammar: 1) the difficulty levels of the grammatical forms relative to learners' needs; 2) the requirements for production of the grammatical forms; and 3) the degree of explicitness in the teaching of the grammar. A fixed list of all grammatical structures in ascending order of difficulty does not exist for teachers to draw upon. Nevertheless, some grammatical systems are ordered, such as the tense system (where present tense would be easier than present perfect) or the clause structure (where simple sentences would be easier than compounds). The difficulty of the task depends on the requirement for production: Tasks requiring learners to produce grammatical forms are typically more difficult than those that require learners to recognize the forms. The third factor, explicitness, refers to the amount of grammar explanation that learners receive in an activity. Activities that introduce the form to learners for the first time are often most explicit. Other activities contain a much less explicit focus on form, instead prompting learners to work with the grammar point while thinking about the meaning of the language. The challenge is to plan activities by considering these factors in the specific situation.

What the research says

Some research suggests that teachers might make appropriate choices for grammar instruction based on the difficulty of the grammar and the levels of the students. One study of CALL that supported this idea showed how form-focused instruction helped learners develop their ability to form relative clauses (Doughty, 1991). A key to observing this improvement was the researcher's analysis of how learners performed on relative clauses of varying degrees of complexity. More research such as this would help to show the varying degrees of difficulty of English grammar and would help in the design of CALL tasks. Similarly, further study on the learners' individual differences in performing tasks would give more data on the relationship between presentation type and success in learning grammar (Abraham, 1985; de Graaff, 1997). Until the research provides teachers with more guidance, teachers must use their judgment in choosing and teaching grammar in a manner that is appropriate for learners at different levels and with various learning styles. This chapter explores how some individualized CALL programs can help.

What the teacher can do

CALL grammar activities can be found for all levels of English learners, and they may follow a wide variety of approaches. Teachers can choose from different types of grammar activities, as illustrated in Figure 2.1 on page 42, but they should realize that many of these activities are rather limited, as context is often at the sentence level and practice is often in the form of recognition. Teachers can look for CALL software that embeds grammatical structures in discourse, and that provides students with production practice like that shown in Figure 2.2 on page 43. In such an activity, it is also helpful to have grammar explanations available as an option for students who are ready and interested in more explicit grammar presentations, as illustrated in Figure 2.3 on

[Handwritten annotations:]
ESLpages.com — better site. Has topics in "Grammar Book" + sentence practice, irreg verb flash cards

has levels + then topics so topics are hard to find

Material	*ESLgold—Grammar*
Level	Low Beginning to Advanced
Description	This free Web site offers a large variety of grammar explanations and exercises that are organized by proficiency levels, as illustrated in the left-hand portion of the screen shot in Figure 2.1. A link titled "How to use ESLgold.com" at the bottom of the Web page advises teachers to try out the materials and select the level that's right for their students. This site is recommended for pre-lesson preparation or post-lesson reinforcement.
Web site	http://www.eslgold.com/grammar.html/
Notes	By scrolling down the Web page shown in Figure 2.1, teachers can access links to recommended textbooks, grammar quizzes on the TESL Journal Web site, and quick links.

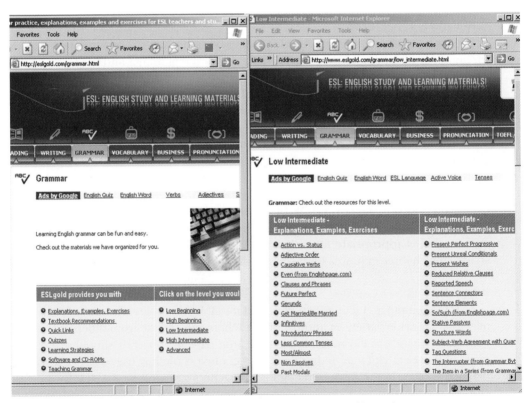

Figure 2.1 *ESLgold* illustrates how teachers can select material based on appropriate difficulty.

page 44. Almost every CALL Web site and program includes grammar, so teachers looking for grammar activities that are form focused and discourse based, that require production, and that include explicit explanations have many choices to consider.

Material	*Understanding and Using English Grammar—Interactive* from Pearson Education, Inc.
Level	Intermediate to Advanced
Description	The screen shot in Figure 2.2 shows software that provides a range of practices for each grammar point across skill areas. A student participates in a role play by listening to part of a dialogue and then producing the target form orally. The student records the response and compares it to the model response provided by the program.
Web site	http://www.pearsonlongman.com/ae/multimedia/programs/uuegi.htm
Notes	The Web site above has both an online tour of the commercial program and a link that allows users to download a free complete sample unit.

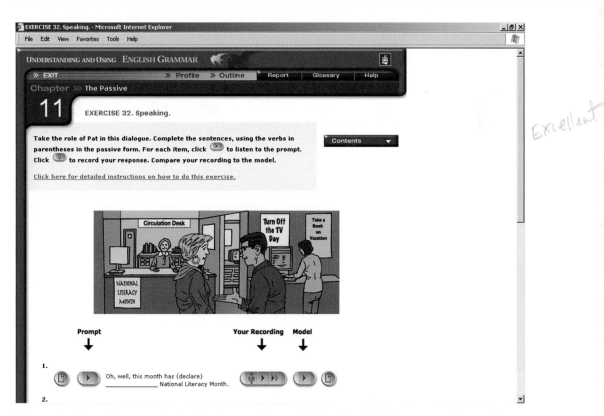

Figure 2.2 Speaking exercise in *Understanding and Using English Grammar—Interactive* requires production of the passive voice.

Material	*Understanding and Using English Grammar—Interactive* from Pearson Education, Inc.
Level	Intermediate to Advanced
Description	In the introduction to noun clauses shown in Figure 2.3, explicit information is provided for the student about the formation of noun clauses, through both examples and meta-linguistic explanations.
Web site	http://www.pearsonlongman.com/ae/multimedia/programs/uuegi.htm
Notes	This chart is available to students if they click on "Chart." The grammar points in this software are presented aurally and followed by exercises, games, and skill-based activities, such as those illustrated with the passive voice in Figure 2.2. The Web site above has both an online tour of this commercial program and a link that allows users to download a free complete sample unit.

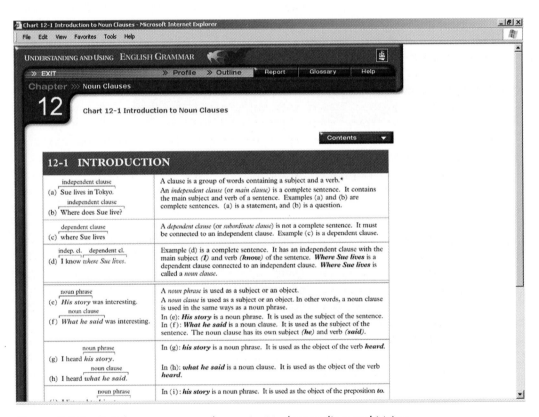

Figure 2.3 Explicit focus on noun clauses in *Understanding and Using English Grammar—Interactive.*

Provide learners with opportunities for interaction with the computer that include explicit teaching, discovery, analysis, and production of grammar.

A variety of computer tools can be used to construct interactive learning activities that focus on particular grammatical points. The key to providing valuable interaction is to choose activities that require learners to respond to questions and receive evaluation, to identify and analyze grammatical patterns and write down their analyses, and to produce the grammar and receive evaluation.

What the research says

Research and practice suggest that students must actively engage in learning in order to increase their knowledge of grammar. One study of CALL for grammar teaching showed the importance of including grammar production by comparing instruction in two programs, one requiring learners to produce the grammatical forms and the other providing input containing the forms but not requiring production (Nagata, 1998). The production group outperformed the input group, demonstrating the need for learners to produce the grammatical forms in order to learn them. Another study showed that engagement with grammar practice in an online French program could be better than the learning that occurs in class (Chenoweth & Murday, 2003). The online French course included grammar presentation that was coordinated with the topics covered in each section of the course and in practice exercises. Students in the online sections of the course attained test scores in grammar comparable to those attained by students in the parallel face-to-face course, but the writing scores for the online students were higher, in large part because of their superior grammatical accuracy, complexity, transitions, and writing development. In other words, for the more demanding, productive use of grammar, the highly interactive and individual work in the online environment produced the best results. This should not come as a surprise in view of the intense interaction that a student engages in during online instruction.

What the teacher can do

Teachers of beginning-level students can use CALL programs that embed grammar in meaningful contexts, such as cartoons or movies, and then follow them with activities. One such program, shown in Figure 2.4 on page 46, requires learners to produce sentences by dropping and dragging words into the correct order. Teachers of intermediate to advanced students can look for activities that ask students to analyze the grammatical patterns in sentences, such as in the examples given in Figures 2.5 and 2.6 on pages 47 and 48. Still another interactive activity for the computer is shown in Figure 2.7 on page 49, in which a student chooses to examine the distribution of a grammatical feature across registers. Teachers could ask students to search for grammatical features they have discussed in class.

Great   *Download CD-R unit?*

Material	*Side by Side Interactive* from Pearson Education, Inc.
Level	Beginning
Description	The scrambled sentence practice illustrated in Figure 2.4 is a common type of exercise provided in CALL. It is based on a video in which people say what they like to do in their spare time. The first exercise practices listening comprehension with pronouns (he or she likes to do something); the second exercise practices typing *like* or *likes*. The exercise in Figure 2.4 practices forming simple sentences using *like*. If a word is put in the correct order, it stays in place. If a word is put in the wrong order, the word returns to its starting place above the numbers.
Web site	http://www.pearsonlongman.com/ae/multimedia/programs/SbS.htm
Notes	Grammar-toons provide cartoons with animation of the target form in charts in each lesson segment.

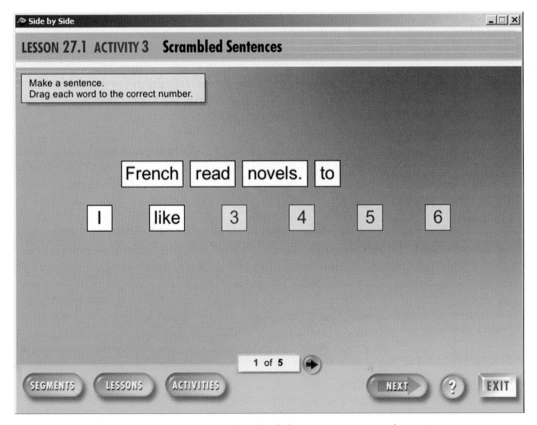

Figure 2.4 Interactive grammar activity in which learners construct the correct form in *Side by Side Interactive.*

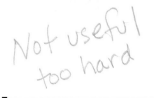 Not useful too hard

Material	*Chemnitz Internet Grammar* from the Chemnitz University of Technology Web site
Level	Intermediate to Advanced
Description	The free Web site in Figure 2.5 offers learners a three-way approach to the study of English grammar—discovery, explanation, and exercises—as illustrated by the colored wheel on the right-hand side. If learners click on "Discovery," groups of sentences taken from three corpora are shown. Learners must discover the grammar patterns that are represented in example sentences, as illustrated at the top of Figure 2.6. Then, learners check their understanding of the appropriate form for each clause type by clicking one of the four choices provided. Learners are shown if their choices are correct on the right-hand side of the screen.
Web site	http://www.tu-chemnitz.de/phil/english/chairs/linguist/real/index.html
Notes	This Web site represents a research project in progress that can be accessed for free. At the Web address above, click on "Learner behaviour—the Chemnitz Internet Grammar" and create a log-in by typing a user name and password. To navigate to the page shown in Figure 2.5, go to the "Content Menu" on the left and select "Conditional Structures." Then, click on "Conditionals—Basics" and "Patterns and Tenses."

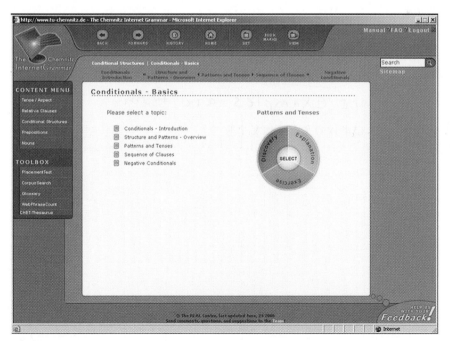

Jraskin english

Figure 2.5 Discovery, explanation, and exercise structure of *Chemnitz Internet Grammar*

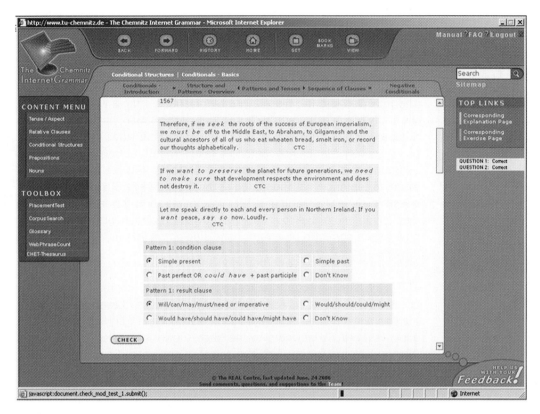

Figure 2.6 Discovering the pattern of conditional structures using *Chemnitz Internet Grammar.*

Site is incomplete. No content under phrasal verbs. The sentence examples are from really hard acacademic texts.

Material	*Chemnitz Internet Grammar* from the Chemnitz University of Technology Web site
Level	Intermediate to Advanced
Description	The screen shot in Figure 2.7 shows the results of a corpus-based analysis of the distribution of the target feature across registers. Under the "Toolbox" heading on the left, "CorpusSearch" was selected. Then, the target feature "must" was typed in. The registers included academic texts (ac), public speeches (doc), European Union documents (eu), and tourist brochures (tou). Only statistics were chosen to be displayed. Here, we can see that "must" often occurs in academic texts and public speeches, but rarely occurs in tourist brochures. Such analysis of selected linguistic features could heighten a student's awareness of the importance of registers in understanding the use of grammatical features in English.
Web site	http://www.tu-chemnitz.de/phil/english/chairs/linguist/real/index.html
Notes	Other output display options are keyword in context (KWIC) and complete sentences. At the Web site above, click on "Learner behaviour on the Internet—the Chemnitz Internet Grammar" and create a free log-in by typing a user name and password.

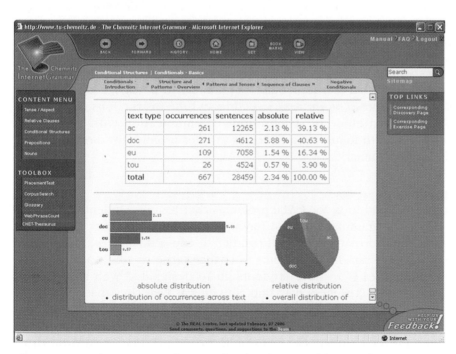

Figure 2.7 Analysis activity showing the distribution of the word "must" across registers in *Chemnitz Internet Grammar.*

3   **Let grammar tasks spark interaction among learners.**

The computer can be used to get students to *talk about* grammar or to *talk using* grammar. By placing students in pairs to complete a grammar exercise on the computer, the teacher can focus learners' attention and direct their conversations to specific grammar points. Meaning-focused computer tasks might prompt learners to use particular grammatical structures in their discourse.

What the research says

Researchers suggest that the first type of conversation—talking about grammar—provides a means of raising learners' consciousness about grammatical forms. When learners collaborate in conversations about grammar, they assist each other in getting the correct answers. This has been shown with grammar exercises in some classroom collaborations (Ohta, 2000; Swain, 1998). Research has shown that CALL grammar tasks can be completed by a group of two or three students who collaborate to get the job done (Abraham & Liou, 1991). The computer keeps the conversation goal oriented and productive, and the learners work together to complete each part of the task, receive feedback from the computer, discuss the feedback, and continue.

The second type of grammar conversation prompts learners to talk about a topic that lends itself to the use of particular grammatical forms. For example, "what I did last weekend" would prompt use of the past tense. Loschky and Bley-Vroman (1993) suggest that communication tasks can be developed in such a way as to make the use of particular grammatical structures essential during task completion. CALL research has shown that if students are prompted to do so, they will focus on form during communication tasks, but it is difficult to know which forms will be the focus of learners' attention. Fiori (2005) and Pellettieri (2000) have shown that learners focus on grammar in pedagogical tasks when they are guided to do so by the task structure and the instructions given by the teacher. The written mode of synchronous communication with the teacher prompting learners to focus on form seems to offer promise for directing learners' attention to grammar.

What the teacher can do

Teachers should look for CALL programs that require students to discuss and use particular grammar forms in fun and meaningful contexts. One idea is to group students so that they work together to edit a document, as shown in Figure 2.8. Teachers can direct students to change tense or voice, or to simplify clauses. Another idea is to have students go to designated Web sites to find answers to questions. Teachers may find activities at Web sites that accompany their textbooks. Figure 2.9 on page 52 shows a jigsaw activity intended to focus attention on question formation. In both of these examples, teachers can create opportunities for their students to focus on form and practice grammar in structured, yet fun, activities.

Material	*Newspaper Editor* from Clarity Language Consultants, Ltd.
Level	High Intermediate to Advanced
Description	The program shown in Figure 2.8 gives teachers the opportunity to have students work in groups to edit articles from the archive, and publish their articles within the preset time limit. Students have to deal with incoming news flashes, discuss the articles with their teammates, persuade, and negotiate. Teachers could use this kind of software to have students work on specific grammatical features. For instance, the article in the screen shot may be used to have students work in groups and practice writing less complex sentences.
Web site	http://www.clarity.com.hk/program/newspapereditor.htm
Notes	A demo version can be downloaded from this Web site. Users must send an e-mail message to receive an access code.

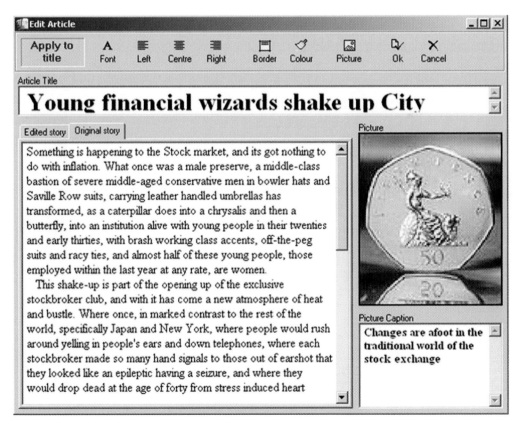

Figure 2.8 Meaning-focused editing activity in *Newspaper Editor* can include focus on form.

Material	*Focus on Grammar 2—Course Companion* from Pearson Education, Inc.
Level	High Beginning to Low Intermediate
Description	This online Web site complements the course *Focus on Grammar*. In Figure 2.9, the "Courseware Companion" has a group activity to accompany the unit on *Wh*–questions. Students are assigned to either group A, B, or C. In Part One of the activity, students go to a Web site about a place and answer *Wh*–questions about the place in complete sentences. In Part Two of the activity, students bring their worksheets to class and work with students from different groups. They ask their classmates questions and try to guess their places.
Web site	http://www.pearsonlongman.com/ae/fog_level2/SR/pdfs/2_07web_sh.pdf
Notes	The site opens a .pdf file that includes Web addresses for students to research. Students cannot type directly into the document; they must first print it out and then write in their answers.

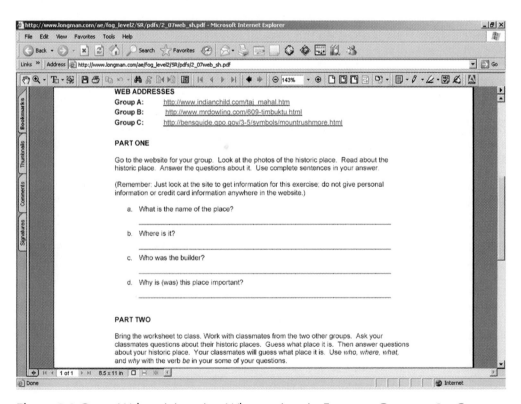

Figure 2.9 Group Web activity using *Wh*–questions in *Focus on Grammar 2—Course Companion.*

Include evaluation of learners' responses and regular summaries of their performance.

Developing grammatical accuracy requires that learners receive feedback about the correctness of their grammatical knowledge. CALL activities can be particularly useful for giving learners this individualized written feedback.

What the research says

Second-language researchers point out that when students receive feedback on their performance, they have the opportunity to notice the gaps between their knowledge and correct grammar (Lyster & Ranta, 1997; Swain, 1985). A number of studies have found that evaluation and feedback are valuable for learning grammar. For example, Chenoweth and Murday's (2003) study, in which online grammar instruction resulted in the highest grammatical accuracy in writing, included self-tests as part of the learning materials. In other words, the assessments were built in to the instruction. In a study looking at different types of feedback, Nagata (1993) found that explicit feedback for learners about why their responses were correct or incorrect produced the best results for grammar learning, compared to feedback that simply pointed out the location of learners' errors. These two studies show the importance of any type of assessment, but they also should help to remind teachers to look for feedback that is informative to learners, and to help learners make sense of all the feedback they receive from the computer.

What the teacher can do

Not all CALL materials provide clear feedback for learners, but teachers can find CALL software for grammar that does. Teachers can look for software that provides grammar assessment and feedback about correctness both before and after instruction. An example of a diagnostic grammar quiz is shown in Figure 2.10 on page 54. The feedback tells students to review specific forms in their textbooks or CALL programs. An example of evaluation and feedback on a grammar quiz that follows each set of practice items is shown in Figure 2.11 on page 55. Specific units can be assigned to students as homework following the introduction of grammatical topics in class. Teachers can encourage individual learners to monitor their own progress and knowledge of grammatical forms by checking their results on the quizzes.

Material	*Study Skills Success* from Clarity Language Consultants Ltd.
Level	High Intermediate to Advanced
Description	The grammar section of this program begins with two assessments: Diagnosing Your Grammar Errors and Grammar Test. Figure 2.10 shows the learner the results of the grammar test. Color is used to show correctness—blue for correct, red for incorrect, and green for corrected. By clicking on "Feedback" at the bottom right on the screen, the learner is informed of the type of mistakes made, and directed to go to the textbook or grammar software program for more work in the problem areas—in this case, articles, the passive, and count/noncount nouns.
Web site	http://www.clarity.com.hk/program/studyskills.htm
Notes	An online demo at the Web site above focuses on preparation for the reading and speaking sections for the IELTS™ exam. You can send an e-mail to request a demo CD-ROM that includes grammar.

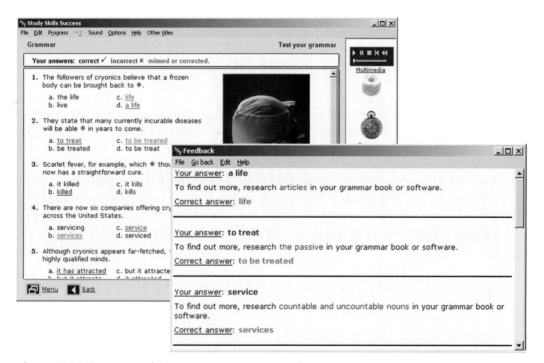

Figure 2.10 Correct and incorrect answers on a diagnostic grammar test in *Study Skills Success.*

Material   *Understanding and Using English Grammar—Interactive* from Pearson Education, Inc.

Level   Intermediate to Advanced

Description   The screen shot in Figure 2.11 shows a pop-up window that displays the results of an end-of-unit test. The "Progress Report" gives the students their scores on each of the four noun clause forms presented and practiced in Chapter 12: Noun Clauses. It also tells students which charts in the chapter explain each grammar point. The student can return to the test to see which questions were answered correctly or incorrectly. A green check indicates a correct answer (#1) and a red X indicates an incorrect answer (#2). Clicking on an "e" after the correct answer provides an explanation. (In this example, #3 and #4 were skipped.)

Web site   http://www.pearsonlongman.com/ae/multimedia/programs/uuegi.htm

Notes   A sample showing a different unit of the program can be downloaded from the Web site.

◉ **For a demonstration of students using this program, see the CD-ROM at the back of this book.**

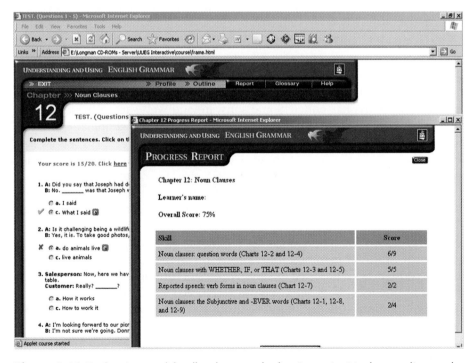

Figure 2.11 Evaluation and feedback on end-of-unit test in *Understanding and Using English Grammar—Interactive*.

Help learners develop strategies for learning grammar from texts on the Web through explicit practice and inductive learning.

The grammar that learners study in class can be the start of a lifelong refinement of their knowledge of English grammar, so grammar study must also include learning how to continue to develop grammatical accuracy and complexity throughout their lives.

What the research says

Based on theory and research on second-language acquisition, Ellis (1995) suggests that students benefit from grammar tasks that require them to interpret specific grammatical forms. Such tasks require learners to move beyond getting the general meaning of an utterance and on to a precise form-function mapping in their minds. In other words, such tasks require that students understand the meaning conveyed by the grammar, rather than inferring meaning from their world knowledge and an understanding of some of the words. A corpus is an ideal place to turn to for examples of interpretation tasks because teachers can consult the actual use of grammatical patterns in choosing examples, as linguists do (Biber, Johansson, Leech, Conrad, & Finegan, 1999). Conrad (2000) suggests that this approach to grammar has the potential for changing the way that grammar is taught. Johns (1994) points out that the students themselves can also use the corpus to find examples of grammatical structures, and some writing classes are integrating such activities into courses in hopes of helping learners to develop the skills that will help them take advantage of the many electronic texts that they have access to on the Web (Cheng, Warren, & Xun-feng, 2003).

What the teacher can do

Teachers can model many strategies for students, in the hope that students will use them after the class has ended. Some software and Web sites provide learners direct access to corpora that they can explore to answer their grammar questions. Teachers might select a Web site such as *VIEW: Variation in English Words and Phrases*, illustrated in Figure 2.12, to show students how they can look at variation in grammatical selection across types of writing, or registers. Grammatical points, such as the one in the example, can come from class discussion. Other grammar might come from the students' own writing. For example, if a teacher sees a student using a form that is too informal for writing, the teacher can show the student how to search for more formal forms across the registers. Questions may arise while students are writing, but the study of grammar itself raises questions such as how particular grammatical constructions are used in various types of writing, or registers. Teachers can introduce students to Web sites, such as *Dave's ESL Cafe*, where they can post their grammar questions to a discussion board, as shown in Figure 2.13 on page 58. Still another tool that teachers can introduce to their students is the use of the "Find" function available in many programs. Teachers can have students search for grammatical patterns by using this feature of *Google*, shown in Figure 2.14 on page 59.

Material	*VIEW: Variation in English Words and Phrases* from the Brigham Young University Web site.
Level	High Intermediate to Advanced
Description	The screen shot in Figure 2.12 shows the results of a corpus-based analysis across registers. The target feature is *whom* and this was typed in on the left side of the screen under "Search String." A chart was selected to display the results. Here we see that *whom* is used much more in academic writing than in speech. If you click the name of a register above the corresponding bar in the chart, the bottom half of the window will show you the actual sentences/instances within the register. The student can observe the use of the target feature in texts that are available on the Web.
Web site	http://corpus.byu.edu/bnc
Notes	This Web site offers a free program. You must register to use it. The first time you visit this Web site, click on the "More information" drop-down menu on the right-hand side in the center and take the "three-minute tour."

For a simulation that guides you through this program, see the CD-ROM at the back of this book.

Good

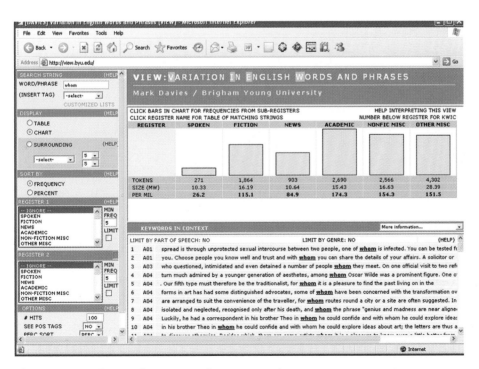

Figure 2.12 Inductive learning and register analysis in *VIEW: Variation in English Words and Phrases.*

Must register

Material	*Student Discussion Forums* from *Dave's ESL Cafe.*
Level	All
Description	On this Web site, a learner can post a question about grammar on a discussion board and talk about it with other learners. In Figure 2.13, we see an example of a self-directed learner who is posting his grammar question about article use with the countable nouns *brother* and *sister.*
Web site	http://www.eslcafe.com/forums/student
Notes	The Web site above takes you to student forums. Scroll down and click on "Learning English" to get to the forum depicted in Figure 2.13.

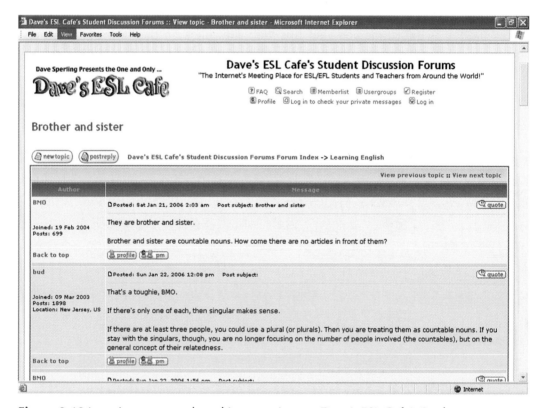

Figure 2.13 Learning grammar by asking questions at *Dave's ESL Cafe's Student Discussion Forums.*

Good for
finding readings
w/ specific grammar

Material	*Google* and *Greenpeace*
Level	All
Description	Learners can search for particular grammatical constructions in texts that interest them by using *Google's* Advanced Search. In Figure 2.14, a learner has specified the words *greenpeace* and *will*. When *Google* returns its results, if the learner clicks on "Cached" at the end of the reference, the key terms will be highlighted in the text. In this way, learners can use this tool to see instances of a grammatical structure in authentic texts.
Web site	http://www.google.com/advanced_search?hl=en and http://www.greenpeace.org/canada
Notes	This technique could be used on any of the *Google* results that have the "cached" option available.

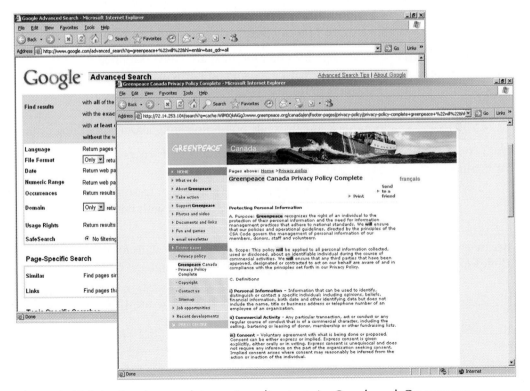

Figure 2.14 Selecting the search terms in online texts in *Google* and *Greenpeace*.

FINDING GOOD GRAMMAR ACTIVITIES

Examples in this chapter illustrate some of the potential for using CALL for grammar, but not all grammar materials offer the language learning opportunities that have been described. By selecting grammar activities using the points outlined in this chapter, teachers can help students use CALL to increase their knowledge of grammar and their ability to analyze grammatical examples. Specific questions that teachers might ask are summarized in the table.

What to look for	Focus questions
Learner fit	Does the structured grammatical input fit the learners in terms of level, topics, and activities?
	Does the program provide a means of matching the learners to the grammatical instruction they need?
Interaction with the computer	Do learners have opportunities for interaction with the computer to provide a variety of explicit teaching, discovery, analysis, and production?
Interaction with other learners	Can the activities be used to spark conversation and collaborative work focusing on particular grammar points that you want to teach?
	Do the activities provide an opportunity for learners to focus on form occasionally while communicating about something else?
Two types of evaluation	Do the activities provide *feedback* to learners about their responses?
	Does the program provide evaluation of learning outcomes through *quizzes* that provide learners with information about their performance?
Strategy development	Do the activities help learners develop skills for using corpora for gathering and analyzing language examples?
	Do the activities provide guidance in assisting learners to develop strategies that will help them work with electronic texts outside of class?

CONCLUSION

Someday soon CALL materials may provide teachers and students with many different ways of presenting and practicing grammatical forms so that appropriate individualized instruction may be available for learners on demand in and outside of the classroom. In the meantime, teachers have a wide variety of materials to choose from for teaching grammar. These materials not only help students learn grammar, but they also help them develop awareness of the use of electronic texts to find examples of grammatical patterns for their analysis and interpretation.

READING

English teachers know that ESL learners need to read English to be successful in their other academic classes and to function as literate people in a global environment. These are obviously central goals for most ESL classes, but to understand the value of CALL materials in reading, teachers must consider the role that written language plays in helping learners acquire English. In other words, reading is not only the goal of instruction. It is also the process by which learners can develop their language abilities and strategies for language use. This chapter shows some of the specific ways that teachers can use CALL activities to help learners develop their reading skills as well as their overall English ability through reading.

Think about what happens when you try to read something in another language. As an unskilled reader, your eyes move along each sentence attempting to decipher the meaning of each word. You hope to construct the meaning of each sentence so you can ultimately get the message from the complete text. The process that you engage in so effortlessly in your first language becomes a puzzle when you read in another language. Every step of the way your meaning making is slow and frustrating as you trip over unfamiliar or partially familiar words, phrases, and grammatical constructions. Your understanding is blocked by limited linguistic knowledge in addition to lack of experience with second-language texts and the contexts in which they were written (Carrell & Grabe, 2002). You do not feel that you understand what is written on the page and cannot predict what comes next, as a skilled reader would. You do not feel you are improving your language ability.

Most researchers would agree that if learners cannot understand what they are reading, they are not likely to learn much, if any, of the language. Many experts would agree that the process of language development can be more efficient if learners read material at an appropriate level, and if they receive help with the language while they are reading. Two goals of teaching reading are to help learners understand the meaning of a text and to help them use the text to develop their overall language ability. The tips in this chapter can help teachers use CALL to focus on these two interrelated goals.

TIPS FOR TEACHING READING WITH CALL

CALL is good for teaching reading. CD-ROMs and texts on the Internet provide learners with a variety of materials to read and interact with. The seven tips described in this chapter, listed below, help the teacher to get students working productively with electronic texts.

TIPS

1. Select CALL materials with appropriate reading texts. 🔘
2. Look for important words and phrases to be emphasized on the screen.
3. Provide learners with opportunities to interact with the computer for getting help with the language in the text.
4. Let the text on the screen spark interaction among learners.
5. Choose CALL materials that teach English through reading.
6. Include evaluation of learners' comprehension and language knowledge. 🔘
7. Help learners develop their strategies for reading online.

Throughout the rest of the chapter, each of these seven tips is explained with

- a description of *what it means* for the teacher who is using CALL for reading,
- a summary of *what the research says* about the tip, and
- a suggestion of *what teachers can do* in the classroom.

Along with each tip, illustrations of CALL activities from published CALL software and Web sites are provided. The Web addresses are given so that readers can visit them to try out the activities.

FEATURE: Examples of how to use one type of reading software and one reading Web site are on the CD-ROM at the back of this book. They include a demonstration of Tip 6 and a simulation of Tip 1.

1 Select CALL materials with appropriate reading texts.

It goes without saying that teachers attempt to choose materials that are appropriate for their students. That is, teachers always strive for good learner fit. Learner fit is especially important for CALL reading texts because of the opportunities for matching the right texts with individual learners. The variety of electronic texts and CALL activities make it easy to find texts that are at the appropriate level of difficulty, that cover topics of interest to learners, and that include tasks that engage learners (Chun, 2006). Learner fit becomes more feasible when using CALL reading texts because of the opportunities for matching the right texts with individual learners.

What the research says

Research that has focused on the effects of using texts at appropriate levels was originally based on Krashen's (1982) idea that the language input that learners are exposed to should make them stretch their language knowledge just the right amount. In other words, if the language in texts is too easy for learners, the texts will not provide any language for them to learn. On the other hand, if the texts are too difficult, learners will become frustrated at not being able to understand them, and again, the language of the texts will not offer any opportunity for learning. Research results support the suggestion that particular types of texts are best for second-language acquisition. Texts must contain language that is sufficiently difficult for learners to learn something from, but they should contain elaborations to help learners comprehend the meaning (Oh, 2001; Yano, Long, & Ross, 1993). Another useful perspective on learner fit comes from the work of van Lier (1996), who describes the importance of learners engaging with the learning materials. Such engagement can potentially develop if the teacher selects interesting and appropriately challenging materials.

What the teacher can do

Teachers should keep learner fit in mind when reviewing and selecting CALL materials. When teachers select a CALL program with texts for the whole class, they should read the texts, complete a sample of the activities, and prepare to discuss the texts with the students in class. For example, a teacher may visit a Web site to find readings that are graded according to level, such as those shown in Figure 3.1 on page 66. A teacher of a beginning to intermediate ESL class may choose to include readings from *Adult Learning Activities*. As illustrated in Figure 3.2 on page 67, a teacher can select interesting readings according to topics that are covered in class. The teacher can also look for CALL materials that are *adapted* to the level and interests of the students. A Web site that provides such adapted texts is illustrated in Figure 3.3 on page 68.

Material	*ESL Independent Study Lab*—Reading from the Lewis and Clark College Web site
Level	All
Description	Readings are categorized for students by level, ranging from Level 100 for beginners to Level 400 for advanced, as shown at the top of Figure 3.1. Readings at this site include student compositions, folktales, comics, and adult education topics such as working, law, and government, as well as follow-up activities including cloze, matching, and multiple-choice questions about main ideas, details, and vocabulary.
Web site	http://www.lclark.edu/~krauss/toppicks/reading.html
Notes	This site is free. It contains a large number of links that may be confusing to learners, so teachers should guide students. Also, some of the sites listed here do not indicate the level of the readings, so teachers will have to look them over to decide whether the readings are appropriate.

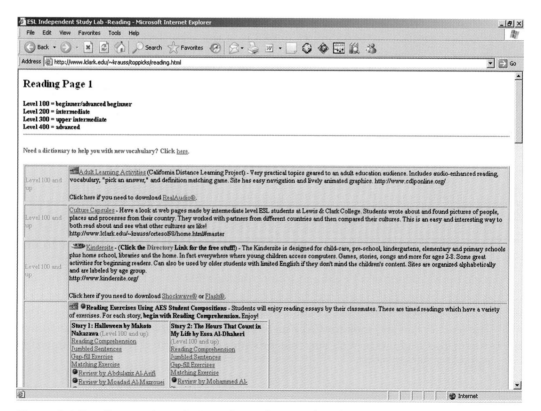

Figure 3.1 Reading section of *ESL Independent Study Lab.*

Material	*Adult Learning Activities* from the California Distance Learning Project
Level	Beginning to Intermediate
Description	Readings about a variety of topics (working, law and government, family, school, health and safety, housing, money, science and technology, services, going places, and nature) are available at the Web site shown in Figure 3.2. Each topic has several readings (some with audio), and each reading has vocabulary and comprehension activities. A teacher may choose these readings if the topics are thematically tied to class activities.
Web site	http://www.cdlponline.org/index.cfm
Notes	This free Web site features links to other sites for beginning readers.

For a simulation that guides you through this Web site, see the CD-ROM at the back of this book.

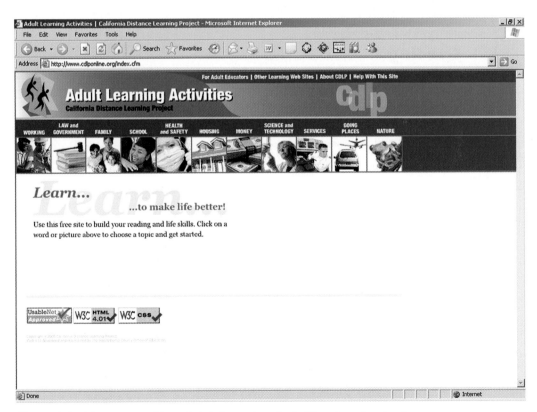

Figure 3.2 Menu page from *Adult Learning Activities* showing topics.

Material	*ESL Reading*
Level	Beginner to High Intermediate
Description	This Web site has a small selection of texts that have been adapted so that they are graded by vocabulary, grammar, and readability. Some selections begin with a prereading exercise, followed by the text. The texts are divided into parts, and students make predictions about what will come next.
Web site	http://www.gradedreading.pwp.blueyonder.co.uk/index.html
Notes	Some readings, such as "Ghost Stories," are described by level, length, Flesch reading ease, and Flesch-Kincaid reading level, but others are not described. Some readings are followed by exercises. This Web site is free.

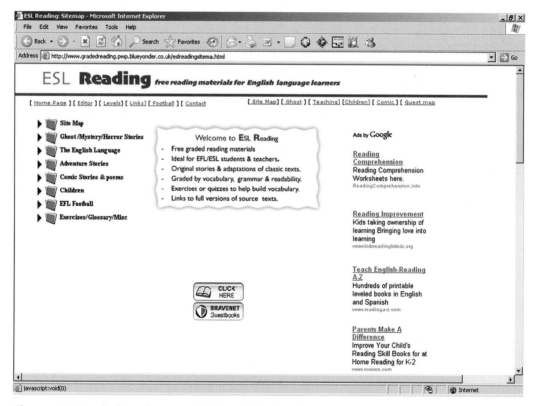

Figure 3.3 Graded readings available at *ESL Reading*.

Look for important words and phrases to be emphasized on the screen.

One purpose of reading is to help learners develop their English. Therefore, teachers need to look for written texts that include important words and phases for students to learn—these will make good language lessons. CALL programs should help by emphasizing particular aspects of the language on the computer screen. In other words, the input must be made *salient* so the learner's attention will be directed toward it.

What the research says

Based on his own research and experience, Schmidt (1992) argues that learners are more likely to learn vocabulary and grammar if they notice these forms in the texts they read. One way that language in a text becomes *salient* to learners is when they have trouble understanding it. Another way that particular vocabulary and grammar becomes *salient* is by highlighting the words in the text, as many researchers have suggested (Sharwood Smith, 1993; White, 1998). A third way that language can be made *salient* is by exposing learners to the words many times (N. Ellis, 2002). This type of repetition has been called an input flood (Doughty & Williams, 1998) because learners are flooded with the target vocabulary and grammar. Finally, language in a text can be made *salient* because of what the learner has been taught before reading or what the learner is expected to do after the reading. More research is needed on the value of *salient* input from reading, but in the meantime most researchers agree that it is a good idea to draw learners' attention to specific vocabulary and grammar in texts if learners are expected to remember and learn it. Research on CALL reading materials has shown that students learn vocabulary in reading texts if they are given help in understanding the *salient* forms (Chun & Plass, 1996). In other words, a combination of *salience* and help is good for language learning.

What the teacher can do

Teachers can look for CALL reading materials that have clear linguistic objectives, and that attempt to draw learners' attention to examples of relevant vocabulary and grammar in the reading. Learners' attention can be directed to specific language through the use of color, font size, and animation. Figures 3.4 and 3.5 on pages 70 and 71 illustrate texts that have specific language highlighted. The examples show the type of help that has proven effective for learning vocabulary. Unfortunately, many of the texts in CALL reading materials do not have this type of *salient* input for the learner. What can the teacher do? The teacher can draw learners' attention to specific vocabulary and grammar in the text by preteaching particular language, by asking students to write down language that they do not understand in the text, and by constructing a follow-up activity such as a summary of the text. We hope that you learned the word *salient* in this chapter, and that you remember how useful it is for a reader to have important linguistic points clearly marked in the texts.

Material	*Longman English Interactive 3* from Pearson Education, Inc.
Level	Intermediate
Description	This integrated skills CALL program contains twelve units, and each unit has a section on reading. The reading shown in Figure 3.4 uses color and underlining to draw attention to the words and phrases that the students are intended to learn. These words and phrases, such as "a matter of life and death," are linked to definitions that are displayed when learners request them by clicking on the words. The program also uses images to help situate readers.
Web site	http://www.pearsonlongman.com/ae/multimedia/programs/lei3_4.htm
Notes	There are British and American versions of this commercially available program. This example is from the American English program. A sample unit of this commercial program can be downloaded from the Web site above. Click on "Try a sample CD-ROM" and then click on "Longman English Interactive (*American English*)." Finally, click on "Level 3 US sample." This reading exercise is in the sample unit. Try it and see if you notice the highlighted words and phrases. Click on them to see what happens.

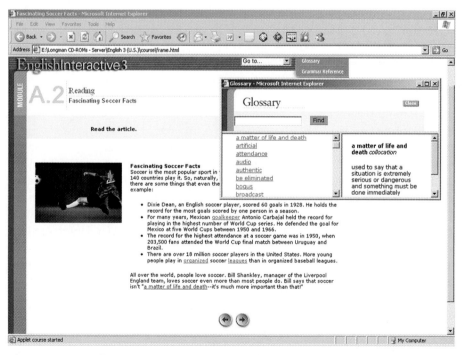

Figure 3.4 Reading passage with key vocabulary highlighted from *Longman English Interactive 3.*

Material	*Issues in English* from Protea Textware
Level	Beginning—Level 1
Description	This integrated skills program begins each unit with people presenting an issue or an opinion on topics of interest to adults (e.g., euthanasia, gambling, smoking, the environment). Learners' attention is drawn to key vocabulary in short reading passages that also have video so the learners can listen. In the screen shot in Figure 3.5, the salient language in a short paragraph on smoking is emphasized with red-colored font. The presentation of the issue is followed by several types of exercises, such as comprehension, fill in the blank, spelling, and dictation.
Web site	http://www.proteatextware.com.au/iie.htm
Notes	This commercial CALL program is in Australian English; it includes eight modules at each of four ability levels. The activities in each unit build off of a video clip. Students and teachers can request a demo CD-ROM at the Web site above.

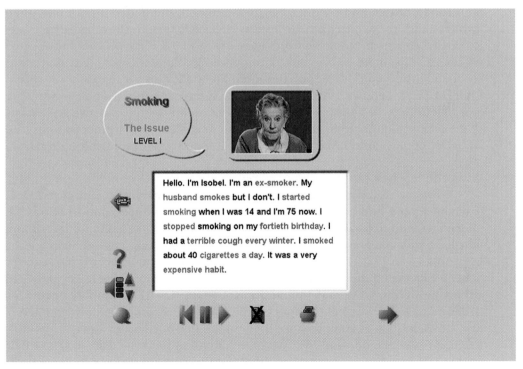

Figure 3.5 Reading passage from *Issues in English.*

Provide learners with opportunities to interact with the computer for getting help with the language in the text.

Learners interact with the computer in CALL reading materials when they click on a phrase for help with meaning, select help from a menu to obtain grammar or culture explanations, or respond to a question and receive feedback on the response. Such interactions before, during, and after reading are potentially valuable for second-language acquisition because they direct learners' attention to language (i.e., make the language salient), they raise awareness of what learners do not know, and they provide learners with help in comprehending the language.

What the research says

Researchers agree that language development is enhanced through interaction, but in most of the research on second-language acquisition, interaction refers to the back-and-forth of conversation among people. Ellis (1999), however, emphasizes that this is only one of the meanings of interaction. When learners interact with computers as they click for help and respond to questions, this is the human computer version of interaction, and Cobb and Stevens (1997) describe many other ways that learners can interact with electronic texts.

There is reason to believe that such interaction with electronic texts has benefits for second-language learners (Chapelle, 2003). Several studies have shown that when learners interact with the electronic texts by clicking for help with vocabulary, the likelihood of their remembering the words increases (Yoshii & Flaitz, 2002). Some research suggests that the more ways in which learners access the vocabulary (e.g., oral representation, image, and definition), the more likely they are to remember it (Plass, Chun, Mayer, & Leutner, 1998). The research on interaction in reading is clear: The more interaction, the more likely the learner is to acquire the language that is the focus of the interaction. However, this research also finds that many learners do not take advantage of the help available in CALL, which suggests an important role for teachers.

What the teacher can do

What can teachers do to increase their students' interaction with texts? First, teachers should look for CALL reading activities that provide opportunities for interaction with texts and the program. The amount of opportunity for interaction in reading differs among programs. Two programs containing valuable help appear in Figures 3.6 and 3.7. Second, teachers should explain to students how they can get help by clicking on the appropriate links. They also should prompt learners to take advantage of the help and interactive activities that the computer provides (Hubbard, 2004). Using help is not cheating! Third, teachers should assign interactive activities, such as comprehension questions, that accompany the text (as illustrated in Figure 3.8 on page 75). These questions and the immediate feedback that learners receive on their responses can prompt learners to go back to the texts to review and pinpoint language and ideas that were not completely clear to them the first time they were presented. In other words, they prompt additional interaction with the texts. Not all CALL reading programs provide good opportunities for inter-action, but students can be encouraged to interact with the texts if the teacher uses them for additional classroom discussion and as the basis for writing activities.

Material	*Dilemma* from Educational Activities Software
Level	Beginning to Intermediate
Description	This multimedia reading program contains stories that would be of interest to high school students and young adults. Each story begins with a short video that sets the scene for a dilemma or choice a person might face. As illustrated in Figure 3.6, learners can interact with the computer by click-ing on the icons at the bottom of the screen. For example, by clicking on the picture of the ear, learners hear key vocabulary. Notice that this program also highlights key words, as discussed in Tip 2.
Web site	http://www.ea-software.com/reading5.shtml
Notes	The review of this commercial program in TESOL's *CALL-IS Software List* states that it is "useful for ESL false beginners and above" (Healey & Johnson, 2004). Again, note the inclusion of multimedia—video is a key part of this program. The Web site above provides product information. Click on "Links" to see sample Web activity worksheets for other software programs.

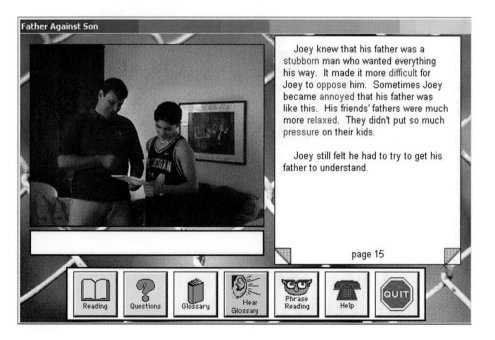

Figure 3.6 Interactive vocabulary in a reading passage from *Dilemma*.

Material	*OpenBook ESL* from OpenBook Learning
Level	Beginning to Advanced
Description	The beginning curriculum of this phonics-based software program includes "chapters" on basic literacy, stories, vocabulary, and assessment. Each chapter is made up of many pages that contain several different kinds of activities. In Figure 3.7, learners interact with the computer by typing in letters in this cloze-type activity. Learners could be encouraged to read each sentence aloud. Learners who find it difficult to decode the words can click on an individual word to hear it pronounced and to see a phonemic transcription of the word in the text. Learners can click in the boxes on the left to hear the individual sounds.
Web site	http://www.openbooklearning.com/ESL-instruction.html
Notes	The transcription method used in this commercial program may not be exactly the same one that students have studied earlier, but this program presents and practices each phoneme individually before students move on to the activity. The Web site above provides product information only.

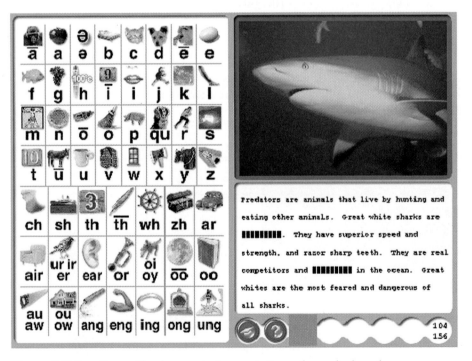

Figure 3.7 Reading with phonemic transcription of vocabulary from *OpenBook ESL*.

Material	*WebLadder* from *ReadingEnglish.net*
Level	Intermediate to Advanced
Description	This free Web site provides students with *Voice of America (VOA)* news texts that have been modified in order to have every word linked to an online dictionary. The program keeps track of every word that students click on for a translation or definition, and uses that information to rate subsequent texts for difficulty based on the number of new words a student will encounter. On the far left of Figure 3.8, all of the words in a reading are listed and linked to a dictionary. In the center, the adapted *VOA* reading text is shown. On the right, the dictionary pop-up is shown, displaying the English definition of *agriculture* because that word was clicked on in the text.
Web site	http://www.readingenglish.net/students/
Notes	To use this free program, click on "Search" or "Review" on the home page. Then, new users click on "Here" to set up a user name and password. Dictionary translations are available in Arabic, Chinese, English, French, Japanese, Korean, Russian, Spanish, and Thai. Another version of this program, *TextLadder*, can be downloaded for free at http://www.readingenglish.net/software.

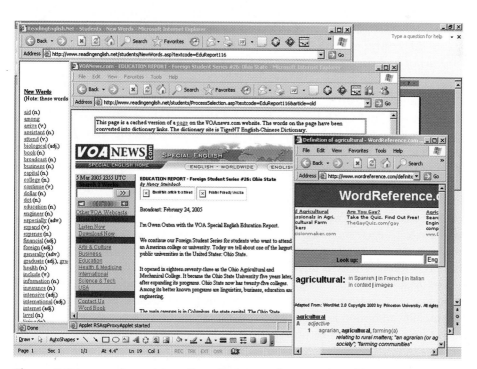

Figure 3.8 Interaction with online dictionary from *WebLadder*.

Let the text on the screen spark interaction among learners.

Reading a text is often the starting point in a series of activities. The reading selection provides the initial language and ideas that the learners summarize, discuss, or reformulate through writing or discussion. Reading at the computer is often ideal for starting discussion among small groups of learners as they sit around the computer screen. Many CALL programs provide texts that learners can read together, and the teacher can provide an assignment that requires learners to discuss the text and work with the language of the text. Learners can work together to check predictions, seek additional information and help, cut and paste the text to produce a glossary, and outline a new text.

What the research says

Reading can be a social activity entailing a combination of reading from the screen, talking to others in the class, and e-mailing others outside the class (Kern, 2000). Teachers and researchers find that the types of assistance learners receive in such reading-based conversations are valuable for their language development (Klingner & Vaughn, 2000). Research suggests that CALL activities are particularly interesting in this respect because the computer provides a dynamic contribution to the learners' conversations (Abraham & Liou, 1991; Jeon-Ellis, Debski, & Wigglesworth, 2005; Mohan, 1992). For example, if two or three learners are working together at a computer, when the computer poses a question or problem, the students can begin to answer by discussing the solution. They can enter their solution and see how the computer responds. This response, in turn, creates another opportunity for discussion. Any type of reading activity that learners might do individually at the computer can be turned into a helping conversation by adding another learner or two.

What the teacher can do

Teachers can find CALL reading activities that lend themselves well to group reading and collaborative activity and provide prereading, reading, and postreading activities. Some CALL programs and Web sites include guidance for such activities, but if they do not, teachers can supplement the CALL reading with pair or small-group work, having students make predictions, summarize, or relate the reading to their personal experiences. In such activities, particularly in larger groups, guidance is needed to ensure that all members of the group participate. This can be done by assigning a role to each member of the group (e.g., typist, note taker, and reporter) and having students take turns performing each role. One site that encourages discussion as a prereading activity is illustrated in Figure 3.9. Postreading activities may ask students to discuss what they have read and produce a consensus opinion or a set of images and key points from the reading. The teacher can look for CALL reading materials that include an option for students to post their opinions to a "discussion board." One such site is illustrated in Figures 3.10 and 3.11 on pages 78 and 79.

Material	*English Language Centre Study Zone* from the University of Victoria Web site
Level	Intermediate
Description	This Web site has several activities associated with five different readings about "wild children." The screen shot in Figure 3.9 shows a prereading activity about Emily Carr. Before reading the story, students are given opportunities for interaction. They activate their background knowledge by asking each other if they know who Emily Carr is. They activate their observation skills by guessing what kind of person she was and why she was a "wild child." Students can work in small groups to discuss or write down their ideas, and then share them with other groups in class so that they don't just click and go.
Web site	http://web2.uvcs.uvic.ca/elc/studyzone/
Notes	This free Web site has reading activities at different levels. This one is from Level 490, Wild Children, Part Four.

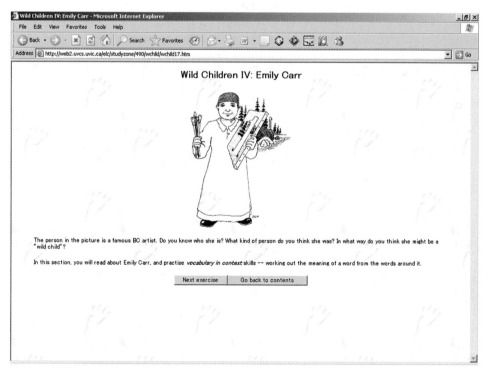

Figure 3.9 Prereading "Wild Children" exercise provides opportunity for interaction.

Material	*TOPICS*, Online Magazine
Level	Intermediate
Description	*TOPICS* is an online magazine written by ESL students for ESL students, and it contains content that is generally of interest to students. Figure 3.10 shows the title page of a section on academic dishonesty that contains links to articles written by a number of students. Students can read and discuss the articles in class and then collaborate to compose an entry for the forum section of this Web site, thereby interacting with other students outside of their classroom. Note that one of the links in Figure 3.10 is "Send us your opinion." Once submitted, students' comments are subsequently available for review by others by clicking on "Readers Respond," a link on the magazine's title page. Figure 3.11 shows a screen shot of students' opinions about academic dishonesty.
Web site	http://www.topics-mag.com/readers/cheating-forum.htm
Notes	The student forum page is accessed through the Web address above. Click on "Issue 13," Academic Dishonesty, to access the articles. This free Web site provides students the opportunity to write personal responses to a variety of the articles.

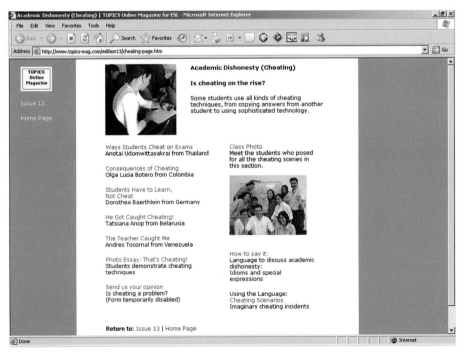

Figure 3.10 *TOPICS* issue about academic dishonesty.

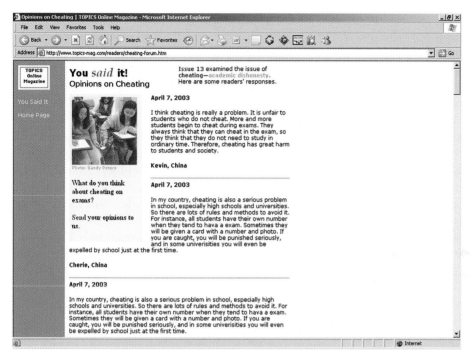

Figure 3.11 Students' responses to articles about academic dishonesty from *TOPICS*.

5 **Choose CALL materials that teach English through reading.**

Learners read English for many different purposes, such as to find information, to enjoy a story, and to find out about current events. In an English class, however, the most important purpose of reading is to help learners increase their knowledge of English. For this purpose, teachers should choose CALL reading materials that explicitly teach language to the students.

What the research says

A lot of research has been conducted to investigate whether or not learners can simply pick up the language without explicit teaching. The results are clear, and they are good news for teachers: Explicit teaching is better than simply letting students sink or swim on their own in reading. DeKeyser (2003) reviewed the research that investigated whether students can learn simply by exposure to the vocabulary and grammar they need to know. He found no evidence that exposure alone can positively affect learning. Moreover, research investigating whether or not learners can guess their way through the vocabulary in a reading found that readers often do not guess correctly, and end up with a poor understanding of the text and no opportunity to acquire the guessed words (Nassaji, 2003). These results support the use of some explicit instruction that can draw learners' attention to the language and help them understand new vocabulary and grammatical constructions.

What the teacher can do

Teachers should look for CALL activities that provide explicit teaching and practice with the language they want students to learn from a text. Many CALL readings have vocabulary exercises to preteach key words in the reading passage, as illustrated in Figures 3.12 and 3.13 from *Longman English Interactive*. A teacher can also choose CALL readings that focus on grammar, as shown in Figure 3.14 on page 82. However, many CALL activities fail to include sufficient explicit teaching. In such cases, the teacher should supplement the lesson by preteaching the vocabulary and foregrounding the reading in the CALL materials. Follow-up activities that the teacher might include can focus on the vocabulary, syntactic structures, derivational affixes, and cohesive devices found in the texts. Even when the CALL activities have some explicit language instruction, the teacher can always add to them, thereby increasing the odds that the students will remember the language they learned.

Material	*Longman English Interactive 3* from Pearson Education, Inc.
Level	Intermediate
Description	The reading section in this integrated skills program has prereading activities that focus on vocabulary learning. In Figure 3.12, the learner matches each key word from the main reading selection with its appropriate sentence-level context. The words in the exercise are included in the main passage, as shown in Figure 3.13. Additionally, learners can click on "Vocabulary Help" for more information (in this case to see a definition).
Web site	http://www.pearsonlongman.com/ae/multimedia/programs/lei3_4.htm
Notes	There are British and American versions of this commercially available program. This example is from the American English program. A sample unit with a similar example can be downloaded from the Web site above.

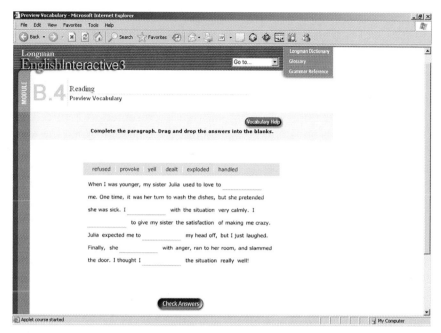

Figure 3.12 Explicit instruction of vocabulary in a prereading exercise from *Longman English Interactive 3*.

Figure 3.13 Reading that includes vocabulary from a prereading exercise from *Longman English Interactive 3*.

Material   *Click into English* from Clarity Language Consultants, Ltd.

Level   Intermediate

Description   This integrated skills program has several activities in each unit. One activity focuses on listening and reading, and it includes explicit grammar instruction. A reading passage is presented in Figure 3.14 with some words and phrases highlighted in a blue font. When the word "has" is clicked on, a dialog box opens with an explanation of why the simple present tense is used. Then the program instructs the learner to find six other verbs in the present tense. Also, explanations are available to the learner by clicking on the "Grammar" icon on the right.

Web site   http://www.clarity.com.hk/program/clickintoenglish.htm

Notes   This commercial program was produced in partnership with Australia's Adult Multicultural Education Service. It has three different levels. The Web site above provides product and purchase information only.

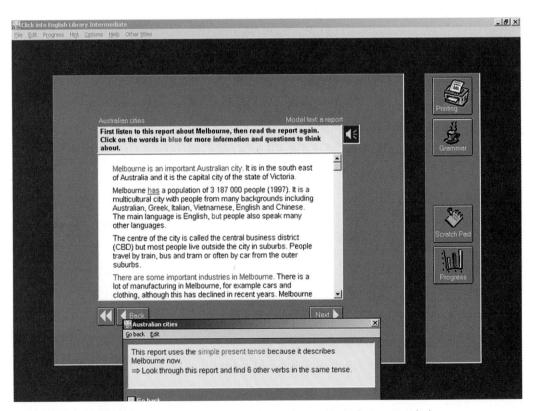

Figure 3.14 Explicit explanation of verb tense usage in *Click into English.*

6 **Include evaluation of learners' comprehension and language knowledge.**

Evaluation in a CALL program helps focus learners' attention on what they should be learning while they are reading and points out what they do not know after they have worked on reading activities. Teachers should look for two types of evaluation in CALL for reading. The first type of evaluation takes place at the point the learner responds to questions and other activities. Such evaluation should provide feedback about correctness, and ideally more information to help learners understand their errors. The second type of evaluation occurs at the end of a unit of instruction, where a summary score about performance on that unit can be given. Both types of evaluation should help learners and teachers make decisions about subsequent choices for instruction, and they are expected to help in the process of learning.

What the research says

Most researchers would agree that evaluation plays an important role in learners' acquisition of the vocabulary and grammar that they are taught through reading. Feedback on individual responses is important for learning because it directs learners' attention to parts of the reading that they do not understand, and therefore, such feedback helps to identify gaps in learners' second-language knowledge (Swain, 1998). When students realize that they do not know something, they are in the position to seek the answer and ultimately attain the knowledge that they lack. Ideally, CALL programs would provide feedback on why responses are incorrect, and some do, but the majority of them simply indicate that a response is incorrect. This should help prompt learners to try to figure out where the problem lies.

Evaluation that occurs at the end of a unit as a quiz or test is valuable because of the effects it can have on students' learning. Researchers who study the washback effects of tests find that students and teachers are influenced in what they learn and teach by the fact that they know a test is coming up (Alderson & Hamp-Lyons, 1996). This research has focused on the potential negative effects of high-stakes tests, whereas in CALL, we are interested in the potential positive effects of low-stakes tests. In other words, evaluation can be used to motivate students to study the material and guide them to review what they did not learn the first time. Nevertheless, what is important is the idea that assessment during or after instruction can affect learning.

What the teacher can do

Teachers should carefully examine how evaluation takes place in CALL reading programs because they vary considerably in the extent to which they provide useful and timely feedback. Learners' immediate knowledge of the correctness of their answers should heighten their perceptions of their reading abilities. One example of immediate feedback on an exercise from *Click into English* is illustrated in Figure 3.15 on page 84. Another example is provided in Figure 3.16 on page 85 from

Material	*Click into English* from Clarity Language Consultants, Ltd.
Level	Intermediate
Description	This Australian integrated skills program also includes reading-for-main-idea exercises in which students' answers are immediately evaluated. In Figure 3.15, the wrong answer results in three actions: a sound that indicates a mistake was made, a pop-up box in which the correct answer is explained, and a change in the color of the incorrect selection from black to red. The learner may return to the item and make the correct selection.
Web site	http://www.clarity.com.hk/program/clickintoenglish.htm
Notes	This commercial program was produced in partnership with Australia's Adult Multicultural Education Service. It provides immediate feedback on incorrect answers, with detailed reasons why the answers are incorrect. The Web site above provides product and purchase information only.

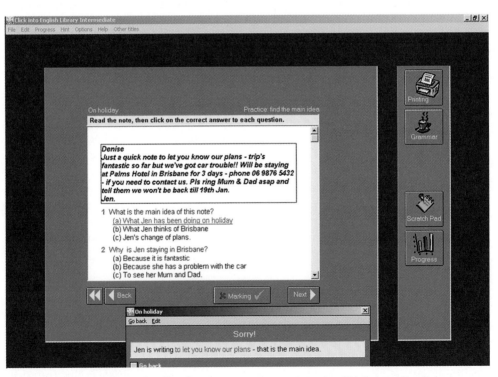

Figure 3.15 Immediate feedback to incorrect response in *Click into English.*

Material	*Longman English Interactive 3* from Pearson Education, Inc.
Level	Intermediate
Description	This integrated skills program provides learners with evaluation of their reading comprehension in a unit quiz. In Figure 3.16, reading is only one part of the quiz; learners are shown the number of items answered correctly and the total number of items in each part. Once the learner sees the progress report for the entire quiz, he or she can click on a part, such as reading, to see the corrected version. In Figure 3.17, the reading quiz shows the correct answers with a green check.
Web site	http://www.pearsonlongman.com/ae/multimedia/programs/lei3_4.htm
Notes	Knowledge of correct answers is important in the learning process, but teachers should encourage students to consider both their answers and the correct answers. Teachers can also follow up this type of quiz with an in-class or homework assignment, such as writing a summary of the reading. Sample units can be downloaded from the Web site.

For a demonstration of students using this program, see the CD-ROM at the back of this book.

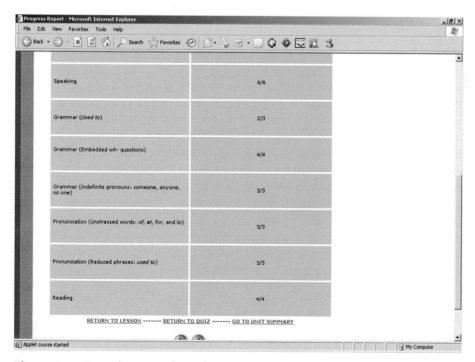

Figure 3.16 Partial screen shot of quiz progress report for *Longman English Interactive 3*.

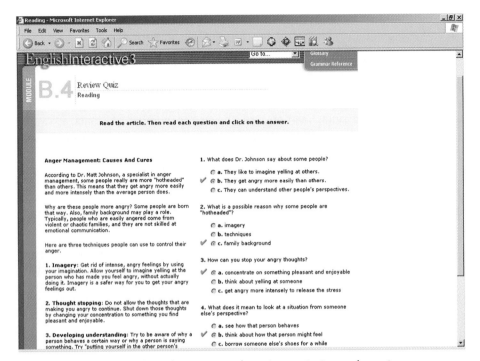

Figure 3.17 Corrected reading comprehension quiz items from *Longman English Interactive 3.*

Longman English Interactive 3. Evaluation in terms of successful completion of a unit of instruction or a program is illustrated in three ways: 1) a progress report from an end-of-unit quiz, as shown in Figure 3.16 on page 85; 2) feedback on reading comprehension questions, as shown in Figure 3.17; and 3) a cumulative progression through a reading program, as shown in Figure 3.18. The teacher should plan to use the evaluation included in CALL to complement the other forms of evaluation completed in class in which there is typically a time lag between when students take a quiz and when they obtain knowledge about the correctness of their responses. The teacher can also ask learners to write down the responses that they answered incorrectly along with the correct responses. This helps learners spend more time reflecting on their errors, particularly in cases where the CALL program provides no explanations about incorrect responses.

Material	*Reading Upgrade* from Learning Upgrade, LLC
Level	Adult Literacy/Beginner
Description	This very beginning reading program offers ongoing evaluation of progress across levels. Learners work through a series of fifty levels, as shown in Figure 3.18. Students must get 100 points to be able to move on to the next level. Points are awarded when students give correct answers in the activities; students get seven points if they get the answer right on the first try, four points if they get the answer right on the second try, and one point if they get the correct answer on the third try or more.
Web site	http://www.learningupgrade.com/readup
Notes	While feedback at this level is appropriate for beginners, more advanced learners may want more detailed information about why their answers are incorrect. One way for teachers to add qualitative as well as quantitative feedback is to sit a bit behind learners who are using the program, watch their reactions to the feedback, and ask them questions at the end of the lesson.

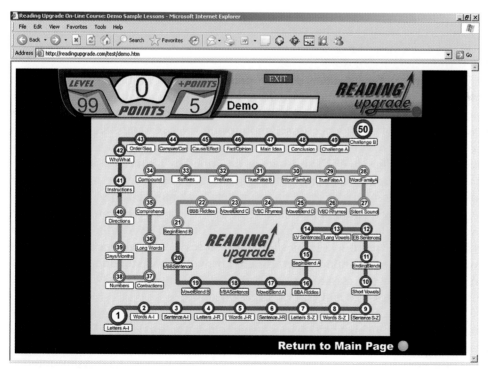

Figure 3.18 The fifty levels of *Reading Upgrade.*

Help learners develop their strategies for reading online.

Most English teachers recognize that English language learners are preparing for a life of reading in English through a variety of modes including both paper and electronic texts. Many of the strategies that learners develop through reading in CALL activities will serve them well as they read from electronic texts and paper texts in the future. Therefore, teachers should attempt to help learners develop not only good learning and reading strategies, but also the range of strategies required for reading and working with texts online. These strategies include using online tools for help comprehending online texts.

What the research says

Research in this area is not very advanced. Rather than finding effective ways to teach online reading strategies, researchers have been attempting to identify what those strategies are (e.g., Chun, 2001). Many literacy researchers refer to multimodal literacy to express the range of literacy abilities that learners need (Kress, 2004; Tyner, 1998). Warschauer (2000) points out that what we used to think of as reading might better be called reading/research, to express the reality that reading online has a strategic dimension. Reading on the Web means searching and evaluating the results of searches, quickly scanning lists of results to decide if a search was successful, clicking on several of the results to look at them quickly, and finally, choosing one or more pieces that satisfy the search. These are some of the skills that are used routinely when reading on the Web.

What the teacher can do

Teachers can help students develop strategies that they can use in the future for learning through CALL on their own, for reading in general, and for reading online. One of the strategies that students can learn is self-monitoring. To help students develop a sense of confidence in self-monitoring their reading skills, teachers can encourage them to estimate how many questions they answered correctly before having the computer check their results, as described by Tarone and Yule (1989).

Reading strategies that are useful for both paper and online reading include understanding the main idea and important details, skimming and scanning, restatement and inference, and summarizing. One way that a teacher can help students develop their reading strategies is by making use of language learning software that accompanies their textbooks, as is shown in Figure 3.19. Heightened awareness of how to go about skimming texts effectively will serve students well beyond the boundaries of the classroom. An example of skimming in a Web exercise is illustrated in Figures 3.20 and 3.21 on pages 90 and 91.

Strategies that are useful for online reading include using readily available monolingual and bilingual dictionaries, using translation services, and copying notes from a passage and storing them in word processing files. The last strategy must be taught through the use of electronic resources; one such application is illustrated in Figure 3.22 on page 92.

Material	*Shining Star* from Pearson Education, Inc.
Level	Intermediate—Secondary School
Description	The CD-ROM that accompanies this ESL literacy textbook series explicitly involves students in strategy training. In the activity illustrated in Figure 3.19, students' metacognitive awareness is heightened as they consider the activities involved in skimming.
Web site	http://www.pearsonlongman.com/ae/shiningstar/index.html
Notes	This is an example of companion software, for which a multimedia CALL program has been developed to accompany a textbook. The program could be used separately. Teachers can click on "Contact Us" to order a desk copy at the Web site above.

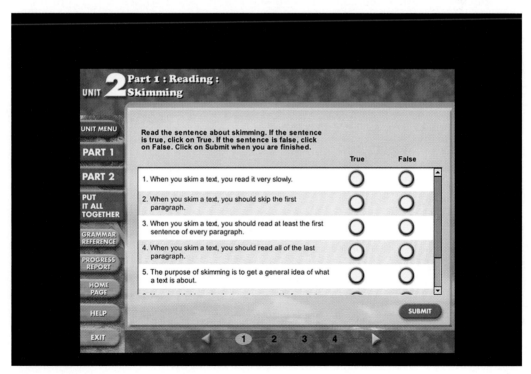

Figure 3.19 Exercise to develop awareness of skimming strategies from *Shining Star.*

Material	*English Language Centre Study Zone* from the University of Victoria Web site
Level	Intermediate
Description	This Web site contains a variety of exercises on different reading topics. An example of practice with reading strategies is shown in Figure 3.20. In this skimming exercise, students are given two minutes to identify the main idea in each of the five paragraphs of a reading. When the student clicks the "Start the exercise" button in the top right-hand pane of the screen, the passage will appear in the left-hand pane, with a clock at the top of that pane that counts down from two minutes, as shown in Figure 3.21.
Web site	http://web2.uvcs.uvic.ca/elc/studyzone/
Notes	This free Canadian Web site has reading activities at different levels; this one is from 570. This activity, like many available on the Web, was made with a program called HotPotatoes, also from the University of Victoria at http://hotpot.uvic.ca/.

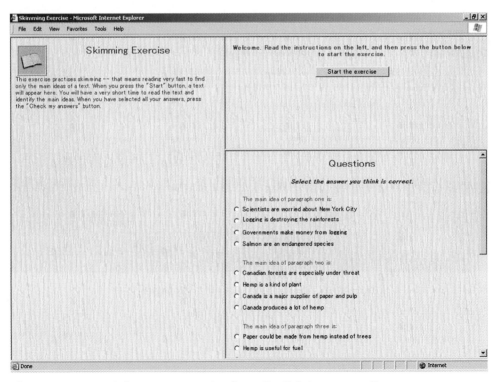

Figure 3.20 Timed skimming exercise from *English Language Centre Study Zone*.

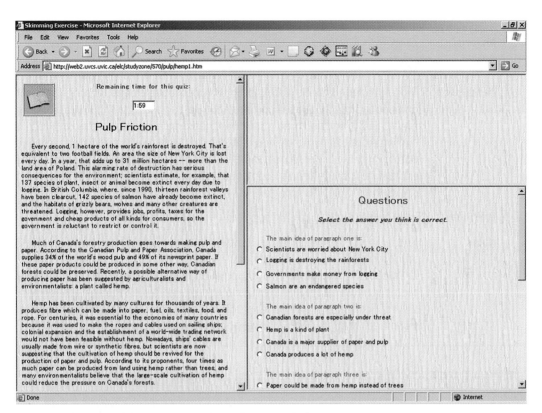

Figure 3.21 Timed skimming exercise from *English Language Centre Study Zone.*

Material	*Click into English* from Clarity Language Consultants, Ltd.
Level	Intermediate
Description	This integrated skills CALL program also encourages strategy use for online reading. It does so by providing a "scratch pad." The display in Figure 3.22 shows three screens: a reading passage on the top left; a summary of the unit on the bottom left; and the scratch pad on the bottom right. Students can use the scratch pad to take notes. Directions explain how students can copy and paste exercises into the scratch pad (by highlighting and using CTRL + C and then CTRL + V).
Web site	http://www.clarity.com.hk/program/clickinto english.htm
Notes	The Web site above provides product and purchase information only. If students click on the "File" menu in the scratch pad, one of the choices is "Ideas." The teacher could encourage students to implement metacognitive strategies such as planning, goal setting, and assessment by responding to the questions under these ideas, or by making a similar worksheet that students can respond to in their journals.

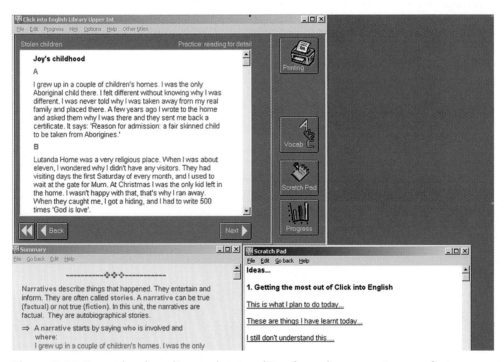

Figure 3.22 Example of reading and note taking from the upper-intermediate level of *Click into English.*

FINDING GOOD READING ACTIVITIES

Examples in this chapter illustrate some of the potential for using CALL for reading, but not all reading materials offer the language learning opportunities that we have described. If learners are expected to apply the language learning benefits of CALL for reading, teachers might select reading software that reflects the points outlined in this chapter. Teachers can use the tips in this chapter to choose the most appropriate reading software by using the questions summarized in the table.

What to look for	Focus questions
Learner fit	Does the language of the reading activities fit the learners in terms of level, topics, and activities?
	Does the program provide a means of matching the learners to the appropriate level of language?
Vocabulary and grammar	Do the activities help learners focus on particular linguistic aspects of the reading?
Interaction with the computer	Do the activities provide opportunities for learners to interact with the computer to receive help?
Interaction with other learners	Do the activities guide learners to work with classmates and contribute to online discussions?
	Can you imagine other collaborative activities you could develop based on the materials?
Explicit language teaching	Do the activities provide explicit instruction to teach specific linguistic points found in the texts?
	Does the program come with materials to help you preteach and develop follow-up activities?
Two types of evaluation	Do the activities provide *feedback* to learners about their responses?
	Does the program provide evaluation of learning outcomes through *quizzes* that give learners information about their performance?
Strategy development	Do the activities promote good language learning strategies?
	Do the activities promote good reading strategies?
	Do the activities provide guidance in helping learners develop strategies that will help them work with electronic texts outside of class?

CONCLUSION

The examples in this chapter show some of the ways that teachers can use CALL reading activities to improve the process of language development through explicit focus on relevant linguistic features of texts, offering learners new forms of interaction, providing individualized instruction and evaluation, and helping to develop their strategies for working with texts. These techniques for language instruction offered by CALL have the potential to add significantly to the quality of the time that learners spend reading in English by enriching the language experience that is possible through paper materials while acculturating them to the world of electronic texts. Learners will have the opportunity to expand their reading strategies through the foundation of electronic reading skills that they have learned in class. As not all CALL materials include every opportunity for learning described in this chapter, the teacher can usually augment the materials with additional activities, working with the texts that are provided in the materials.

CHAPTER 4

WRITING

Writing is an important skill for ESL students because it is used in everyday communication (such as e-mail), as well as for academic work at all levels. Most ESL students work on their writing all of their lives—even after they have studied at an English-medium university. Helping students become effective writers is the goal of many ESL classes around the world. Many researchers point out that in addition to being an end goal, effective writing is valuable for language acquisition. The discussion of CALL for writing in this chapter focuses on both the learners' needs to increase their abilities to communicate effectively through written language and the potential of writing practice to develop learners' language abilities.

Effective communication requires the writer to think about the audience and the purpose of the writing in order to choose appropriate language. In the process of choosing what to say to get a message across to a particular audience, a writer stops to think about the form of the language that is needed to express the idea, a process that is important for language development. When writers stop to find the word they need or struggle to get a verb form correct, for example, they are engaging in the type of reflection that most teachers and researchers would say is essential for language development.

Another benefit of writing is that it requires students to test their knowledge of the precise orthographic and morphological forms of the language. Writers cannot write down a word if they have only a partial memory of how it is written (e.g., it starts with "c"). What happens when writers do not know how to write something correctly? Their attention is drawn to the linguistic features that they do not know or have not mastered. This chapter presents six tips for using CALL in writing instruction and highlights the factors about writing that make it particularly valuable for language development.

TIPS FOR TEACHING WRITING WITH CALL

The six tips described in this chapter are drawn from the more general points of intersection between second-language (L2) acquisition and CALL, as outlined in the Introduction. Each of the tips is explained and illustrated by CALL activities for writing.

TIPS

1. Select appropriate writing texts as models.
2. Choose CALL that teaches genre as well as linguistic knowledge and strategies.
3. Teach learners how to benefit from interactive help and feedback from the computer.
4. Create opportunities to expand knowledge of English through writing and to write for a real audience.
5. Include explicit evaluation.
6. Help learners develop their writing strategies.

Throughout the rest of the chapter, each of these six tips are explained with

- a description of *what it means* for the teacher who is using CALL for writing,
- a summary of *what the research says* about the tip, and
- a suggestion of *what teachers can do* in the classroom.

Along with each tip, illustrations of CALL activities from published CALL software and Web sites are provided. The Web addresses are given so that readers can visit them to try out the activities.

FEATURE: Examples of how to use one type of writing software and one writing Web site are on the CD-ROM at the back of this book. They include a demonstration of Tip 6 and a simulation of Tip 1.

1 Select appropriate writing texts as models.

The model texts that may be of most value to ESL writers contain examples of the language and genre-specific conventions of English writing from the appropriate levels. If students are attempting to write e-mails requesting tourist information, letters of application, or essays about what they did last weekend, for example, they can see some examples of these genres and study the vocabulary and grammar that the writers used for each purpose. If a student is attempting to write a letter of request, it does not help him or her much to look at an essay about what someone did over the weekend. Further, it is not very useful for low-level students to look at the complex language of a technical book. The teacher must examine and select the written models in CALL activities that fit the learners' linguistic levels. The challenge is to identify materials that contain language that is useful for constructing the genre that is being taught and that contain language the learner is ready to learn.

What the research says

Model texts must reflect the genre that the students are being taught. Paltridge (2001) explains a genre approach to language teaching that seems particularly useful for the teaching of writing. *Genre* refers to the linguistic conventions that are used to perform particular functions. For example, "I am writing to apply for the job that was advertised" must be modeled for learners if they are to learn to write a letter for a job application. Paltridge (2001) refers to a number of studies that show the value of this approach, and asserts that learners' analysis of model texts makes such texts easier for them to understand and, therefore, to learn from. Bhatia (1993) refers to such analyses by learners as *easification* of the text. Easification is a learning strategy that helps learners gain access to texts that contain genre-specific language they need to learn, but that is too difficult for them.

What the teacher can do

At the beginning levels, it may be difficult to find writing models intended to help students with particular genres of writing, but teachers can find programs that vary according to difficulty level. For example, Figure 4.1 on page 98 shows a Web site with essays labeled "easier," "moderately difficult," and "the most difficult." For more advanced students, teachers might also search for Web sites that have models of particular rhetorical organizations of writing, as shown in Figures 4.2 and 4.3 on pages 99 and 100. For advanced learners studying English for academic purposes, excellent models of genre-specific language, such as that used to write an abstract in biology, or to introduce a methods section in anthropology, can be found in the many electronic journals on the Web. The teacher must provide guidance to help learners identify the specific language that authors use in the various genres of writing.

Material	*Easy Writer*
Level	Low Intermediate to Advanced
Description	This software program color codes over eighty-five essays that were written by ESL students, so that students can select texts that match their linguistic levels. Figure 4.1 displays a screen shot from *Easy Writer's* Web site. The essays contain different types of grammar and spelling errors that students must find—and at the more advanced level, correct. Each unit ends with a section in which students can reference the model as they write their own essays. Students are encouraged to have their classmates edit their writing.
Web site	http://www.softwareforstudents.com/
Notes	The software has an optional textbook: *Grammar HELP! Student Handbook.* Both of these commercial products can be seen at the Web site. Scroll down and click on "Easy Writer" sample pages to get a feel for this program.

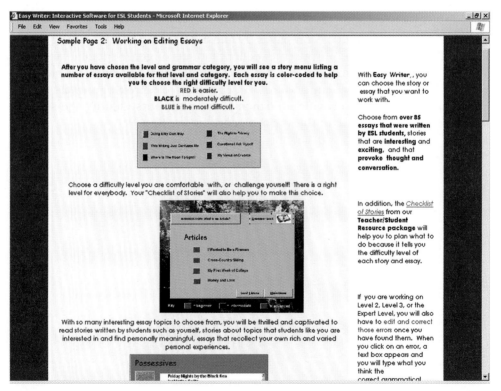

Figure 4.1 Example of *Easy Writer's* essay choices.

Material	*WriteFix* from The Argument and Opinion Essay Writing Web site
Level	High Intermediate to Advanced
Description	The home page in Figure 4.2 illustrates the structure of this Web site. Students can read about how to write argumentative essays and what the parts of an essay are, and they can view a number of model essays, as illustrated in the drop-down menu. The lengths of the model essays are between 250 and 400 words. Figure 4.3 shows a model essay about the value of education. The drop-down menu listing the parts of an essay provides learners with explanations and example sentences of language that is used in argumentative essays.
Web site	http://www.writefix.com/argument/
Notes	The target audience for this free Web site is IELTS™ or TOEFL® test-takers, and it can also be adapted for classroom use. A downloadable version is available at the Web site above.

⊙ **For a simulation that guides you through this program, see the CD-ROM at the back of this book.**

Figure 4.2 Example of *WriteFix's* models of argumentative essays.

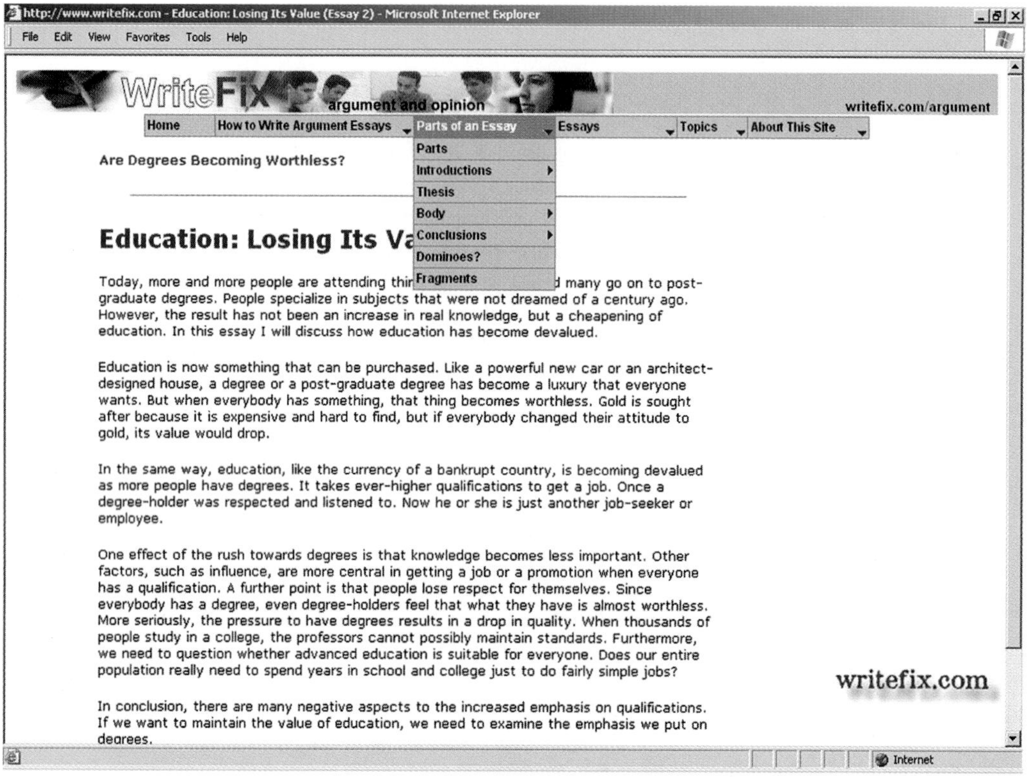

Are Degrees Becoming Worthless?

Education: Losing Its Va

Today, more and more people are attending thir[...]d many go on to post-graduate degrees. People specialize in subjects that were not dreamed of a century ago. However, the result has not been an increase in real knowledge, but a cheapening of education. In this essay I will discuss how education has become devalued.

Education is now something that can be purchased. Like a powerful new car or an architect-designed house, a degree or a post-graduate degree has become a luxury that everyone wants. But when everybody has something, that thing becomes worthless. Gold is sought after because it is expensive and hard to find, but if everybody changed their attitude to gold, its value would drop.

In the same way, education, like the currency of a bankrupt country, is becoming devalued as more people have degrees. It takes ever-higher qualifications to get a job. Once a degree-holder was respected and listened to. Now he or she is just another job-seeker or employee.

One effect of the rush towards degrees is that knowledge becomes less important. Other factors, such as influence, are more central in getting a job or a promotion when everyone has a qualification. A further point is that people lose respect for themselves. Since everybody has a degree, even degree-holders feel that what they have is almost worthless. More seriously, the pressure to have degrees results in a drop in quality. When thousands of people study in a college, the professors cannot possibly maintain standards. Furthermore, we need to question whether advanced education is suitable for everyone. Does our entire population really need to spend years in school and college just to do fairly simple jobs?

In conclusion, there are many negative aspects to the increased emphasis on qualifications. If we want to maintain the value of education, we need to examine the emphasis we put on degrees.

Figure 4.3 Model essay about the value of education from *WriteFix*.

Choose CALL that teaches genre as well as linguistic knowledge and strategies.

Teaching students how to write particular genres is accomplished ideally by emphasizing the language used to perform the functions of those genres. If learners are trying to write a letter of application, for example, they should not have to guess which opening sentence to choose for signaling the appropriate politeness! The linguistic forms used to express particular functions should be emphasized through explicit teaching, highlighting, and repetition.

What the research says

Research and experience suggest that learners do not simply pick up the important linguistic expressions that they need, so emphasis on the relevant language is important for learning. Much of the research on teaching genre-specific language was motivated by the need to help international scholars gain access to the "discourse community" of academic writers. Swales's (1991) analysis of the research article demonstrated the specific generic conventions that must be taught explicitly through examination of the language used to accomplish specific purposes. Today most researchers and linguists would agree that learners must be taught to write by focusing on the language that is required for accomplishing specific purposes.

What the teacher can do

Teachers can use CALL programs that provide models that highlight forms used in a particular type of writing, such as language use in postcards, as illustrated on page 102 in Figure 4.4 from *Click into English*. The postcard writer chooses incomplete sentences to convey news in the shortest form possible, including only the essential words and grammatical forms. Figure 4.5 on page 103 from *Click into English* shows an example of an opinion essay that a teacher might use to draw the students' attention to specialized language in preparation for an opinion writing assignment. Figures 4.6 and 4.7 on pages 104 and 105 show activities that explicitly guide students to write a paragraph. Teachers can find many Web sites offering individual lessons about the organization of essays. Such lessons emphasize the grammatical choices that writers make to express particular rhetorical purposes. These might serve as good models for particular types of writing assignments. The Web is a source for many examples of the language used to express specific purposes. Teachers can find examples of newspaper articles, opinions, advertisements, and academic papers—all of which are potential language lessons for teachers who can select and explain the language that is important to the genre.

Material	*Click into English* from Clarity Language Consultants, Ltd.
Level	Intermediate
Description	In this CALL program, students begin each unit by reading and listening to a model text. As is shown in Figure 4.4, the relevant language of a postcard is emphasized in blue font, which can be clicked on. When the letter "v" is clicked on, the use of abbreviations in postcards is explained in a new screen shot. Students use the information in the model to write their own postcards and print them out for their teacher. Another feature of the explanations given in this software is that the student is asked to look for other examples of the language in the model text.
Web site	http://www.clarity.com.hk/program/clickinto english.htm
Notes	The Web site above provides product and purchase information only.

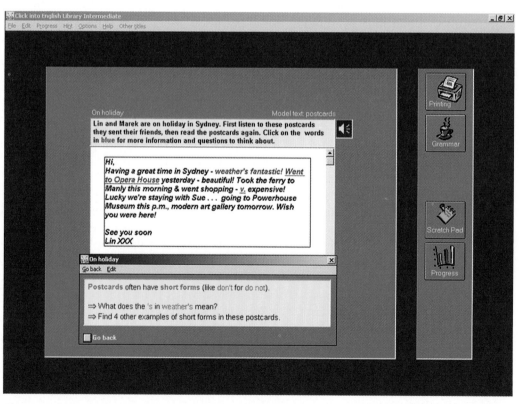

Figure 4.4 Example of relevant language usage in postcards from *Click into English.*

Material	*Click into English* from Clarity Language Consultants, Ltd.
Level	Intermediate
Description	One of the exercises available to learners in all of the units in this program is called "Text Structure and Grammar." Genre and linguistic help is provided to enhance the model opinion text in Figure 4.5. In this example, the learner clicked on the grammar icon on the right of the screen to open the pop-up box that explains the functions of the paragraphs and the use of particular linking words and phrases.
Web site	http://www.clarity.com.hk/program/clickintoenglish.htm
Notes	This commercial program was produced in partnership with Australia's Adult Multicultural Education Service. It has three different levels. The Web site above provides product and purchase information only.

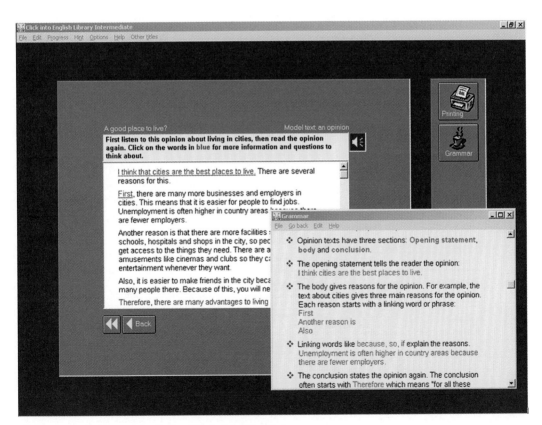

Figure 4.5 Grammar help in *Click into English.*

Material	*English-Zone.com*
Level	Intermediate
Description	This Web site offers many activities that are organized by language skills. In Figure 4.6, one lesson in the "Writing Zone" is about the parts of a paragraph, which are explained in a table at the bottom of the page. Above the table is a model paragraph. When the student clicks on a part of the paragraph, the relevant language is emphasized in a red font.
Web site	http://english-zone.com/writing/para-strctr.html
Notes	This Web site allows guests to have free access to limited materials, and paid members are allowed access to all materials.

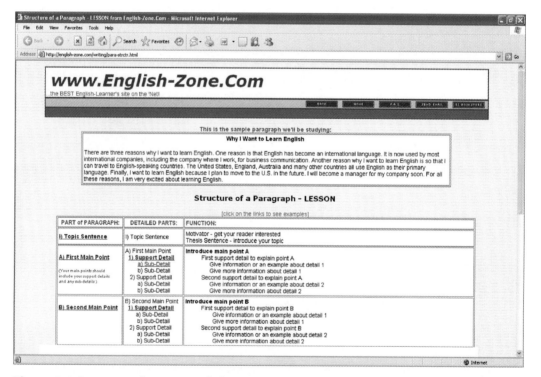

Figure 4.6 Structure of a paragraph from *English-Zone.com*.

Material	*Paragraph Punch* from Merit Software
Level	Beginning to Intermediate
Description	This program takes the student through the steps of writing a paragraph. It prompts the writer to provide words or phrases to answer questions, then to create sentences, and finally to create a paragraph. In Figure 4.7, the learner has already responded to a set of questions and is now prompted to put the words into a sentence. The program teaches linguistic and genre knowledge as it reminds the learner of the parts of a sentence, and it encourages the learner to give appropriate details.
Web site	http://www.paragraphpunch.com/
Notes	Downloadable free samples of this commercial software are available at the Web address above.

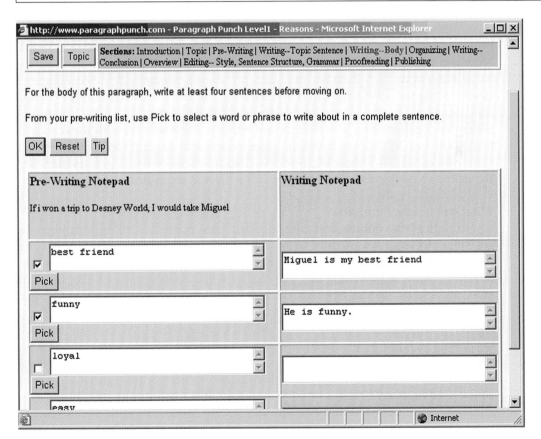

Figure 4.7 Generating sentences in *Paragraph Punch.*

**Teach learners how to benefit from interactive help
and feedback from the computer.**

When learners write at the computer, they have access to a variety of types of feedback and help. With the right software and guidance, students can get help with spelling and grammar, as well as guidance in typing word forms at the computer. The process of writing with help and feedback is beneficial for language learning because it draws learners' attention to the specific language that they are attempting to use. In particular, the vocabulary and grammar that learners do not know well become salient during the process of writing with help and feedback.

What the research says

Researchers haven't found clear evidence on the value of the feedback that teachers typically write on students' papers, but Ferris (2004) points out that under the right circumstances error correction would be expected to be effective. The right circumstances include the immediacy and quality of the feedback for making learners' errors salient, and then having the opportunity to correct these errors. The process of noting errors and working to correct them appears to be valuable for increasing learners' language ability (Doughty & Williams, 1998). Moreover, many second-language researchers would agree that a critical time for error correction is when learners are producing meaning-focused language (Swain & Lapkin, 1995). Research investigating the use of automatic error correction for second-language writing has shown that students can use the computer-generated feedback to correct errors and improve their writing with the teacher's help (Burston, 2001; Liou, 1991). In other words, it is not a good idea to restrict error correction to grammar exercises. It should also occur while learners are struggling to construct creative language to express their ideas.

What the teacher can do

Teachers can choose software that provides learners with opportunities to get help and feedback as they write. Help is available in most word processing programs. As the learner types, the spelling corrections can appear automatically. But often learners have difficulty coming up with the words they want, and so a more aggressive form of help has been developed to provide writers with word choices as they type, as illustrated with *WordQ* in Figure 4.8. For very low-level learners, teachers can find immediate feedback at the word level in programs such as *OpenBook English*, illustrated in Figure 4.9 on page 108. Teachers can also help learners use the grammar feedback in word processing programs, but more appropriate learner feedback is offered in editing tools such as *MY Access!*, shown in Figure 4.10 on page 109. It is important for teachers to remember that these writing tools offer a new form of potentially useful feedback on students writing at precisely the time in the writing process when students need it. However, most students do not know how to use such tools, so the teacher's guidance is essential.

Material	*WordQ* from Quillsoft
Level	Beginning
Description	This program is an interactive writing tool that can be used together with any word processing software. As the student types each word, a text box with choices pops up, as illustrated in Figure 4.8. The student can then refer to these choices. When a period or a question mark is typed to indicate the end of a sentence, the text-to-speech software pronounces that sentence.
Web site	http://www.wordq.com/
Notes	This commercial software predicts words and makes suggestions, but it does not correct grammar. *WordQ* includes text-to-speech, and it also has a speech recognition plug-in. A free thirty-day evaluation version can be downloaded from the Web site.

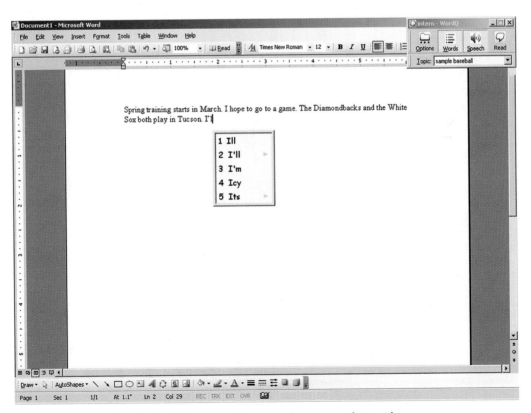

Figure 4.8 Example of *WordQ* pop-up boxes with Microsoft Word.

Material	*OpenBook English* from OpenBook Learning, Inc.
Level	Literacy–Beginner
Description	In this program, learners are taught to develop sound-symbol correspondences. One interactive writing activity is keyboarding practice, as illustrated in Figure 4.9. Here, the learner hears a voice say "Type the word *turtle*. T-U-R-T-L-E." If the student makes a mistake, the fingers on the screen move to the correct key (in this case, T), which is also highlighted in red, and the voice repeats the letter sound.
Web site	http://www.openbooklearning.com/English-Instruction.html
Notes	This commercial program also has an ESL version available at http://www.openbooklearning.com/ESL-instruction.html.

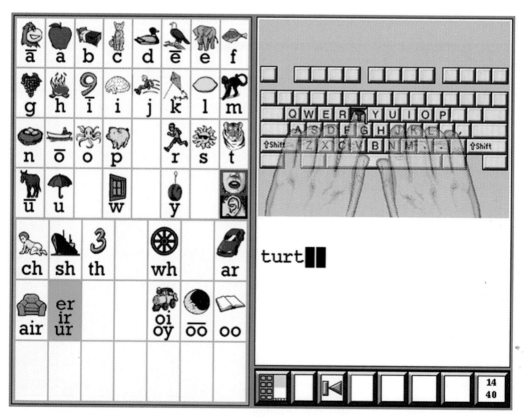

Figure 4.9 Example of a keyboarding activity for beginners in *OpenBook English.*

Material	*MY Access!* from Vantage Learning
Level	High Intermediate to Advanced
Description	This is an online program in which learners write essays based on prompts that their teachers have selected from the program's bank of writing prompts. After a learner drafts an essay, there are opportunities for interaction with the computer. A learner can check the form of the essay with an editing tool. The editing function of the program indicates words and phrases that the learner might want to change, as shown in Figure 4.10.
Web site	http://www.vantagelearning.com/myaccess/
Notes	This commercial software allows learners to work with a variety of tools, such as a thesaurus, a dictionary, and a translator (with English, Spanish, or Chinese definitions and synonyms). A free online demo and free Web demonstrations (webinars) are available at http://www.vantage.com/pdfs/demos/robo-myaccess.html.

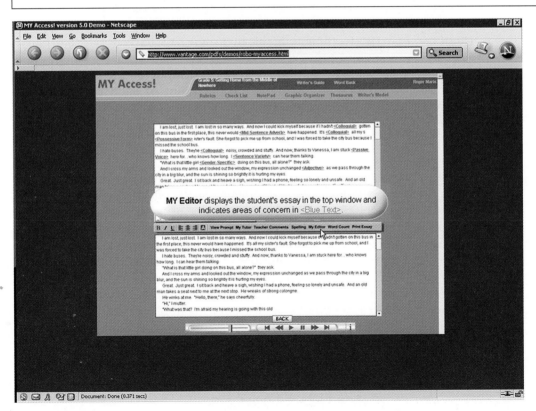

Figure 4.10 Edited version of a learner's essay from *MY Access!*

Create opportunities to expand knowledge of English through writing and to write for a real audience.

Teachers can use writing in CALL activities as a means of getting students to expand their knowledge of English and to interact among students and other people outside the classroom. Students can work on their own to put their ideas into English or work together at the computer to produce an e-mail message, a Web page, or other documents created with a word processing program. These activities typically work best if the text requires the participation of all of the learners in the group and if they can anticipate that someone will be reading what they are writing.

What the research says

Some researchers look at writing as essential for language development because it creates an opportunity for producing "comprehensible output" (Swain, 1985). Comprehensible output is not simply any production of language, but rather language production that is intended for someone to understand. Such language production is different from language produced simply for practice, or to display knowledge of language. Researchers point out that CALL opens up a lot of new opportunities for learners to write to real audiences (Egbert & Hanson-Smith, 1999; Warschauer, 1997). Researchers looking carefully at the language that learners use to write to their long-distance pen pals have noted that native speaker peers sometimes provide good feedback to learners about the level of politeness of their language, but they tend to concentrate on the message rather than offering much correction. However, the point of such exchanges—to provide a real audience for the writing—seems to work well, especially with the guidance of the teacher.

What the teacher can do

The teacher's role of facilitator is essential for bringing together students within a framework for language development. Such collaborations can begin in the classroom, where the teacher can choose a program such as *Daedalus* (shown in Figures 4.11 and 4.12), which allows students to see and edit each other's papers. Teachers can also draw upon international sites on the Web that have been set up precisely for the purpose of bringing English learners together. On such sites, each learner can be encouraged to find a pen pal, as shown on page 113 in Figure 4.13 for *Linguistic Funland*. The subsequent exchanges can be nurtured by the teacher who might ask students to bring to class examples of what they have written to and received from their pen pals. Similar to pen pals, tandem learning, which is illustrated in Figure 4.14 on page 114, pairs people who want to learn each other's languages. In all of these programs, the teacher's participation and interest in the exchange can help keep it going as a serious commitment in which learners try to put their best English forward.

Material	*Daedalus Integrated Writing Environment,* or *DIWE*, from The Daedalus Group, Inc.
Level	Intermediate to Advanced
Description	As shown in Figure 4.11, *DIWE 7* is a writing software program that has six different functions: Invent, Write, Respond, Mail, InterChange, and BiblioCite. One way learners can interact with others is by using the Respond function. One student edits another student's paper by responding to a set of questions that are presented by the computer program. In Figure 4.12, an ESL activity that describes a place is shown. The reviewer is asked to write about the place that the writer has described. If the reviewer is not sure what to do, he or she can click on the "Explain" button, as illustrated, where he or she will be prompted to just "write the basics about the location in a sentence or two." The final questions ask the reviewer to give the writer advice.
Web site	http://www.daedalus.com/
Notes	A free fully-functional thirty-day version of this commercial program can be downloaded from the Web site. Although originally designed for native speakers, *DIWE 7* has a detailed *Teacher's Guide for ESL–EFL Students*, available free. Just click on "Resources/Documentation."

Figure 4.11 Image of *DIWE 7* functions.

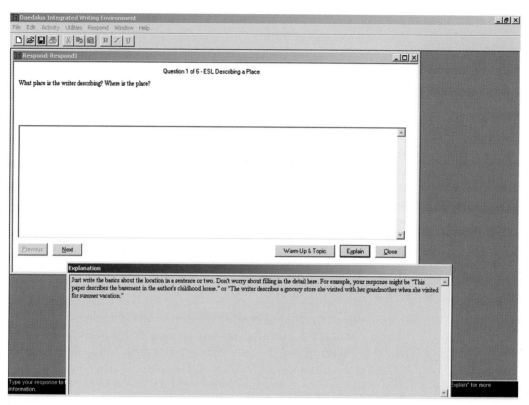

Figure 4.12 Example of the "Respond" function in *DIWE 7*.

Material	*Linguistic Funland TESL Pen Pal Center*
Level	All
Description	This Web site allows teachers to find pen pals for their students, creating opportunities for them to write for a real audience. As illustrated in Figure 4.13, a teacher in Poland is looking for English pen pals for her twelve- to fourteen-year-old students. To respond, the teacher can click on the contact's name, and then reply in a message that *Linguistic Funland* forwards to the contact. The contact then has the option to respond.
Web site	http://www.tesol.net/penpals/penpal.cgi
Notes	Information about pen pals on this free Web site can be sorted by age or language.

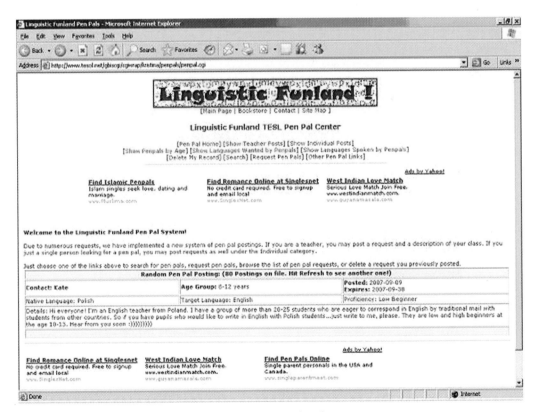

Figure 4.13 Setting up pen pals at *Linguistic Funland.*

Material	*eTandem* from the University of Sheffield Web site
Level	All
Description	As a tool for autonomous language learning, *eTandem* facilitates a partnership between two people who want to learn each other's languages. Partners spend half of the time in each other's first language. Teachers can have learners incorporate material studied in class in e-mails as they interact with their partners outside of class time, as explained on the screen shown in Figure 4.14. Because both partners are serious about learning a language, this site provides a great opportunity to write for a real audience. This site offers a free search for *eTandem* partners.
Web site	http://www.shef.ac.uk/mirrors/tandem/etandem/etlehrer-en.html
Notes	This site also provides explanations, tips, and links for using *eTandem*. The site is hosted by another server as well: http://www.slf.ruhr-uni-bochum.de/etandem/etlehrer-en.html.

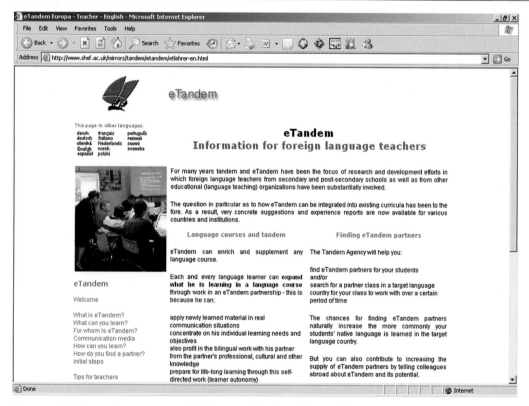

Figure 4.14 Introductory material about *eTandem* for teachers.

Include explicit evaluation.

Explicit evaluation refers to a score that is given to inform learners about the quality of their writing. It can come from other students, the teacher, or the computer. Each source of evaluation has strengths and weaknesses, but the important similarity is that they all motivate learners to write with attention directed to the quality of their language.

What the research says

Researchers in language assessment and second-language acquisition agree on the important role of assessment in the learning process (Cheng & Watanabe, 2004). Focusing on effects of individual learning, Skehan (1998) identifies evaluation as one of the factors that has been found to affect the quality of learners' production positively. The expectation that writing is going to be evaluated is likely to prompt learners to plan their time and correct their own language, both of which have been found to be positive for language development (Crookes, 1989). In short, the reflection and careful attention to language that is prompted by evaluation is important for language development.

What the teacher can do

Teachers can help learners understand how to improve their writing by helping them understand how their writing is evaluated. Teachers should make the evaluation rubric clear to students. Teachers should also provide time for students to plan for writing and to revise their writing according to the evaluation that they receive. Teachers can choose software that evaluates students' writing and then can help students revise their writing on the basis of the feedback they receive from the software. The programs shown on the following pages, in Figures 4.15, 4.16, and 4.17, provide informative feedback to the learner in categories such as grammar and organization. Most students need help in understanding how to use this feedback to improve their writing.

Material	*Criterion Online Writing Assessment* from Educational Testing Service
Level	Intermediate to Advanced
Description	This is an online program. Students write essays on topics selected from a bank. They can write the essays online or cut and paste them from another application. They then submit the essays and receive immediate feedback in the form of a holistic score, as illustrated in Figure 4.15. Diagnostic analysis is done for grammar, which is shown in Figure 4.16, as well as for usage, mechanics, style, and organization and development. The errors are highlighted; as a student moves a mouse over an error, a pop-up box gives more information about that error.
Web site	http://www.ets.org
Notes	To see a free online demo of this commercial product, scroll down the ETS home page to "Products" and click on "Criterion; Online Writing Evaluation." Then, click on "Online Tour." Free Web-based seminars are also available. The screen shots are taken from the online tour. English-language learning topics are geared to TOEFL® test-takers.

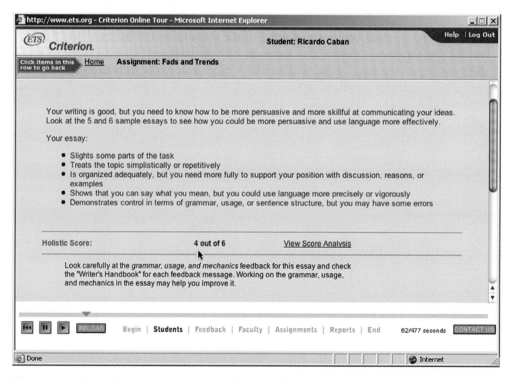

Figure 4.15 Sample screen of essay evaluation from *Criterion.*

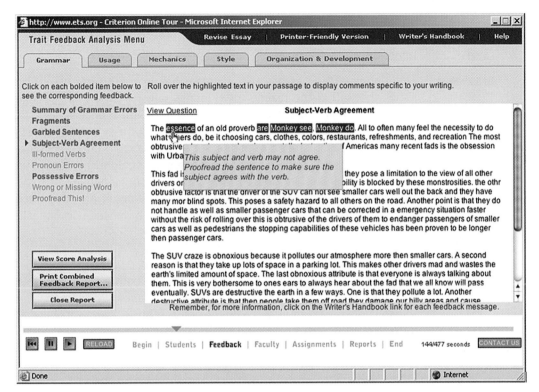

Figure 4.16 Detailed feedback on sample essay from *Criterion*.

Material	*MY Access!* from Vantage Learning
Level	Intermediate to Advanced
Description	This online writing assessment program has learners write essays on topics that either the teacher or students select from a bank. Before submitting their essays, learners are provided with a checklist of the qualities that their essays will be graded on so that they can self-assess their essays, as illustrated in Figure 4.17. The program provides immediate feedback on strengths and weaknesses in five domains: focus and meaning, organization, content and development, language use and style, and mechanics and conventions. In addition, it provides three levels of feedback—developing, proficient, and advanced—in English, Spanish, or Chinese.
Web site	http://www.vantagelearning.com/
Notes	Targets English language learners in K–12. An online demo and free Web-based seminars are available for this commercial program. The screen shots are taken from the online demo at http://www.vantage.com/pdfs/demos/robo-myaccess.html.

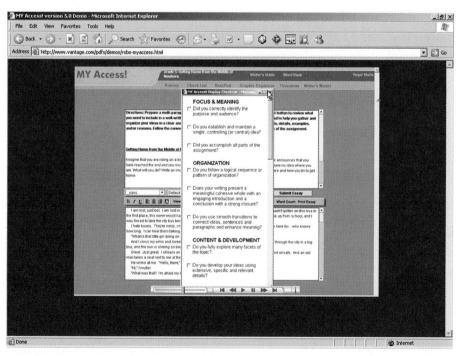

Figure 4.17 Checklist for self-assessment in *MY Access!*

6 **Help learners develop their writing strategies.**

Every writing teacher knows that good writing develops over a long period of time from the learner's growing expertise in using writing strategies. Teachers cannot teach everything, but they can teach students strategies that will help them write and improve their writing over time. Communication strategies, such as assessing the audience, planning, and evaluating the extent to which the goals are met, must be developed by beginning L2 writers if they are ultimately to learn to meet the demands of a variety of writing situations. At the same time, developing strategies for self-evaluation is essential for language acquisition through writing. Ideally, learners will use the opportunities for production of written language to reflect on the correctness of their language and to note the meanings they are not able to construct to their satisfaction.

What the research says

Researchers study writing strategies from three different angles (Grabe & Kaplan, 1996). From a psychological perspective, they focus on the process of invention and creation that learners go through in constructing ideas that they transform into language. From a sociological perspective, they study the way that the processes of negotiation, collaboration, and audience consideration affect the writing. From a linguistic perspective, researchers are interested in processes learners undertake to analyze existing texts as models, and monitor their own texts to conform to conventions of genre and correctness. All three perspectives provide insight into the demands of the writing process, and they point to the need for several different types of help from CALL.

What the teacher can do

Teachers can help learners develop all three types of strategies. Teachers can choose software that prompts learners in the process of invention, such as the examples shown in Figure 4.18 on page 120. This is particularly useful for learners who have trouble getting started with writing. The example shown in Figure 4.19 on page 121 helps learners use strategies for planning and organizing. Teachers can also help learners write and revise by using the tools provided in Microsoft Word, which provides immediate feedback about words that may be misspelled or may be grammatically incorrect. Such feedback can make learners stop and look at what they wrote. In addition to the feedback that is produced automatically by the word processor, the learner has the option of calling on help from the thesaurus, or going to the large corpus of texts on the Internet in search of examples of words and expressions of interest. The example in Figure 4.20 on page 122 provides a model essay that the learners can use as a basis for their own essays. The strategy of copying specific phrases and then modifying them will be useful for learners beyond the classroom as they learn to take advantage of the texts available on the Web. Teachers should teach students how to analyze, copy, and

Material	*Daedalus Integrated Writing Environment,* or *DIWE 7*, from The Daedalus Group, Inc.
Level	Intermediate to Advanced
Description	One useful writing strategy involves generating ideas to write about. In Figure 4.18, we see this strategy practiced as part of the "Invent" function. A set of ESL questions for describing a place is illustrated. Learners are encouraged to have an audience in mind and to write as much as they can about each question, not worrying about spelling or grammar. If they are not sure about a question, the "Explain" button will open a pop-up box for more information. When finished, students can save this file and refer to it, or cut and paste from it, when they write their essays.
Web site	http://www.daedalus.com/

For a demonstration of students using this program, see the CD-ROM at the back of this book.

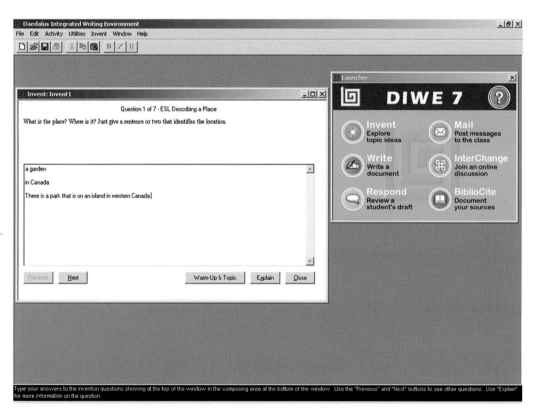

Figure 4.18 Generating ideas through the "Invent" feature of *DIWE 7*.

learn from other texts without plagiarizing. In fact, examination of linguistic models on the Web provides an ideal opportunity for teachers to explain the seriousness of plagiarism and provide guidelines about how to avoid it through the use of quotations and paraphrases.

Material	*MY Access!* from Vantage Learning
Level	Intermediate to Advanced
Description	In this program, writers are encouraged to use strategies when planning and editing their work. One writing strategy for organizing ideas is to diagram the relationships by using graphic organizers. A variety of types of graphic organizers like the one illustrated in Figure 4.19 are available for learners.
Web site	http://www.vantagelearning.com/
Notes	The screen shot in Figure 4.19 is from an online demo available at http://www.vantage.com/pdfs/demos/robo-myaccess.html.

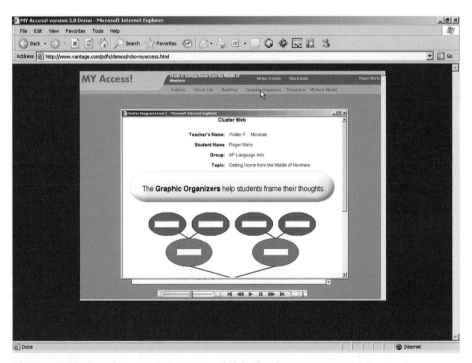

Figure 4.19 Graphic organizers available for learners at *MY Access!*

Material	*Click into English* from Clarity Language Consultants, Ltd.
Level	Intermediate
Description	In this program, the model presented to learners at the beginning of each unit can guide their writing in future exercises. One strategy for writers is to copy language from the model and the prompt, paste it into a new essay, and then make changes. This strategy is shown in Figure 4.20 from *Click into English*, where the learner is creating an opinion essay in the "Scratch Pad."
Web site	http://www.clarity.com.hk/program/clickintoenglish.htm
Notes	This commercial program was produced in partnership with Australia's Adult Multicultural Education Service. The Web site above provides product and purchase information only.

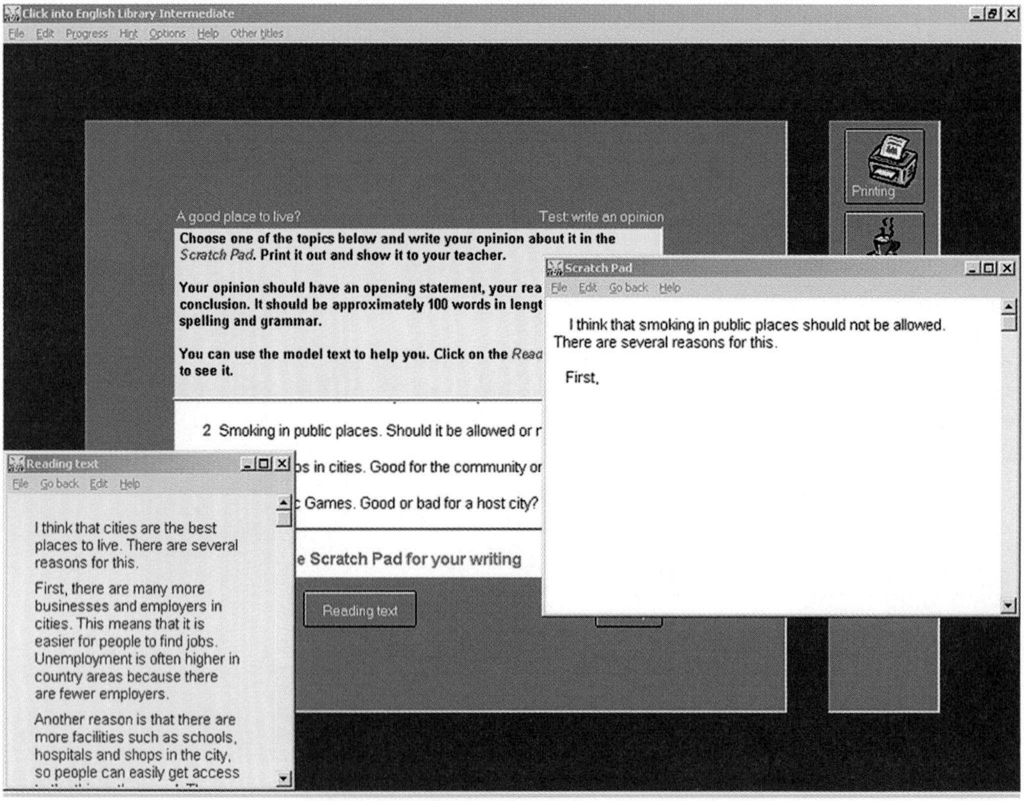

Figure 4.20 Using cut and paste as a writing strategy in *Click into English.*

FINDING GOOD WRITING ACTIVITIES

The tips provide advice for using CALL to help learners develop their writing. Some of the tips require only a word processing program and access to the Internet, but many CALL programs offer the language learning opportunities that we have described, especially for lower-level learners. Teachers selecting CALL for writing will find the points summarized in the table useful. The specific questions that one might ask are included under "Focus questions."

What to look for	Focus questions
Appropriate models	Does the program provide a means of matching the learners to the appropriate level of writing models?
	Does the language of the writing activities fit the learners in terms of level, topics, and genres?
	Does the program have sufficient examples of written forms that students need to work with?
Explicit instruction emphasizing genre and language	Do the activities help the learners focus on particular linguistic aspects that they can use in writing?
	Do the activities provide explicit instruction to teach specific linguistic points of the texts?
Interactive help and and feedback	Does the writing program have spelling and grammer checkers?
	Does the program suggest word or phrase charges?
Opportunities for a real audience	Do the activities provide opportunities for interaction between the learner and another person?
	Do writers receive help and obtain feedback from someone else?
	Do the activities provide the opportunity for learners to write texts that someone else will read and respond to?
Evaluation	Does the program provide evaluation of learning outcomes by giving learners information about their performance?
	Are there checklists to help learners self-evaluate?
Developing strategies for writing	Do the activities provide guidance for learners to develop strategies that will help them write and continue to improve outside of class?

CONCLUSION

The examples in this chapter show some of the ways that CALL can improve the process of language development through explicit focus on relevant linguistic features of texts. The activities offer learners new forms of interaction by providing them with help upon request while they are writing. CALL writing programs can provide students with individualized instruction and evaluation, and develop strategies for working with texts. While enriching the language experience that students can get from using paper materials alone, CALL writing activities also introduce students to the world of electronic texts, such as blogs and e-mail. In adding these activities to their lesson plans, teachers introduce varieties of writing that students will continue to engage in beyond the classroom.

CHAPTER 5

LISTENING

Most students complain that listening is difficult for them. Spoken language is temporary and fleeting. Unlike readers, listeners typically cannot go back to review or look ahead to preview. Spoken language does not contain distinct segments that mark words, phrases, and sentences. Instead, some phrases are marked by pauses. Speech is less clearly segmented than writing and may be colloquial, lacking in fluency, and subject to phonetic modification (Bejar, et al., 2000; Lynch, 1998). These facts, in addition to the reality that many students in non-English-speaking environments have limited time to listen to spoken English, make listening to spoken English more difficult than reading written English for most students.

The limited exposure to spoken English contrasts with what many learners will find if they study in an English-medium school or work in an English-medium business. Listening is the most frequently employed language skill—people listen twice as much as they speak, over three times more than they read, and over five times more than they write (Morley, 1984, 2001). Because listening is so prevalent, most second-language curricula include the goal of developing students' listening abilities. This is not an easy undertaking, because listening is also the least explicit of the four skills (Hulstijn, 2003). As Rost (2002) points out, some teachers and students perceive listening as a receptive process that involves decoding, comprehension, and interpretation, all influenced by memory and background knowledge. Others perceive listening as constructive, because it entails constructing and interpreting meaning, or collaborative, because it means negotiating meaning with the conversation partner. Still other teachers and students define listening as transformative because meaning is created through involvement, empathy, and imagination.

Whatever the perspective, listening is a challenge because learners have to recognize the linguistic information from an acoustic signal in real time and make meaning from it. Teaching this skill must include extensive practice in decoding and making meaning. But in normal listening, learners cannot see speech or the boundaries between words; they cannot stop it or slow it down, and they must deal with it in real time. CALL activities can slow down the process, capture the oral language in text, and show word boundaries.

TIPS FOR TEACHING LISTENING WITH CALL

Our discussion of teaching listening with CALL focuses on the many ways that computers can be used to help learners develop, practice, and improve their listening abilities. The tips and examples included here are compatible with a variety of perspectives of listening in a second language.

TIPS

1. Select CALL materials that are appropriate for students to listen to.
2. Look for listening materials that include both top-down and bottom-up activities.
3. Provide learners with opportunities for selective listening activities based on what they are hearing. ⊚
4. Choose CALL activities that include video. ⊚
5. Include evaluation of responses and a summary of performance at the end of each unit. ⊚
6. Help learners develop their strategies for listening online. ⊚

Throughout the rest of the chapter, each of these six tips is explained with

- a description of *what it means* for the teacher who is using CALL for listening,
- a summary of *what the research says* about the tip, and
- a suggestion of *what teachers can do* in the classroom.

Along with each tip, illustrations of CALL activities from published CALL software and Web sites are provided. The Web addresses are given so that readers can visit the sites to try out the activities.

FEATURE: Examples of how to use one type of listening software and one listening Web site are on the CD-ROM at the back of this book. They include a demonstration of Tip 3 and a simulation of Tips 4, 5, and 6.

Select CALL materials that are appropriate for students to listen to.

Listening involves both the listener and the spoken text. When we consider a text's appropriateness, we must take affective factors, as well as cognitive and linguistic factors, into account. The interest level and the difficulty level of the spoken texts are important considerations when choosing CALL listening materials.

What the research says

Sketching a pedagogical model of listening, Flowerdew and Miller (2005) include the affective dimension that accounts for a student's decision to listen. They say, and others such as Buck (1995) and Mendelsohn (1994) agree, that comprehension can take place only if individuals are relaxed and motivated to listen. Prelistening activities can lower students' anxiety in addition to providing context and activating background knowledge (Buck, 1995; Sadow & Sather, 1998). These activities, along with considerations of what makes listening to texts difficult, will help focus instruction on the process of listening.

Brown (1995) summarized previous research on cognitive dimensions of difficulty into six principles: It is easier to understand any text that 1) involves fewer rather than more individuals and objects; 2) involves individuals that are clearly distinct from one another; 3) includes simple spatial relations; 4) tells events in the order in which they occurred; 5) requires few inferences to relate one sentence to what preceded it; and 6) is self-consistent and fits in with what the listener already knows. Bejar et al. (2000) summarized previous research on *linguistic* dimensions of difficulty to include pause rate, accent, infrequent vocabulary, syntactic complexity, and discourse complexity.

What the teacher can do

Of course, what is interesting to one teacher may not be of interest to all of his or her students, but in general, teachers have a good idea of topics that students will find interesting. One approach to finding interesting materials is to use news stories, as illustrated in Figure 5.1 on page 128. Another approach to selecting materials is to use audio material that has already been categorized by level, that has relevance to ESL learners, and that has prelistening activities intended to activate a student's background knowledge, as in the example in Figure 5.2 on page 129. Authentic examples such as popular songs provide material that will relax most students and address their motivation to learn. One Web site that provides songs with lyrics is illustrated in Figure 5.3 on page 130.

Material	*NewsVOAcom: Special English* from *The Voice of America*
Level	Beginning to Intermediate
Description	Lower-level students may be motivated to listen to stories on the site shown in Figure 5.1 because the materials (e.g., radio programs, TV programs, and transcripts) are based on real-world, everyday news, but the news is rewritten/retold with 1,500 basic words. The familiar vocabulary, the single voice of the announcer, and the interesting topic should combine to create a comprehensible text. A range of topics are available for teachers/learners to choose from.
Web site	http://www.voanews.com/specialenglish/index.cfm
Notes	The stories on this site are updated weekly. To view a story from 2001 through the present, click on "Transcript Archive" at the top of the screen, and locate the story by its date. Special English *VOA* podcasts are also available on this site.

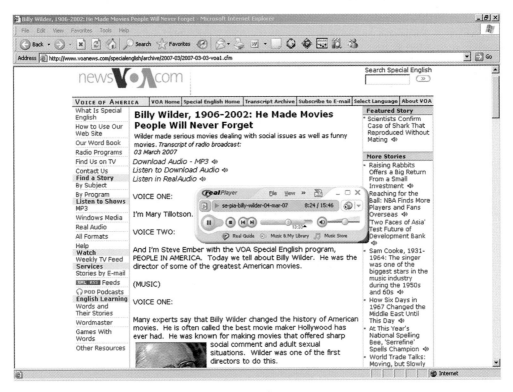

Figure 5.1 Sample news story from *Voice of America*.

Material	*Randall's ESL Cyber Listening Lab*
Level	Beginning to Advanced
Description	This site provides listening materials for students at different levels, as is shown in Figure 5.2. On the right side, a screen lists listening quizzes by topic—1 is "Introductions," 2 is "Education," and 3 is "Work." On the screen on the left side, one of the listening passages from Unit 2, "Taped Library Tour," has been selected. Note how background knowledge is activated in the prelistening exercise. The listening exercises consist of multiple-choice comprehension questions that are scored immediately. Also, a postlistening exercise gives a discussion question that could be used by the teacher for small-group work or for homework as a written response.
Web site	http://www.esl-lab.com
Notes	In addition to listing by topic, this site lists listening materials from other related Web sites by language function and difficulty level (www.trainyouraccent.com, www.ezslang.com, www.dailyesl.com, and www.tips4students.com).

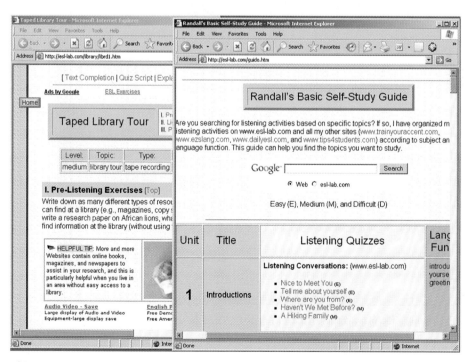

Figure 5.2 Listening categorized by level and topic at *Randall's ESL Cyber Listening Lab.*

Material	*ELLLO: English Language Listening Lab Online*
Level	All
Description	This Web site provides popular songs along with a line-by-line display of the lyrics. Students click on a song title and are redirected to a screen with the title, a graphic picture, and a play button. When they click the play button, the words of the songs are displayed phrase by phrase in large font. The fact that the songs are current and popular may motivate students to listen and learn the lyrics and songs.
Web site	http://www.elllo.org/english/Songs.htm
Notes	This free Web site has many other types of activities and authentic listening materials, such as interviews, listening games, and newscasts.

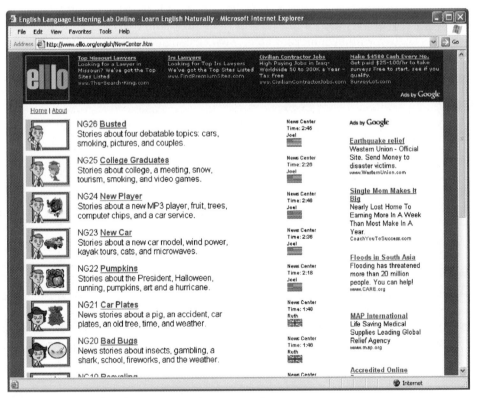

Figure 5.3 Example of songs page from *ELLLO*.

Excellent

2 Look for listening materials that include both top-down and bottom-up activities.

From the perspective of listening as a receptive process, decoding, comprehension, and inferencing are most important. Successful listening involves both bottom-up and top-down processing simultaneously. Bottom-up processing refers to decoding individual morphemes, words, and syntactic meanings. Top-down processing refers to using world knowledge and prediction strategies to anticipate and construct the meaning of the aural language.

What the research says

In many cases listening is equated with comprehension and learning, but before students can listen to learn, they must learn to listen (Vandergrift, 2004). Listening is a goal-oriented activity that makes use of both bottom-up and top-down processing (Rost, 2005, p. 503). With bottom-up processing, the listener attends to the incoming sound signal to decode the sounds of speech. With top-down processing, the listener uses background knowledge and expectations to develop understanding. These processes occur simultaneously and operate on five levels of language: phonology, vocabulary, grammar, propositions, and discourse. Focusing on bottom-up processes, Hulstijn (2003) argues that CALL can be used for the development of word recognition skills; he sees vocabulary acquisition and automatic word understanding as two of the most important factors in second-language acquisition. Peterson (2001) and Helgesen and Brown (2007) outline different goals and exercise types for bottom-up, top-down, and interactive listening processes for learners at beginning, intermediate, and advanced levels.

What the teacher can do

The teacher can look for CALL listening materials that foster different types of processing. Some materials begin with a bottom-up focus on vocabulary and grammar, creating sound and meaning correspondences, as illustrated in Figure 5.4 on page 132. Other materials begin with a top-down focus, providing prelistening questions as warm-up activities that provide context and elicit background knowledge, as shown in Figure 5.5 on page 133. The last example, Figure 5.6 on page 134, includes both top-down and bottom-up processes, in a manner similar to that advocated by Hulstijn (2003). Here, students first watch and listen to a video, then on a second viewing, they also see the transcript to help them realize what they should have understood, as they play the video again.

Material	*Rosetta Stone*
Level	Beginner to High Intermediate
Description	In the lesson shown in Figure 5.4, students both read and listen to the sentence "the girl is eating," and must click on the correct picture. This bottom-up approach focuses the learner's attention on sound, its representation in letters, and the meaning conveyed through pictures. If students click on the correct picture, a check mark appears and a pleasant tone plays; if they click on an incorrect picture, a red X appears and a different tone plays.
Web site	http://www.rosettastone.com/en
Notes	The commercial software is available in thirty different languages and it contains a variety of activities, including listening, speaking, reading, and writing. The Web site for *Rosetta Stone* has two demos, a brief one online and a fully functional one in all thirty languages that can be downloaded upon completion of the online demo.

Figure 5.4 Matching written and spoken sentences with pictures in *Rosetta Stone*.

Material	*Study Skills Success* from Clarity Language Consultants, Ltd.
Level	High Intermediate to Advanced
Description	In the prelistening exercise illustrated in Figure 5.5, the list of questions given to the student before hearing the conversation (e.g., *What is the general topic of conversation? What do you know about this subject?*) is intended to activate prior knowledge. This illustrates a top-down approach to listening.
Web site	http://www.clarity.com.hk/program/studyskills.htm
Notes	This site provides information about the program and an online demo, but the listening section of the program is not illustrated. The program can be used for academic preparation as well as test preparation, such as for IELTS™ International. North American English versions are available.

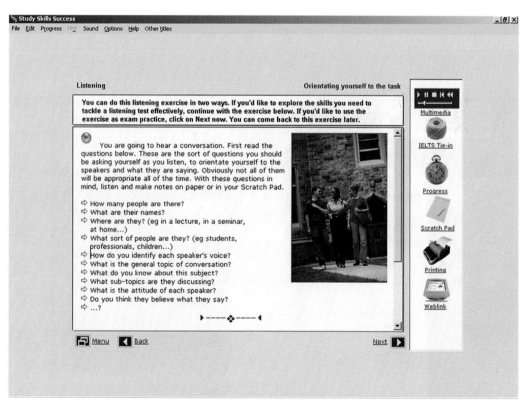

Figure 5.5 Top-down listening exercise in *Study Skills Success.*

Material	*Lingualnet*
Level	Intermediate to Advanced
Description	The screen shot in Figure 5.6 is from a Web site built around learning English through movies. It includes both top-down and bottom-up features. Students select a genre such as narrative or travel. A synopsis is available to provide the listener with background information. This example is for a travel movie, *Expedition 360*. Using a tri-view method, students are encouraged to watch the film one time, and then watch it the second time with subtitles, and then watch it a third time while answering intermittent comprehension questions. At the end, students are encouraged to rate the movie and write a brief review, which can be shared with others.
Web site	http://www.lingual.net/lingualproductitems/
Notes	The film shown here can be found in the "Documentary" category. The other categories are "Drama," "Animation," "Cine-Poetry," "Home made," "Travel," and "Commercials."

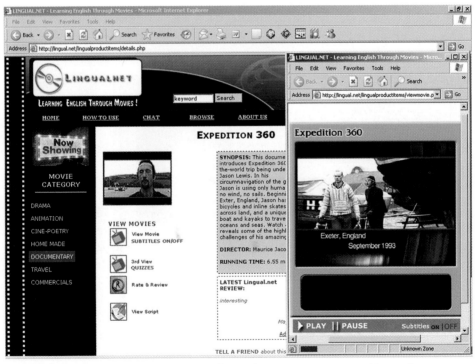

Figure 5.6 Combining bottom-up and top-down processing at *Lingualnet*.

Provide learners with opportunities for selective listening activities based on what they are hearing.

Two important and interrelated factors in developing listening ability are purpose and memory. In real life, people have a purpose for listening to something. The purpose focuses their attention and allows them to identify salient information from the incoming stream of speech in their short-term, or working, memories. However, the focus of this attention can be held in memory only for a limited amount of time. Rost (2005) claims that the ability of a learner to deal with salient input in real time in short-term memory is a key factor of second-language listening proficiency.

What the research says

Based on the work of the psychologist George Miller in the 1950s, it has long been acknowledged that humans tend to "chunk" information in memory and can remember about seven of these chunks at any one time. Spoken texts that a listener must process consist of short, clause-like units that are about seven words long and that last about two seconds. Each "burst" is first passed through echoic memory (where sounds are briefly held); then it is acted on in working memory by fast (automatic) or slower (controlled) processes; and then it is passed into long-term memory where it is compared with other knowledge, and a feedback loop updates the representation (Bejar, et al., 2000; Buck, 1997, 2001; Rost, 1994, 2005). Learners of English have a limited capacity for this normal process because they are simultaneously working to process the second-language signals, which also draw upon cognitive resources. Because of this limited capacity for listening processes, they must use selective attention in order to comprehend meaning (Rost, 2002).

What the teacher can do

The teacher can look for CALL software that contains listening activities that focus students' attention on specific information and require listeners to do something meaningful with that information (Mendelsohn, 1994; Morley, 1984, 1995, 2001). Due to memory constraints, it is important that these activities occur *during* the listening, and not after it. Comprehension-checking activities help learners monitor their understanding of a text while they are listening to it, and also help to chunk the text into more manageable units (Flowerdew & Miller, 2005; Helgesen & Brown, 2007). Three types of tasks that provide different levels of focus are dictation (Figure 5.7), identifying specific information (Figure 5.8), and note taking (Figure 5.9). All of these types of tasks aim to improve the linguistic processing in the listener's working memory.

Material	*Real English Online* from The Marzio School and Real English, LLC
Level	Beginning to Intermediate
Description	In this Web-based program, students use dictation exercises to work on retaining language in short-term memory. They type different people's answers to the question *What time is it?* They must pause the video in order to type the answers.
Web site	http://cla.univ-fcomte.fr/english/dictations/realenglish/realindex.htm
Notes	Students must type the exact answers they hear. If they click on "Check" and the response is correct, it appears as typed. If not, nothing appears or the learner can click on "Show Answer."

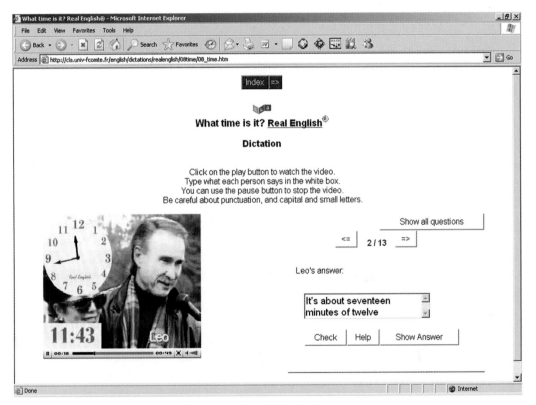

Figure 5.7 Dictation exercise from *Real English Online.*

Material	*Planet English*
Level	Intermediate
Description	The activity in Figure 5.8 has learners engage in a functional, selected-attention listening activity. They first listen to a recorded message from a bank; then they follow the directions and provide the required information. Learners will use the illustration of the cell phone to enter the required information. They will receive feedback on their comprehension, will be able to try the activity again, and will then continue with the remaining audio script and exercises.
Web site	http://www.planetenglish.com/page.aspx
Notes	This commercial program uses Australian English. A demo can be downloaded from the Web site. This listening example is not available on the demo.

⊙ **For a demonstration of a learner using this program, see the CD-ROM at the back of this book.**

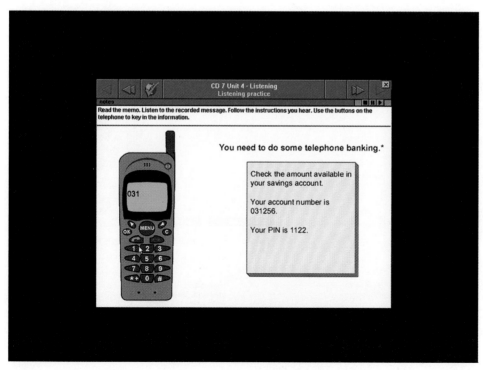

Figure 5.8 Functional, selected-attention activity from *Planet English.*

Material	*Study Skills Success* from Clarity Language Consultants, Ltd.
Level	Intermediate to Advanced
Description	Some CALL software provides both the opportunity to take notes while listening and instruction on how to take notes. One such program is illustrated in Figure 5.9. Here we see a screen shot illustrating notes from the first part of the lecture "The Cornell System." On the bottom right-hand side of the screen, the scratch pad had been opened by the student, and her notes are shown.
Web site	http://www.clarity.com.hk/program/studyskills.htm
Notes	This site provides information about the program and an online demo, but the listening section of the program is not illustrated. The program can be used for academic preparation as well as test preparation, such as for IELTS™ International. North American English versions are available.

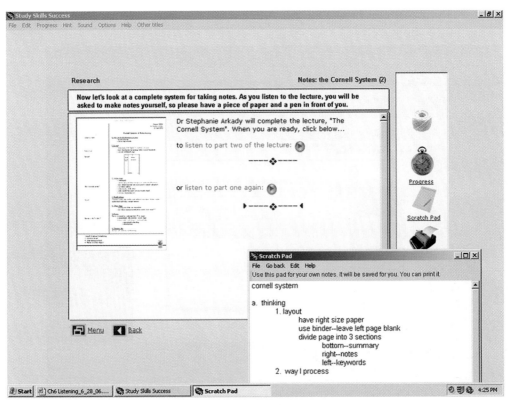

Figure 5.9 Listening to lectures and taking notes in *Study Skills Success.*

Choose CALL activities that include video.

Not all of the input to a listener is aural. Most of the time, the listener also sees the speaker and the speaker's surroundings. CALL with video can help to simulate the visual dimension of listening with paralinguistic and extralinguistic information (Mendelsohn, 1994; Ur, 1984). Paralinguistic information includes body language, gestures, facial expressions, pausing, and intonation; these features contribute to a listener's understanding of a speaker's attitudes. Extralinguistic information includes clues about the setting, the number of participants, and their relative status.

What the research says

Visual information helps to call up background knowledge and schemata and to build context for understanding. It creates redundancy, which facilitates comprehension by putting less pressure on memory, and it provides a basis for discussion of the sociolinguistic dimension of listening (Vandergrift, 2004). Psycholinguists consider listening to be a bimodal skill that involves both auditory and visual senses (Rost, 2005, p. 512). Brett (1997) provided support for this claim in a study of CALL. He compared the recalls and listening comprehension of English language learners using three different types of materials: audio, video with pen and paper for notes, and multimedia. Brett found that multimedia materials provided the best results. He attributed this success to the fact that the learner received ongoing visual support, which may have helped make the input comprehensible.

In other studies, the use of video has been found to raise listeners' motivation and attention levels, and to improve their comprehension (Lynch, 1998). Citing the importance of reduced anxiety, Morley (2001) stated that it is essential that students be able to control the source of the input so that they can start, stop, or replay it at will. Students today expect to receive information through both audio and video. It makes them comfortable; it addresses the needs of both visual and auditory learners; and it aids their understanding of the cultural contexts in which language is used (Brinton, 2001; Flowerdew & Miller, 2005; Rubin, 1995).

What the teacher can do

Listening activities that include video are readily available to classroom teachers. Teachers can look for CALL programs and Web sites that include references to the paralinguistic and extralinguistic information that is available in the activities associated with the video, as shown in Figure 5.10 on page 140. Also, as illustrated in Figure 5.11 on page 141, teachers can try to capitalize on learners' motivation by selecting videos that will connect to their real-life experiences. Teachers should make sure that there are controls so that the learner can pause and replay segments of the videos.

Material	*Longman English Interactive (LEI) 3* from Pearson Education, Inc.
Level	Intermediate to High Intermediate
Description	The video listening activity in Figure 5.10 contains many of the features teachers should look for. Note the controls under the picture where the student can control the pace of the activity. The student can answer and check comprehension. He or she can click on the "e" (for "explanation") after an incorrect response to listen to the part of the video that contains the correct information. Finally, in this example there is an explicit inclusion of an explanation for the paralinguistic hand signal of double quotes in "Culture Notes."
Web site	http://www.pearsonlongman.com/ae/multimedia/programs/lei3_4.htm
Notes	The videos in *LEI 3* and *LEI 4* tell an ongoing story revolving around a soccer scandal. A free sample unit can be downloaded from the Web site.

For a simulation that guides you through this program, see the CD-ROM at the back of this book.

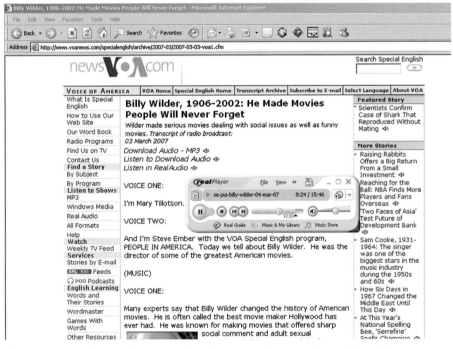

Figure 5.10 Video with comprehension questions and paralinguistic cues in *LEI 3*.

Material	*Real English* from *English Online*
Level	Beginner to Intermediate
Description	This site provides a range of authentic video clips shot on the street, involving real passersby. Learners—even beginners—can be exposed to a range of grammatical and functional topics embedded in real conversations. In Figure 5.11 a screen shot of a beginning level video shows people on the street saying their names and spelling them. Note that there are also several exercises to support skills development.
Web site	http://www.real-english.com/
Notes	Teachers and learners can try free sample lessons from this commercial Web site by subscribing online.

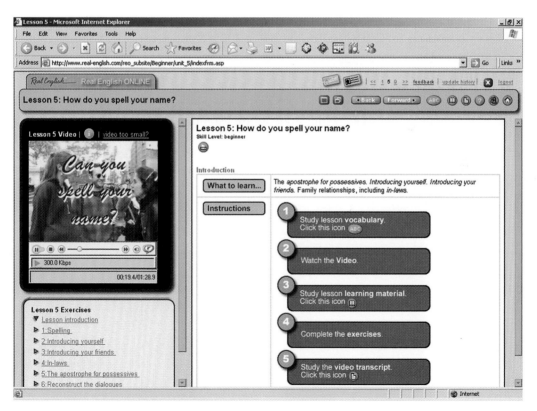

Figure 5.11 Authentic video from *Real English.*

5 **Include evaluation of responses and a summary of performance at the end of each unit.**

Evaluation of students' listening can be either product oriented (occurring after they have listened) or process oriented (occurring while students are listening). The former may focus on comprehension of the important points of a message, whereas the latter can assess the details and the language of the message.

What the research says

Traditionally, instruction has exposed students to listening rather than teaching students how to listen (Mendelsohn, 1994). The usual format is to play an audio recording and then follow up with comprehension questions. Sometimes this format is appropriate, particularly in the testing of listening comprehension. The results provide useful information that can assist teachers in assigning grades or placing students into different levels (Buck, 2001; Helgesen & Brown, 2007; Rost, 2002). More recently, teachers have been focusing on the process of listening. They encourage students to develop their listening skills by evaluating themselves through comprehension-checking activities, thus bringing the process of listening to a conscious level (Flowerdew & Miller, 2005; Mendelsohn, 1995; Morley, 2001; Rubin, 1995).

What the teacher can do

Teachers can look for CALL listening programs that provide intermittent comprehension questions while students are listening, as shown in Figure 5.12. The immediate feedback in this type of program should heighten students' awareness of their understanding. Another type of program provides students with scores showing the percentage of correct answers, and more global feedback at the end of a lesson, as shown in Figure 5.13 on page 144.

Material	*Planet English*
Level	Intermediate
Description	The program provides true-false questions together with a video clip to help learners check their comprehension. In the screen shot shown in Figure 5.12, students are told to read the questions, play the video, and then click on "True" or "False."
Web site	http://www.planetenglish.com
Notes	This commercial program uses Australian English. A demo can be downloaded from the Web site.

Figure 5.12 Comprehension questions interspersed throughout video in *Planet English.*

Material	*ESLRADIO.NET* from Monash University
Level	Intermediate
Description	The site shown in Figure 5.13 is provided by the staff and students at Monash University's English Language Center in Australia. The program includes dramas and speeches produced by ESL students. The screen shot here shows a student's score on the comprehension questions that go with one of the programs. Note that the student received a low score and was urged to listen again and try the questions again.
Web site	http://www.eslradio.net/radio.htm
Notes	This free Web site uses Australian English.

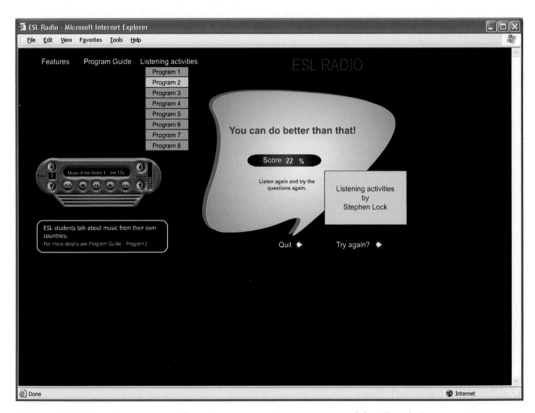

Figure 5.13 Listening comprehension percentage score and feedback from *ESLRADIO.NET.*

Help learners develop their strategies for listening online.

Listening strategies are conscious efforts that students use to control or check their comprehension (Peterson, 2001). Much of what has been included with our earlier tips could also apply to helping students develop listening strategies.

What the research says

Influenced by second-language acquisition research, Rost (2002) proposed three principles concerning listening strategies: 1) Consistent use of strategies helps students learn more efficiently; 2) strategies can enable students to exceed their current capacities, which may be both motivating and instructive; and 3) strategies used by successful learners can be modeled for less successful learners. What are these strategies? Numerous researchers (e.g., Oxford, 1990; Rost, 2005; Vandergrift, 1996, 2003) have provided us with lists to serve as resources. Making predictions before listening, making inferences based on incomplete information, monitoring one's own performance, clarifying areas of confusion, and providing a personal response to what one has understood are five strategies used by successful listeners (Rost, 2002).

What the teacher can do

Two approaches to helping learners develop their listening strategies are to use CALL materials that have incorporated strategies into their instructional designs and to use CALL activities that explicitly teach listening strategies. Figure 5.14 on page 146 illustrates the strategy of predicting before listening. The second approach of direct instruction of listening strategies is illustrated in Figure 5.15 on page 147.

Material	*Longman English Interactive (LEI) 3* from Pearson Education, Inc.
Level	High Intermediate
Description	The prelistening activity shown in Figure 5.14 presents the strategy of predicting what will happen before listening to and watching a video. Students are instructed to look at the picture and predict what is on the tape from three choices. Then, they are told to click the "Play" icon, watch the video, and check their predictions.
Web site	http://www.pearsonlongman.com/ae/multimedia/programs/lei3_4.htm
Notes	The videos in *LEI 3* and *LEI 4* tell an ongoing story revolving around a soccer scandal. A free sample unit can be downloaded from the Web site.

⊙ **For a simulation that guides you through this program, see the CD-ROM at the back of this book.**

Figure 5.14 Predicting before listening in *LEI 3*.

Material	*DynEd Advanced Listening*
Level	Advanced
Description	The screen in Figure 5.15 is part of the introduction to an interactive listening exercise. Students are told in the preceding screen that they will be asked three different kinds of questions: ones that ask for one piece of information, those that ask for details such as facts or the speaker's attitude, and those that ask students to express the relationships between ideas. The video pauses about every ten seconds so that students can take notes, and they are encouraged to replay segments if they have trouble finding the answers to questions.
Web site	http://www.dyned.com/products/al/
Notes	The Web site for this commercial program provides product information only.

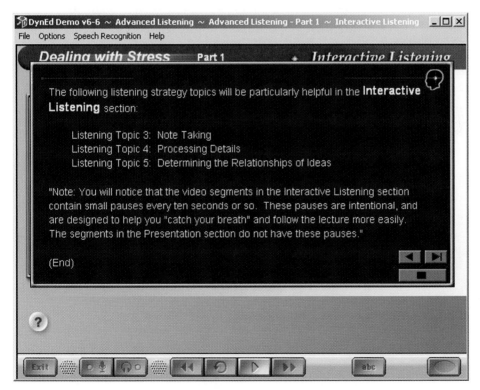

Figure 5.15 Summary of strategy topics in *DynEd*'s Interactive Listening exercise.

FINDING GOOD LISTENING ACTIVITIES

The tips and screen shots provide some advice for using CALL to help learners develop their listening skills. Some of the tips require only audio, but many CALL programs offer video as well. Teachers selecting CALL for listening might find the points summarized in the table useful. The specific questions that one might ask are included under "Focus questions."

What to look for	Focus questions
Learner fit	Does the program present English at a level that is appropriate for learners? Does the program present interesting material?
Bottom-up and top-down processing	Do the activities help the learners focus on particular linguistic aspects?
	Does the program provide prelistening questions to activate background knowledge and to fill in context?
	Are there opportunities for the students to practice both bottom-up and top-down processes?
Selective listening activities	Does the program provide students with a purpose for listening?
	Do the activities provide the opportunity for learners to practice holding information in their short-term memories?
Video	Does the program present listening with video?
	Do the activities include attention to paralinguistic and extralinguistic clues for understanding?
	Are there controls for the student to pause and replay the video?
Two types of evaluation	Does the program include exercises for students to complete while they are listening?
	Does the program include comprehension *quizzes* at the end, with scores and appropriate *feedback?*
Strategy development	Does the program incorporate opportunities for students to practice the strategies of predicting, inferring, monitoring comprehension, clarifying confusion, and providing a personal response?
	Does the program explicitly teach listening strategies?

CONCLUSION

The examples in this chapter show many ways that CALL can be used to practice the process of listening. By utilizing the vast array of audio and video materials that are available on the Web and that may be intrinsically interesting to students, teachers can offer students listening materials that may be transformative. The activities that often accompany these materials provide focused practice with both receptive and constructive listening. By using the content as a starting point for in-class discussion, teachers can also implement listening as a collaborative process. Although second-language listeners want to comprehend, as students they also want to develop their listening abilities. Computer technology can contribute enormously to these goals with help from teachers.

CHAPTER 6

SPEAKING

When someone asks you about your language ability, you typically respond by saying, "I speak English," rather than "I read English" or "I listen to English." *Speaking* is the term that covers it all, for good reason. Speakers have to use the phonology, vocabulary, grammar, and rules of conversation to construct utterances in real time. Speaking is a fast-paced mental and physical activity that requires the speaker to process linguistic knowledge automatically. Successful communication also requires speakers to make strategic linguistic choices that convey intentions pragmatically. With so many factors connected to the act of speaking, the information in most chapters in this book is relevant to understanding how to improve learners' speaking. This chapter, in particular, focuses on CALL that helps learners improve their knowledge and abilities to produce the sounds of the language. Many CALL programs are designed specifically for this purpose. This chapter also discusses using CALL to teach intonation and phrases used in oral communication. Chapter 7, "Communication Skills," covers the more global aspects of speaking.

There are two types of sounds in English: the sounds of segments of the language (such as the sound for "p" in *potato* or "th" in *this*) and the sounds of the stress, timing, and intonation (such as the rising pitch at the end of a question, as in *Do you want to go?*) For most students pronunciation creates a huge challenge for learning English, and the challenge is made even greater by the fact that many teachers and learners are trying to sound like native speakers of English. Most researchers would agree that a more reasonable goal for learners is to attain pronunciation that makes them intelligible. In other words, learners should work to make their English understandable to the people they talk to. Chun (2002) suggests that to teach the sound system of a language, specific sounds must be separated out from the rich contexts in which they are heard. Some research suggests that learners' pronunciation can improve through instruction, but at least two impediments keep researchers from finding positive results from such studies. One is that few teachers receive any instruction on how to teach pronunciation (Derwing & Monro, 2005). In contrast to grammar, for example, pronunciation is not an area covered in many teacher-education programs. The other problem is that pronunciation is difficult to teach in large classes, where in many cases teachers themselves are not completely confident about their own English pronunciation. Can CALL help?

Eskenazi (1999) summarized the pedagogical principles in pronunciation teaching that seem to require the use of CALL. In order to develop an intelligible phonological system

- learners must produce large quantities of sentences on their own;
- learners must receive pertinent corrective feedback;
- learners must hear many different native models;
- prosody (amplitude, duration, and pitch) must be emphasized; and
- learners must feel at ease in the language learning situation.

This chapter provides guidance on how CALL can help satisfy these requirements for learning some aspects of speaking, thereby overcoming limitations in classroom instruction. This chapter offers five tips to help teachers use CALL to improve their students' speaking abilities, especially by improving their pronunciation.

TIPS FOR TEACHING SPEAKING WITH CALL

The five tips described in this chapter are listed below. They are intended to help teachers use speaking software to increase learners' abilities to produce the sounds of English and increase their confidence in their speaking.

1. Select CALL materials that teach the sounds and accents that are relevant for your students.
2. Choose CALL materials that explicitly teach English speaking skills.
3. Provide opportunities for oral practice through interaction with the computer. ◉
4. Evaluate learners' performance and provide feedback. ◉
5. Help learners develop strategies for explicit online learning of oral language through the use of online reference tools.

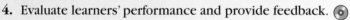

Throughout the rest of the chapter, each of these five tips is explained with

- a description of *what it means* for the teacher who is using CALL for speaking,
- a summary of *what the research says* about the tip, and
- a suggestion of *what teachers can do* in the classroom.

Along with each tip, illustrations of CALL activities from published CALL software and public Web sites are provided. The Web addresses are given so that readers can visit the sites to try out the activities.

FEATURE: Examples of how to use two types of speaking software are on the CD-ROM at the back of this book. They include a demonstration of Tip 3 and a simulation of Tip 4.

 Select CALL materials that teach the sounds and accents that are relevant for your students.

Finding materials with good fit for learners can be a challenge for teachers hoping to teach English speaking skills to their students. One issue is selecting the model or models for English pronunciation. Which dialect of English should be chosen? Another issue is how to select materials that focus on the particular aspects of pronunciation that individual learners need help with. Teachers should examine CALL software with these two issues in mind.

What the research says

Should students learn pronunciation based on American English, British English, Australian English, or one of the many other varieties of English that is used around the world? Should students be taught just one variety, or should they get practice with more than one variety? Some researchers argue that English learners should be exposed to a variety of pronunciations of English and, more generally, should be aware that many varieties exist (Deterding, 2005). This argument is apparent in the principles suggested by Eskenazi (1999). Some researchers point out that nonnative speakers of English outnumber native speakers of English, and therefore, native varieties should not be used as the goalpost. Instead, Jenkins (2002) recommends that the phonological segments taught should be based on what is needed for ESL speakers to communicate with each other. For example, her research has shown that substitutions for the difficult "th" sound do not result in communication breakdowns among ESL speakers. This advice from researchers must be weighed against learners' goals. For individual learners, some of the early research in applied linguistics that focused on the relationship between first-language and second-language pronunciation remains relevant in choosing areas of focus for pronunciation. Contrastive linguistics has helped to identify specific areas of difficulty for learners on the basis of their first language, and more specific hypotheses have been outlined about pronunciation difficulties for learners with particular first languages (Flege, 1995).

What the teacher can do

Teachers can select CALL software that provides a choice of accents to serve as pronunciation models and provides practice on particular speech sounds based on the student's first language. For example, the Web-based program in Figure 6.1 on page 154 provides models from different parts of the United States, Canada, and the British Isles. Teachers can choose one accent that is most relevant for their learners to practice extensively, and then expose their students to other accents. That way, students practice the most useful accent and become more familiar with others.

Material	*Streaming Speech AC* from Speechinaction
Level	Intermediate to Advanced
Description	This online course provides students with training in American and Canadian pronunciations in both discourse features and sound segments. The speech used is unplanned and unscripted. The pronunciation goals for students are to produce clear sounds at speed, to stream the words together, and to vary stress, volume, and speed. After listening to speakers, students work on activities as shown on the left-hand side of the screen in Figure 6.1. Students begin by practicing the sounds in isolation. Then they work with the phonemic transcriptions of the vowel sounds. In the screen shot in Figure 6.1, they are instructed to listen and repeat, at speed. The speed of the speech unit (in words per minute) is shown to the right. Note that students are also directed to assess themselves, which will help them build their self-confidence.
Web site	http://www.speechinaction.com/
Notes	Different programs provide accents from various regions of the United States, Canada, and the British Isles. Demos of these commercial programs can be accessed from the Web site. The example in Figure 6.1 features American and Canadian pronunciations.

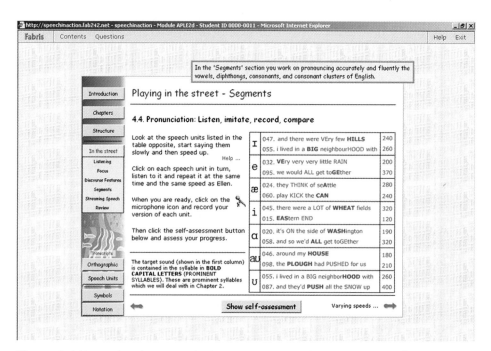

Figure 6.1 Example of pronunciation segments in *Streaming Speech AC.*

Also, teachers can guide students to select the type of practice that is right for them. They can do this by tailoring English pronunciation lessons so that students practice sound segments shown to be difficult for speakers of their languages. The program shown in Figure 6.2 can be customized for learners with different first languages.

Material	*Speech Works 4*
Level	All
Description	The software program shown in Figure 6.2 has twenty-four units that follow a three-stage presentation: listen, repeat, and playback/compare. Each unit contains the following types of exercises: discriminating sounds exercises, word pair drills, sentence exercises, professional vocabulary drills, workplace practice, and extra practice. It has six vocabulary preferences: Adult, High School, K-8, New Immigrant, Medical: Nursing, and Medical: Pharmacy.
Web site	http://www.multilingualbooks.com/speechworks-personal.html
Notes	This commercial program trains learners to speak in fourteen different English dialects, including the standard American accent.

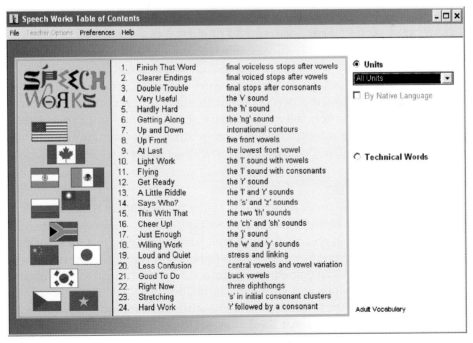

Figure 6.2 Main menu of *Speech Works 4.*

Choose CALL materials that explicitly teach English speaking skills.

The sound system of English is difficult for students because it contains different sounds; combinations of sounds; and stress, timing, and intonation than learners' first languages. Students often cannot hear the differences between sounds that are similar in their native and second languages. Even if they can hear the differences, they do not know what the differences are. Teachers should provide learners with explicit instruction on how the sounds of English are produced, and what the rules are for using them.

What the research says

Derwing, Munro, and Wiebe (1998) investigated improvement in pronunciation for three groups of ESL learners over the course of a ten-week period. They found that the two groups receiving pronunciation instruction improved their speaking, whereas those that received no explicit instruction in pronunciation did not. These studies have been conducted in classrooms or laboratories without using computers. They are important because they have shown that it is possible to teach specific aspects of pronunciation through instruction.

Typically, pronunciation is better taught one-on-one so the learner can have access to multiple repetitions of the sounds. Some recent studies have tested the effects of teaching with technology for improving pronunciation. Some research on teaching the sound system of a second language suggests that pronunciation without any technological assistance for individualized instruction is not particularly promising, at least in short-term instruction (MacDonald, Yule, & Powers, 1994). Wang and Munro (2004) successfully taught English vowel contrasts to Mandarin and Cantonese speakers, using vowels synthesized or recorded by a computer. Over a two-month period, learners worked on that program at their own pace. This resulted in improved perception of the taught contrasts and improved production relative to learners who did not have such training. Other studies have obtained positive results for explicit teaching of stress and intonation, including results that indicate improved confidence in speaking (Hardison, 2004, 2005).

What the teacher can do

In addition to the programs illustrated in Figure 6.1 and Figure 6.2, teachers can use software with movies or animation that show how sounds are produced, thereby focusing students' attention on articulation. This is particularly effective for beginning students. An example of this type of program is provided in Figure 6.3. Other types of software, such as the software shown in Figure 6.4 on page 158, provide extensive practice on both segmentals and stress and intonation patterns. The teacher can assign different parts of these lessons throughout the course, and follow up with classroom communication tasks that allow students to practice the assigned segmentals and patterns. These can all be recycled throughout the course.

Material	*Openbook ESL* from OpenBook Learning, Inc.
Level	Beginning
Description	Pronunciation of fifty-six sounds in English are modeled in this literacy program. As shown in Figure 6.3, a movie appears in the top right section. It shows how the sounds in the word that the student has clicked on are produced. Phonics practice is reinforced when a student clicks on one of the sounds on the left side of the screen.
Web site	http://www.openbooklearning.com/ESL-instruction.html
Notes	The Web site above provides product information only.

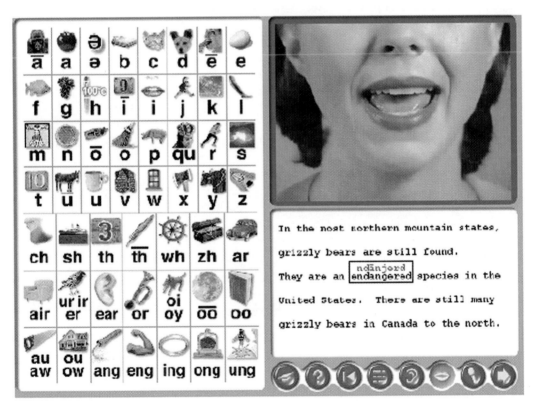

Figure 6.3 Example of articulation of long *a* sound in *Openbook ESL*.

Material	*American Accent Program*
Level	Beginning to Intermediate
Description	The program illustrated in Figure 6.4 provides practice with intonation. Students select the type of practice from a menu, and then work through various exercises. Students are directed to listen to the model, record their voice, and play back and compare.
Web site	http://www.multilingualbooks.com/ameracc.html
Notes	The Web site above provides product information only.

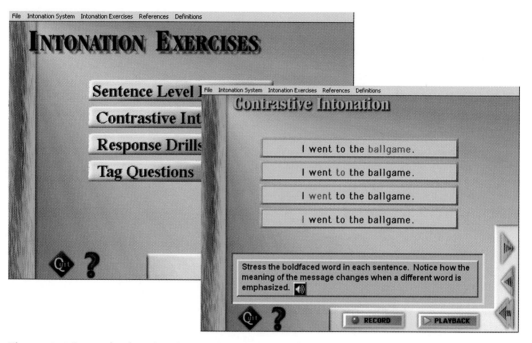

Figure 6.4 Example showing intonation practice in *American Accent Program.*

3 Provide opportunities for oral practice through interaction with the computer.

Software for teaching speaking provides learners with the opportunity to practice listening to a model and then speaking. Such practice provides valuable opportunities for students to listen carefully to the sounds of the language and repeat phrases. This type of practice can offer learners endless opportunities for trying out the sounds in phrases and sentences that will ideally become an automatic part of their vocabulary. Can spoken phrases and sentences be considered vocabulary?

What the research says

The research suggests that people become fluent speakers by remembering groups of words as single units. When we want to use a phrase or sentence, we can access the whole thing at once, rather than piecing it together word by word. In this way, some phrases and sentences are like big words, or formulaic sequences (Schmitt & Carter, 2004). Part of learning how to speak a language is learning what these useful big words are in order to come up with them on demand, or automatically, without having to build them word by word (Skehan, 1998). This type of *automaticity*, which we all have in our first language, comes through hard work and much practice for second-language learners. It also comes from learning phrases that serve as frames for big words in the learners' vocabularies. Phrases such as *How are you? Would you like to*, and *That's very interesting* work in a learners' oral language to help develop fluency. But how does a learner know which phrases are worth remembering, and how do they become automatic? Automaticity of oral language develops through oral practice. CALL activities are designed to provide learners with language worth storing in their collections of frames, in addition to providing practice for making those big words automatic.

What the teacher can do

The teacher can look for programs that provide meaningful contexts for speaking practice, and then build in-class exercises using these formulaic sequences. Some of these speaking programs provide students with more structure for using particular expressions, or frames, than others. For example, the program shown in Figure 6.5 on page 160 provides practice with the set expressions before providing a model and practice-and-repeat exercises. However, many of these types of programs tend to be very open-ended, so students might benefit from teachers' guidance. For example, in the dialogue in Figure 6.6 on page 161, the teacher would identify "would you like to" as a productive frame for the learners, and then ask learners to start a new dialogue asking their partner if they would like to do something. Like exercises in physical fitness class, these dialogues can be used as part of a weekly routine consisting of a specified number of

Material	*Longman English Interactive 4 (LEI 4)* from Pearson Education, Inc.
Level	High Intermediate
Description	In the speaking activity illustrated in Figure 6.5, students can practice first with some set phrases by saying them, as shown on the left, or by selecting them in multiple-choice exercises (not shown). Then students can practice incorporating these phrases into conversations by listening to the speaker (shown on the right), and then creating and recording conversational exchanges according to the directions (for example, "catching up on what's been going on at the office"). Students can play back the entire exchange with their voice, as well as listen to a model.
Web site	http://www.pearsonlongman.com/ae/multimedia/programs/lei3_4.htm
Notes	The videos in *LEI 3* and *LEI 4* tell an ongoing story revolving around a soccer scandal. A sample unit can be downloaded from the Web site.

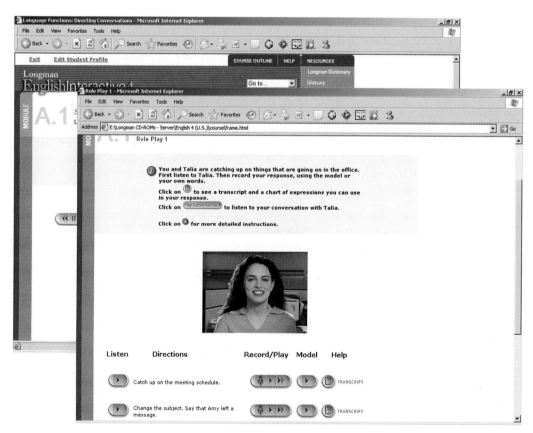

Figure 6.5 Phrases and role play for catching up on things in *LEI 4*.

Material	*TELL ME MORE*® from Auralog
Level	Intermediate
Description	In the program shown in Figure 6.6, the student constructs a dialogue by watching a video and then reading a prompt. In this example, the student has just phoned a friend and must invite the friend and her husband over to dinner. Three ways to say this are shown, including both "would you like to" and "could you" frames. The student has to say one of them. Automatic voice recognition is used to determine which sentence was said.
Web site	http://www.auralog.com/
Notes	Product information and a trial version of a lesson from this commercial program are available at this Web site.

For a demonstration of students using this program, see the CD-ROM at the back of this book.

Figure 6.6 Practice using phrases in conversations in *TELL ME MORE*®.

repetitions. In class, the teacher can provide learners with additional practice, point out to learners where there are good frames, and show some variants of the frames. The CALL program is used to build automaticity of the frame, and then the classroom activity helps to develop the frame into a productive big word by showing its versatility and providing additional practice.

 Evaluate learners' performance and provide feedback.

The sounds of a language are temporary. A learner can say or hear a word and think that the pronunciation is correct, but the word is then gone and so is the opportunity to double-check it. The challenge of correctly articulating the sounds of English is tackled with practice and feedback on performance. O'Brien (2006) describes two types of CALL software that provide pronunciation feedback: software that relies on automatic speech recognition to analyze a learner's language and provide feedback, and software that provides visual feedback by plotting a learner's language on the computer screen.

What the research says

Research and exploration of these two types of CALL software indicate that CALL materials that rely on automatic speech recognition are typically not as good as teachers would like. Pronunciation experts also warn about the limitations of CALL for pronunciation teaching, pointing out the limited speech recognition capabilities of CALL materials and the need for teachers and learners to understand better the goals and methods of pronunciation teaching. CALL technologies are improving all the time, but teachers considering such software should try it out and carefully examine the extent to which it provides valuable and useful feedback for their learners.

On the other hand, software that provides visual feedback that plots the learner's speech signal on the screen has been shown to be useful and effective (Hardison, 2004). Investigating English-speaking learners of intermediate Japanese, Hirata (2004) found that those using CALL with visual feedback improved the pitch and duration contrasts in their Japanese, relative to those learners who had not used a CALL program. Hardison (2005) found that Chinese learners of English improved in their use of stress and intonation as a result of computerized visual feedback. The effects were strongest when the examples and training took place within a discourse context.

What the teacher can do

Teachers can look for pronunciation software that provides feedback. Software that plots intonation can be helpful, but teachers must give learners guidance on how to interpret that type of feedback. Figure 6.7 shows a program that allows students to compare their intonation patterns with model patterns. The feedback shown in Figure 6.8 on page 164 is somewhat easier to interpret, as the number of seconds it took for a student to pause within a phrase is compared to a model, and shown in the form of a line and numbers. Teachers should encourage learners to self-monitor—to use software programs and rate the quality of their

Material	*BetterAccent Tutor* from BetterAccent, LLC
Level	Beginning to Intermediate
Description	The demonstration program shown in Figure 6.7 allows learners to listen to a model, record their utterance, and compare their speech contours to the model's. Learners compare their utterances according to intonation patterns and/or intensity/rhythm.
Web site	http://www.betteraccent.com/
Notes	A demo version of this commercial program can be downloaded at the Web site.

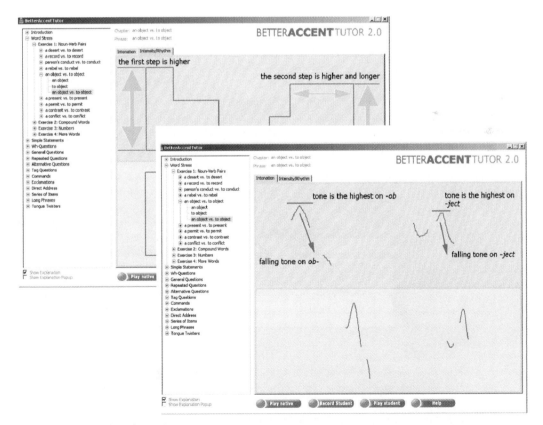

Figure 6.7 Comparison of intonation patterns in *BetterAccent Tutor.*

Material	*Connected Speech* from Protea Textware Pty., Ltd.
Level	Beginning
Description	This software program offers a variety of speaking and listening exercises, focusing on such things as stress, pitch change, and pause groups. In the pause activity, students first listen to a monologue and segment the text into pause groups. Upon completion, the students then record their voice for a few of the segments. Finally, as shown in Figure 6.8, the computer program compares the length of the students' pauses to those in the monologue.
Web site	http://www.proteatextware.com.au/cs.htm
Notes	Readers can request a free demo CD-ROM of this commercial program at the Web site above.

For a simulation that guides you through this program, see the CD-ROM at the back of this book.

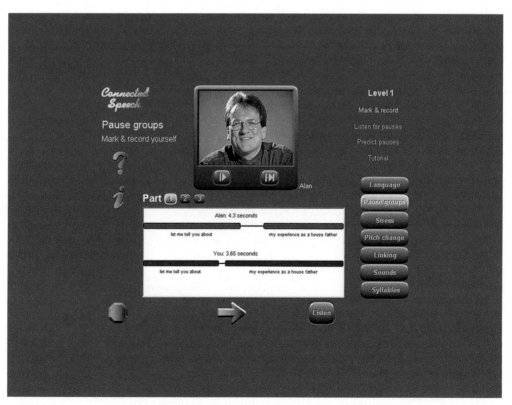

Figure 6.8 Example of the length of pause groups in *Connected Speech*.

production over time. Teachers can also provide opportunities for public display (and rating) of phrases learned in practice sessions, separating them out, but then building them back into context.

 Help learners develop strategies for explicit online learning of oral language through the use of online reference tools.

Learners will always need to learn how to pronounce new words and phrases as they learn more words and specific-purpose words. They will need to move beyond the dialogues from CALL software to, for example, talking about engineering or requesting an extension for a project. Learners can find speech synthesis software on the Internet to provide them with pronunciation guidance long after they have finished their English classes.

What the research says

Research has not been conducted on the autonomous use of text-to-speech software or other aural input for learners, but having the specific help they need when they need it is important for continuous improvement. Students can request to hear the pronunciations of specific words and sentences that they want to use. If text-to-speech software is demonstrated and used in an English class, it will be a resource for students beyond the classroom. For example, students might practice by developing scripts for oral role plays that require them to use new vocabulary. As part of the rehearsal, they can use the computer for help in pronouncing the lines in their scripts. Such classroom demonstrations should help autonomous learners use the computer to help them beyond the classroom. Research can help us better understand how to use the computer for pronunciation help.

What the teacher can do

Teachers can demonstrate text-to-speech tools for their students to use while they are reading on the Web or writing with word processors. These types of programs can be downloaded from the Web and opened before using other programs. One program that reads aloud many Web pages is shown in Figure 6.9 on page 166. Another program that can read aloud any type of page is shown in Figure 6.10 on page 167. Teachers might consider having their students listen to aural input on the Web as homework before a speaking activity in class. Also, teachers can have students create Web pages that address their personal needs by linking them to helpful Web sites (e.g., Web sites with aural language on specific topics or Web sites with aural language and pronunciation help).

Material	*Browsealoud*
Level	Any
Description	This text-to-speech program works on Web sites such as *Google*, which is illustrated in Figure 6.9. Students can download the text-to-speech program, and then open it when viewing Web sites. If the site is compatible with the software, the cursor will turn yellow. The program allows the student to put the cursor over any text on a compatible Web site to hear that text spoken aloud. In this example, the yellow paragraph was read aloud, and the word that was being spoken was highlighted in blue.
Web site	http://www.browsealoud.com
Notes	This free software gives a computer simulation of how words sound.

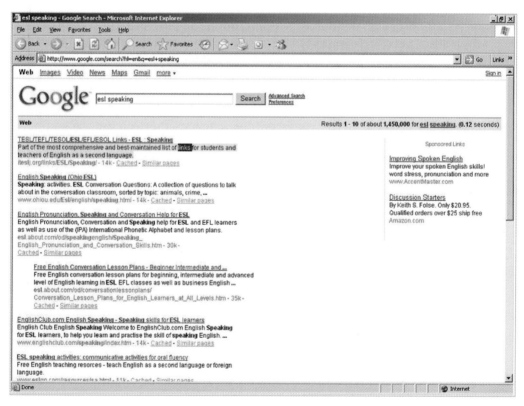

Figure 6.9 Example of *Browsealoud* with a *Google* search page.

Material	*Natural Reader* from NaturalSoft Limited
Level	Intermediate
Description	The mini-box in the upper right corner of the screen in Figure 6.10 is an option in this text-to-speech application that allows the student's Microsoft Word document to be read aloud. The student selects the text, clicks on the sound icon in the left-hand side of the mini-box, and then listens to the selection as it is read aloud.
Web site	http://www.naturalreaders.com
Notes	A free version of the software that gives a computer simulation of how words sound can be downloaded from the Web site. Commercial versions of the software offer better voice quality.

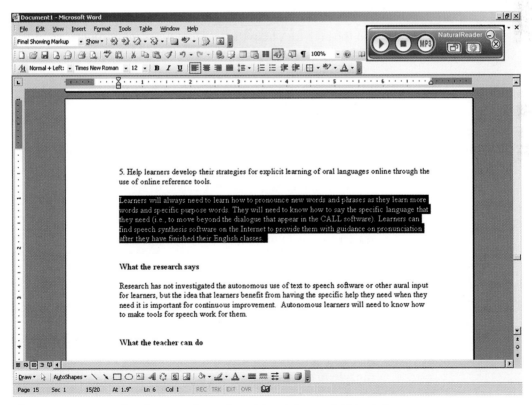

Figure 6.10 Example of *Natural Reader* with a Microsoft Word document.

FINDING GOOD SPEAKING ACTIVITIES

Examples in this chapter illustrate some of the potential for using CALL for speaking with a focus on pronunciation. At the same time, we have noted some areas where using CALL for speaking has fallen short of ideal. If learners are expected to apply the language learning benefits of CALL for speaking, teachers will benefit from considering the points outlined in this chapter when examining software. The specific questions that teachers might ask are summarized in the table.

What to look for	Focus questions
Learner fit	Is the accent used in the CALL activities within the appropriate range of dialects for the learners?
	Does the program provide a means of identifying the oral features with which learners need help?
Explicit teaching	Do the activities help the learners focus on particular sounds, including how they are made and how they contrast with other sounds?
	Does the program come with materials to help preteach and develop follow-up activities?
Interaction with the computer	Do the activities provide opportunities for interaction between the learner and the computer to practice frames in contexts?
	Do these interactions allow learners to speak and record their own voices?
	Does the language of the interactions provide interesting, useful material for learners to use in other activities?
Evaluation and visual feedback	Do the activities provide accurate evaluation and feedback to learners about the correctness of their responses?
	Does the program provide visual feedback that teachers and learners can understand?
Strategy development	Do the activities guide learners in developing strategies that will help them find and use technology for oral language outside of the class?

CONCLUSION

In 1999, Pennington described CALL developed for pronunciation teaching as disappointing but holding great promise. Although room for improvement still remains, many opportunities exist for learners to develop their oral language production through the use of existing software. What once involved embarrassing repetitions in whole-class oral exercises can now be conducted by learners working individually at the computer. Research shows some evidence that such practice can improve learners' oral language skills. What is learned in controlled practice most likely can be integrated into the learners' competence. Derwing, Munro, and Wiebe (1998) point out that the learner who experiences a communication breakdown because of a mispronunciation may be able to focus attention on the cause of the breakdown and successfully repair it because of the focused instruction that he or she has received. However, oral practice at the computer must be introduced by the teacher and integrated into the classroom, where learners will have an opportunity to use the language in other situations. They must be able to use the automatic frames, sounds, and intonation patterns in novel conversations in and out of the classroom. They also must have access to the aural language that they will need in their future conversations and presentations.

CHAPTER 7

COMMUNICATION SKILLS

Many students arrive in their English classes after having spent years communicating through e-mail, text messages, chats, blogs, wikis, and iPods. As Kern (2006) and Thorne and Payne (2005) point out from their research, technology is an important part of normal communication for students. But how can high-tech communication tools that are familiar to students help them learn English?

Many teachers and researchers have been working to answer this question. One of the main principles of communicative language teaching is the idea that students learn English by using English in conversation. Why not use technology to learn English through conversation? Is conversation on the Internet just as good as face-to-face conversation for learning English? Researchers have studied conversation to identify exactly why it helps learners acquire a language. This research suggests that conversations provide good opportunities for learners to hear language that is appropriate for their level, and when they hear something they do not understand, they can ask for a repetition or explanation, and get one.

Conversations also allow learners to try out their language, and in doing so, they find out what they do not know. Learners can understand the basic idea conveyed in language without knowing exactly what the words are, but when learners have to produce the language, they need to know the exact words and their correct forms. All in all, good conversations keep learners interested in talking about something, and make them stop and get help when they need it. Researchers have pointed out that this type of attention directed toward linguistic production can be beneficial for second-language (L2) acquisition (Gass, 1997; Pica, 1994; Swain & Lapkin, 1995).

Computer-mediated communication (CMC) adds some useful dimensions to face-to-face conversation. First, learners have the opportunity to talk to people in distant locations, including proficient speakers of English in English-speaking countries. That seems a lot more interesting to many students than talking to the person sitting next to them in class! Second, many electronic conversations take place through text, which has some special advantages for language learning. Third, students know that they are probably heading for a lifelong experience of using their English through electronic communication, so they know, or can easily be convinced, that practicing their English through electronic communication is worthwhile.

TIPS FOR TEACHING COMMUNICATION WITH CALL

The six tips described in this chapter are listed below. They are based on the ideas that researchers of second-language acquisition have developed about the value of conversation as well as about technology as an aid to conversation.

TIPS

1. Design communication tasks that challenge students to learn more English. ⊚
2. Use written electronic communication to help learners slow down the conversation and notice language.
3. Use written electronic communication for the whole class to provide more opportunities for participation.
4. Provide opportunities for oral interaction among learners. ⊚
5. Encourage learners to use online help during communication.
6. Teach learners strategies for electronic communication.

Throughout the rest of the chapter, each of these six tips is explained with

- a description of *what it means* for the teacher who is using CALL for communication,
- a summary of *what the research says* about the tip, and
- a suggestion of *what teachers can do* in the classroom.

Along with each tip, illustrations of CALL activities from published CALL software and Web sites are provided. In some cases, CALL programs and Web sites are combined to show teachers how they can integrate different resources. The Web addresses are given so that readers can visit the sites to try out the activities.

FEATURE: Examples of how to use two types of communication software are on the CD-ROM at the back of this book. They include a demonstration of Tip 4 and a simulation of Tip 1. In this chapter, additional Web sites and resources are provided in the Notes section of some CALL descriptions.

Design communication tasks that challenge students to learn more English.

Teachers can help learners expand their linguistic abilities by carefully choosing the communication tasks they work on, the people that they communicate with, and the topics that they talk about. The Internet is a place where many different types of conversations can take place. Research indicates that if teachers can help students get into the right kinds of conversations, Internet conversations can extend the opportunities beyond what the learners can do in the classroom.

What the research says

Teachers and researchers who study CMC look at the language that learners use during online conversations. The main question is whether learners appear to be conversing in a way that will help them with their English. For example, do learners use reduced forms and ungrammatical language as they would in a text message outside of class (e.g., using *CU@5* to say "See you at 5:00")? *CU@5* may work well in a text message, but if students spend their time on their English lesson engaged in text talk like that, it may not help them learn English. The question is whether students will pay attention to their English and learn new expressions in order to communicate in English on the Internet. Based on the research, the answer appears to be *yes—if* the teacher plans the communication tasks carefully.

Several studies have shown how important it is for teachers to provide learners with good communication tasks. Researchers contrasted how language learners communicate with and without the teacher's guidance in setting up useful tasks and helping learners to focus on their language. Lamy and Goodfellow (1999) found that students engaged in *reflective* conversations while working on teacher-designed tasks, whereas they engaged in more *social* conversations when they were conversing on their own. The reflective conversations showed that learners were paying attention to the language, whereas the social conversations did not display any evidence that learners were attending to their language. Fiori (2005) tried training two groups of students in different ways for working on communication tasks. The first group was trained to focus on meaning only, and the second group was trained to focus on both form and meaning. The second group learned the grammar from the conversations that they engaged in better than the first group did. Other researchers have found that some tasks help learners to focus naturally on the language (Blake, 2000; Smith, 2004), particularly jigsaw tasks, which require learners to solve a problem by putting together information held by each student. If each learner has different pieces of information, they all must communicate precisely to solve the problem.

Other research has shown the value of getting learners to communicate with peers who are more proficient or with native speakers of the language. Belz and Kinginger (2003) found that if they paired their learners of French and German with French and German students who were learning English, all the students seemed to learn language that was appropriate for talking to peers, rather than only the formal language of the classroom.

What the teacher can do

Teachers can design CALL communication tasks by going to Web sites that have plenty of ideas for using chat in English language instruction. Such sites (like the one shown in Figure 7.1) review chat software and give lesson plans for jigsaw and information-gap types of activities. Once teachers have some models to work with, they can create their own activities using tools that are readily available to them, as illustrated in Figure 7.2 on page 176. Teachers can create interesting and meaningful activities for students to complete in or out of class, with students working together or independently. By working together to reach a solution and send that solution to the teacher, students are likely to pay attention to both meaning and form. To ensure attention to form, teachers can direct students to submit well-written paragraphs that explain their solutions to the activity. Another idea for creating positive CALL learning experiences for students is to match them with electronic pen pals. Figure 7.3 on page 177 shows a Web site for electronic pen pals where learners are paired with peers, especially peers who are studying the students' first language.

Material	*eChatBoX*
Level	All
Description	This Web site provides ESL teachers with forums, resources, and activities for using chats. Forums allow teachers to share ideas and ask questions about how chats work. Resources include evaluations of chat software, as well as links to chat programs. Activities include jigsaw tasks for chats, as illustrated in Figure 7.1. Wikis are also included so that teachers who log on to this site can add their own ideas and activities.
Web site	http://www.echatbox.com/
Notes	Users must register to use this free Web site. An article describing this Web site is at http://www.hltmag.co.uk/may06/mart01.htm.

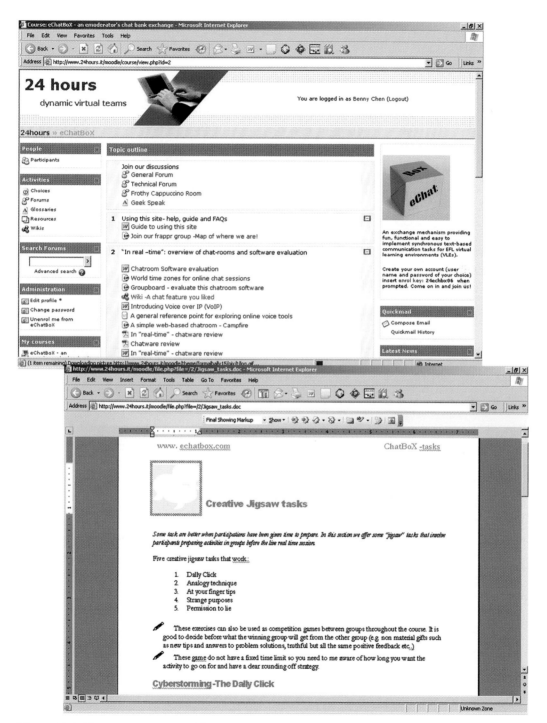

Figure 7.1 Chat resources at *eChatBoX*.

Material	Microsoft® *Windows Messenger*™ and e-mail
Level	Intermediate
Description	Using two types of programs, Microsoft® *Windows Messenger*™ and e-mail, a teacher can create a jigsaw task in which students put together different pieces of information needed to arrive at a single solution. Two students are paired, and each one has different information. In the example in Figure 7.2, the teacher has sent an e-mail with instructions to her class. Students work in pairs to search for an apartment to share. Each student goes to a different Web site to read ads and find three possible places to rent. Then they log on to Windows Messenger to discuss their selections in pairs and rank their top three choices. Finally, they send the teacher an e-mail listing their choices.
Web site	http://get.live.com/messenger/overview
Notes	Microsoft® *Windows Messenger*™ is free and includes video and voice communication. This activity would work with any e-mail and instant messenger programs.

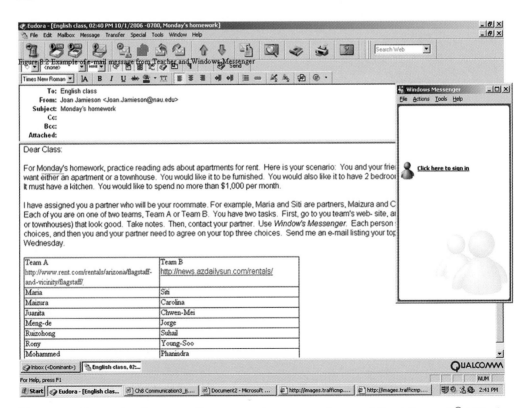

Figure 7.2 Example of an e-mail message from a teacher, and the Microsoft® *Windows Messenger*™ sign-in window.

Material	*Linguistic Funland TESL Pen Pal Center*
Level	All
Description	This Web site provides teachers with the opportunity to pair learners with pen pals who are interested in improving their communication skills. Students can write to their pen pals with simple e-mail programs; the most important thing is that students are engaged in using language for a communicative purpose with peers. Teachers might have students start by asking questions about their pen pals, then about their families, then about their hobbies and interests, and then about a controversial topic. This would provide some structure to the exchanges, and would also provide an opportunity to use the topics to involve the entire class in a discussion about their pen pals.
Web site	http://www.tesol.net/penpals/
Notes	Click on "Request Pen Pals" to get started on this free Web site. Other free pen pal Web sites that provide communication opportunities for language classes include *eTandem* (http://www.slf.ruhr-uni-bochum.de/ etandem/ etindex-en.html), *My Language Exchange* (http://www.mylanguage exchange.com/), and *Tapped In* (http://tappedin.org/tappedin/).

For a simulation that leads you through this program, see the CD-ROM at the back of this book.

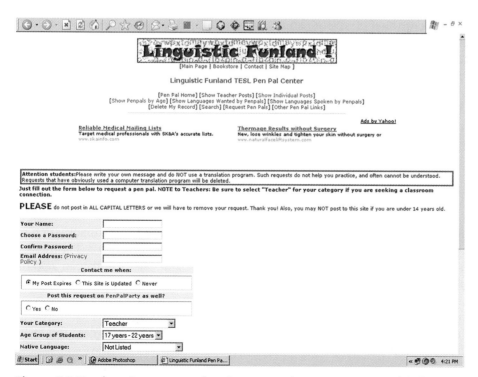

Figure 7.3 Teacher sign-up page for class pen pals at *Linguistic Funland*.

Use written electronic communication to help learners slow down the conversation and notice language.

When language teachers began to look at CMC conversations between learners, the majority of these took place in writing. Teachers and researchers wondered if students could learn to speak by practicing written conversations. Based on research and experience, it did not take long for teachers to realize that the new forms of conversation provided new ways of learning. In fact, written conversations can provide opportunities for learners to slow down the conversation so that they can plan and reflect on what they are trying to communicate. Written conversations also provide a visual record of the interaction, which helps learners focus on the linguistic details that they might miss in oral language.

What the research says

Some researchers have tested the idea that written conversations could provide opportunities for noticing language and for self-correction—opportunities that are not present in oral communication. For one, De la Fuenta (2003) compared oral face-to-face CMC with written synchronous CMC and found that the students who engaged in written communication were the ones who learned the vocabulary in the tasks best. Even though the written CMC is useful, no one would suggest that written CMC should take the place of oral practice. In fact, Payne and Whitney (2002) found that a combination of oral and written interactive communication was better for improvement in oral proficiency in intermediate Spanish than oral practice alone. In a controlled classroom study, Sykes (2005) also found that learners who engaged in written chat increased their oral proficiency more than those who used oral CMC or participated in face-to-face discussion groups. All of the learners in the study had had some oral practice, but those who used written CMC apparently were helped to achieve the objective—to make refusals in Spanish. Other research is less clear about the effects of written language, but some of it does show that learners develop grammatical skills when using written language (Belz, 2004; Stockwell & Harrington, 2003).

What the teacher can do

Chat programs are becoming readily available in many school settings. Some of these programs have been designed especially for second-language instruction and provide teachers with extra tools for student feedback, such as analysis of vocabulary and the number of turns students take. Figure 7.4 shows an example of a language-specific chat program. Chat rooms can also be used to discuss an article that the class read or a movie that they saw, as shown in Figure 7.5 on page 180. By printing logs from chat sessions, teachers can recycle language that students generated, in order to create a variety of different exercises. Teachers can use both oral and written interactive conversation tasks based on the chat room logs.

Material	*L.E.C.S. Language Education Chat System* from the Kanto-Gakuin University Web site
Level	All
Description	This chat program was developed in 2000 to help Japanese students learn English, and it offers some unique features. After a session, each participant can learn how many turns he or she took, the average length of each sentence, whether the words used in the session are included in the JACET 4000 BASIC WORDS, the word collocation, and common mistakes among learners. Teachers can download the text of each chat session so that students can correct their mistakes or rewrite the chat with different expressions.
Web site	http://home.kanto-gakuin.ac.jp/~taoka/lecs/
Notes	This Japanese/English Web site requires the user to set the browser to encode Japanese (shift-JIS). For security reasons, it is recommended that students give chat names on the site instead of real names. This can also help them feel more secure and relaxed.

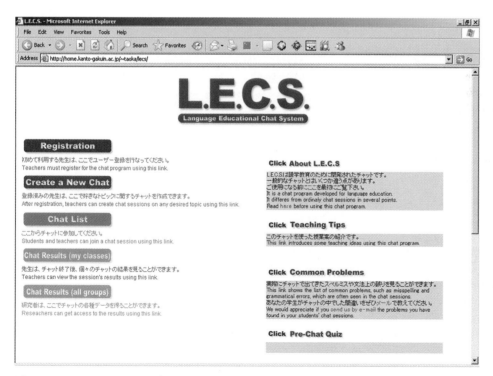

Figure 7.4 Home page of *L.E.C.S. Language Education Chat System.*

Material	*Blackboard's Vista WebCT*
Level	All
Description	The screen shown in Figure 7.5 illustrates some of the functions that a teacher has control over when using chats in a class. When a teacher creates a chat, the program, by default, will keep a log of all entries; the teacher can view the log, print it, and make copies for students. In this example, the chat consists of two parts—a whiteboard and a chat tool. The whiteboard is used for graphics, and the words students type are shown in the chat window following their names. In this example, the teacher of this course could focus on the content (the reasons that Celtic words were not borrowed into Old English), on the language students used to express their opinions, or on the language that was used to react to someone else's idea.
Web site	www.blackboard.com
Notes	This commercial e-learning platform is part of Blackboard.com. The screen in Figure 7.5 can be accessed only by people in the class. The Web site above provides links to some of *Blackboard*'s tutorials. Type "tutorials" in the search box on the top right, click on "Quick Tutorials," and then scroll down and click on "Collaboration Tools."

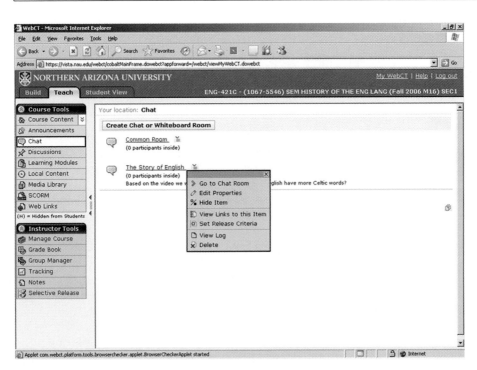

Figure 7.5 Example of chat functions in *WebCT.*

Use written electronic communication for the whole class to provide more opportunities for participation.

One of the frustrations that many teachers in language classes feel is that students have limited opportunities to produce the language. Some teachers have noticed that when the class discussion moves to the computer, two important dynamics change. First, because the teacher is no longer in front of the class directing the discussion, students do a lot of the talking (or typing). The level of students' activity during class increases dramatically as they use the language to express themselves. Second, the level of participation among the students is more evenly distributed because the students who are hesitant to speak in class are more comfortable contributing from their keyboards.

What the research says

Researchers have examined what happens during a CMC activity. In particular, researchers looked at the language that learners produced during CMC class discussions and at their level of participation. Chun (1994) investigated the functions used by first-year German learners in written synchronous CMC in the classroom, finding a number of speech acts, such as asking questions and requesting clarifications. In each of these studies, the researchers speculated that the electronic communication might be instrumental in helping learners develop their abilities to communicate. Kern (1995) studied the vocabulary and grammar that students used in their electronic communications and found that students tended to focus on the meanings of their messages rather than on accuracy, but that they attempted to use language that stretched their language knowledge. This focus on meaning suggests that such discussions can be good for getting learners to use the language in real communication, and this has been noted in other studies, as well (Lee, 2001). Warschauer (1995, 1996) suspected that students would participate more equally in Internet communication, where the effects of personal characteristics such as aggressiveness or shyness are not as strong as they are in the classroom. His research in an English class supported his hypothesis: When the learners communicated through networked computers, they contributed more equally to the discussion than they did in the classroom.

What the teacher can do

CMC provides a new way for teachers to structure classroom conversation, particularly when the goal is to get students to participate by using language to communicate meaning. The best way to structure discussion may differ from class to class, but if learners need opportunities to produce the target language in order to develop more fluency in interpersonal functions, CMC class discussion may be ideal. One program for setting up a classroom management system with a discussion function is shown in Figure 7.6 on page 182. Most software also gives teachers the option of dividing the class into electronic groups. A class of thirty, for example, might be divided into three groups of ten, or six groups of five. Small groups provide more opportunities for students to participate. If the software does not allow subdivisions

Material	*Nicenet*
Level	Intermediate
Description	The Web site shown in Figure 7.6 provides an asynchronous communication tool. In other words, it allows students to contribute to a discussion at any time. These tools are known as discussion boards, or as shown in the figure, conferences. Students can write their responses to prompts developed by the teacher, view their classmates' responses, and respond to others' comments. All of these functions provide opportunities for all the students in a class to participate more fully.
Web site	http://www.nicenet.org/
Notes	This Web site is free.

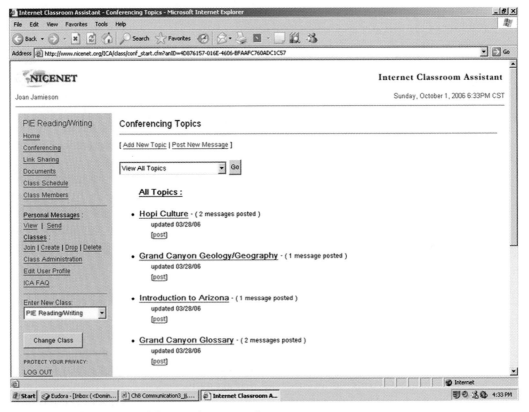

Figure 7.6 Illustration of the conferencing function in *Nicenet.*

blogger.com

of groups, the teacher can simply assign different topics to different groups of students. The important thing is that students will be able to participate at their own pace. Another way to increase student participation is to create an online class journal, or blog. Figure 7.7 shows a Web site that explains blogs and provides examples for setting up blogs for a class.

Material	*TOPICS Online Magazine*
Level	Intermediate to Advanced
Description	Blogs have become very popular as journal writing has gone public. The article shown in Figure 7.7 provides teachers with a thorough introduction to what blogs are, how teachers are using blogs in their classes, and how to create a blog for a class. There are also links to informative articles that illustrate how to involve your entire class in a blog-writing activity.
Web site	http://www.topics-mag.com/call/blogs/ESL_EFL.htm
Notes	Once teachers know how they want to use blogs with their students, they can go to the Web site http://www.blogger.com/start to create a blog.

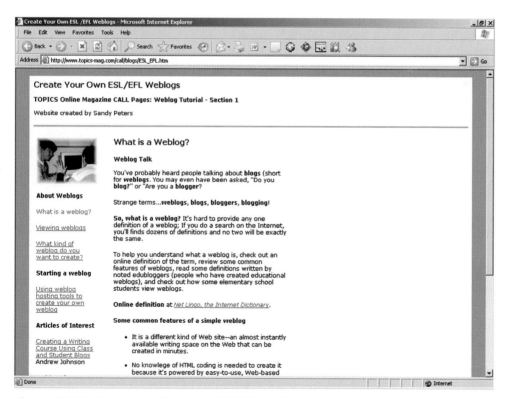

Figure 7.7 Explanation of blogs at *TOPICS Online Magazine.*

Provide opportunities for oral interaction among learners.

Have you ever noticed what happens when two or more people sit at a computer? They talk to each other. They also look at the screen and the keyboard, point to things on the screen, type at the keyboard, watch what happens on the screen, and click the mouse. These actions are intermingled with oral face-to-face conversation. The many activities surrounding various topics that learners can study and complete on the computer provide a variety of interesting stimuli for conversation. Conversations prompted by the computer, the modern-day version of a "describe what's in the picture" task, can take many different forms because of the computer's interactivity and the wide range of available materials.

What the research says

The first studies of learners' conversations around a computer screen focused on what learners say while they are working on various types of programs for learning English (Abraham & Liou, 1991; Mohan, 1992; Piper, 1986). For example, if learners talk to each other while working together on an exercise on the use of articles, what do they say? What happens if they work on a simulation program that asks them to make decisions about running a business? What do they say to each other? The research shows that these types of programs, which respond to learners' choices and therefore always provide something new to talk about, are good for sustaining conversations among learners. Modern versions of this research look at how collaboration develops at the keyboard as learners create multimedia projects (Jeon-Ellis, Debski, & Wigglesworth, 2005). The projects are different, but the same idea applies: The dynamic interactivity of the computer provides lots to talk about.

Some researchers have also looked at the use of oral interaction among learners communicating through the Internet, and their research indicates that oral CMC plays an important role in communication. Researchers find that for some kinds of tasks, the written chat conversations make everything too clear for some learners! If learners always understand the language of a task, they will never have an opportunity to stretch their language knowledge. It is voice communication—whether face-to-face or through CMC—that produces the most misunderstandings and repairs that draw learners' attention to language (Fernández-Garciá & Martínez-Arbelaiz, 2003; Jepson, 2005).

What the teacher can do

Teachers can plan activities, such as WebQuests, that require a pair or small group of students to use the computer to solve a problem. WebQuests are activities that use the computer to stimulate conversation while students are sitting together in front of it. An example of a WebQuest is shown in Figure 7.8. Also, teachers can use oral chat programs, such as the one illustrated in Figure 7.9 on page 186, instead of written chat programs to implement the kinds of meaningful communication

Material	ESL WebQuests
Level	Intermediate to Advanced
Description	The WebQuest illustrated in Figure 7.8 involves two students figuring out how long it will take to travel from Washington, D.C., to San Diego. The partners have to determine where to sleep each night, what to eat during the day, and what sights to see along the way. They also have to create a visual display of their trip and present it to their classmates.
Web site	http://www.call-esl.com/sampleWebQuests/webquestcontents_htm.htm
Notes	This Web site features three WebQuests that were created as a requirement for a master's degree in TESOL. Teachers can also find WebQuests on http://iteslj.org/links/ESL/Treasure_Hunts/ from *The Internet TESL Journal*.

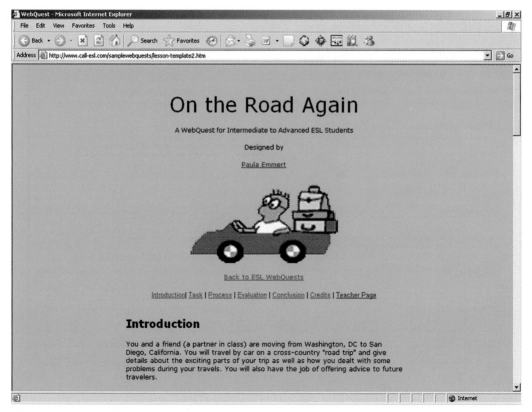

Figure 7.8 Example of an ESL WebQuest.

Material	Microsoft® *Windows Live™ Messenger*
Level	All
Description	The program shown in Figure 7.9 is for making phone calls over the Internet to anyone else who has the program. Most people use a headset, but you can use regular headphones if you have a good microphone. *Windows Live Messenger* supports chats and class conference calls, as well as video calls if you have a camera connected to your computer. It is free and available for anyone to download. This would be a great program for pen pals.
Web site	http://get.live.com/messenger/overview
Notes	This free program allows users to communicate via voice, text, or video. It also allows them to share files, photos, or videos.

For a demonstration of students using this program, see the CD-ROM at the back of this book.

Figure 7.9 Screen from Microsoft® *Windows Live™ Messenger* illustrating how the service works.

activities described in Tip 1. The key for the teacher is to plan activities that require oral communication, such as those involving jigsaw techniques and pen pals, and then use the computer directly or indirectly to get students to talk with one another as they solve problems.

 Encourage learners to use online help during communication.

When learners communicate with other students online, they have the ideal opportunity to get help so that they can express themselves correctly, and in doing so, perhaps learn something. When using written language in e-mail and blogs particularly, learners can take extra time to correct their errors and express themselves in idiomatic language if they use the help and feedback features of the computer.

What the research says

Research has shown that online help from the computer can be at least as useful as help from other learners. Chen, Belkada, and Okamoto (2004) compared the effectiveness of CALL tasks consisting of learner-computer inter-action with CALL tasks based on learner-learner interaction, and found that both were equally effective for learning English. These results are consistent with previous research in which learners tended to get more accurate information and do better when they interacted with the computer than when they engaged in conversation with other students (Chang & Smith, 1991). Other research provides some evidence that learners are capable of using and benefiting from the feedback that they receive from the computer (Burston, 2001; Liou, 1993). These studies, which were conducted in writing classes, indicate that the use of feedback from the computer on language features such as spelling and morphol-ogy benefits students. The challenge in the classroom is to help learners see the use of such feedback and tools as an ongoing part of their communication beyond the classroom.

What the teacher can do

Teachers can encourage students to use the online tools that are available by modeling their use and training students to use them. Teachers can train students to use the help provided in Microsoft products such as *Outlook* as shown in Figure 7.10 on page 188; show them how to use spell checkers; and insist that e-mails from students to their teachers not contain incorrect spellings. Also, teachers can train students to get help from a concordancer by showing them how to use one, and then suggesting ways that students can use concordancers when they are working by themselves, as illustrated in Figure 7.11 on page 189.

Material	Microsoft® *Outlook*
Level	All
Description	Many e-mail programs, such as the one shown in Figure 7.10, have spell checkers that students should be encouraged to use in the classroom. When students become adept at using these tools in the classroom, they can be encouraged to use them outside of the classroom.
Web site	http://office.microsoft.com/en-us/outlook/HA100518161033.aspx
Notes	The Web site contains an online demo of this program.

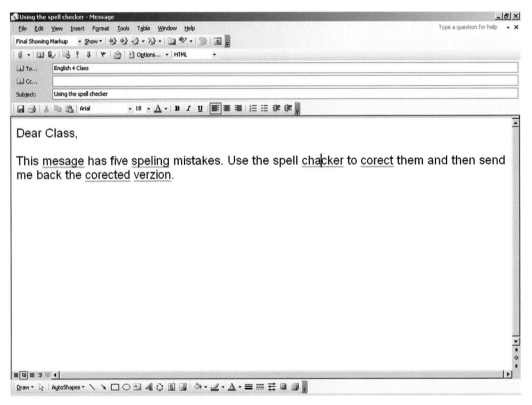

Figure 7.10 Online spell checker in Microsoft® *Outlook*.

Material	Our Class 2006 Blog and *MICASE Concordancer*
Level	Intermediate to Advanced
Description	The left side of Figure 7.11 shows "Our Class 2006 Blog," an ESL blog from Australia. A teacher, Rosa, has been developing blogs for her class since 2005. In this blog, she posted a picture and invited her students to guess what it is. One student, Dan, wrote that it may be a "sort of" salt pond. Another student was curious about Dan's use of "sort of." She opened the *MICASE* concordancing program on the right side of Figure 7.11, searched for examples of "sort of," and incorporated a new use of the phrase into her comment.
Web site	http://ourclass07.blogspot.com/ and http://micase.umdl.umich.edu/cgi/m/micase/micase-idx?type=revise
Notes	Teachers can encourage students to use other online language tools, including concordancers, when responding to blog questions. *MICASE* is the *Michigan Corpus of Academic Spoken English*. It contains over 150 transcripts and can be sorted by characteristics of the speech and the speaker. See Figure 7.7 on page 183 for a discussion of blogs.

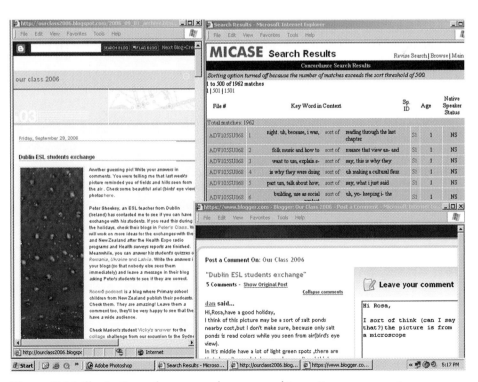

Figure 7.11 Illustration of a concordancer used to write a comment on a teacher's blog.

6 Teach learners strategies for electronic communication.

Most people in the English-speaking world spend large amounts of time each day at their computers sending and receiving e-mail for business and personal reasons. This is the environment that English learners likely will find themselves in during and after their studies. Therefore, an important role of the English class is to help prepare students for their lives as English users in the world of electronic communication. But what are the rules of communication that can help prepare them?

What the research says

Research in this area describes how communication in electronic modes is accomplished, so it is based on observations of technology use. Crystal (2001) examined the language of the Internet across several different modes of communication. He pointed out that the Internet "presents us with a channel which facilitates and constrains our ability to communicate in ways that are fundamentally different from those found in other semiotic situations" (Crystal, 2001, p. 5). Other descriptive work (e.g., Herring, 1996) reveals the patterns of discourse and types of language occurring in these contexts and how ESL learners participate in them (Negretti, 1999). Looking at the big picture, Thorne (2003) noted that the learners' choices of tools in class projects, such as e-mail, instant messenger, and other forms of Internet communication, depended in part on their past experiences with the communication tools. And Lam (2000) found that the choice to engage in communities of electronic communication could itself be significant for learners' development of language and an English-speaking identity.

What teachers can do

Teachers and students can discuss communication on various topics and styles in both written and oral modes. They can use printouts of the chats described earlier to analyze some examples of Internet communication. Teachers can tell students about discussion forums to introduce them to the Internet as a way of practicing English, and in so doing, they can discuss the rules for participation, as shown in Figure 7.12. There are also conventions for chats, as shown in Figure 7.13 on page 192. These rules and conventions invite teacher and student discussions about politeness and intercultural communication.

Material	*UsingEnglish.com*
Level	Intermediate to Advanced
Description	Figure 7.12 shows a discussion forum on the left-hand side. On this site learners can submit questions about English and they will receive answers from teachers. These answers are posted on the Web site rather than being e-mailed to individuals, so that others can comment on them as well. There are rules for posting, as shown on the right-hand side of Figure 7.12, which teachers can explain to their students.
Web site	http://www.usingenglish.com/forum/
Notes	This Web site also includes links to information about online safety issues. Teachers are advised to review posting rules and safety issues with their students.

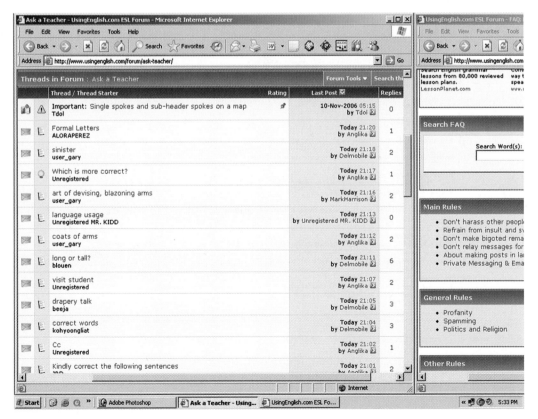

Figure 7.12 *Ask a Teacher* forum and posting rules at *UsingEnglish.com*.

Material	*EnglishClub.com*
Level	Intermediate
Description	The Web page shown in Figure 7.13 provides students with tips for chat etiquette, or "chatiquette."
Web site	http://www.englishclub.com/esl-chat/etiquette.htm
Notes	Because talking online may be new to students, it is recommended that teachers take the time to discuss these politeness conventions before students begin their online tasks. This topic can be reviewed after a few assignments have been completed.

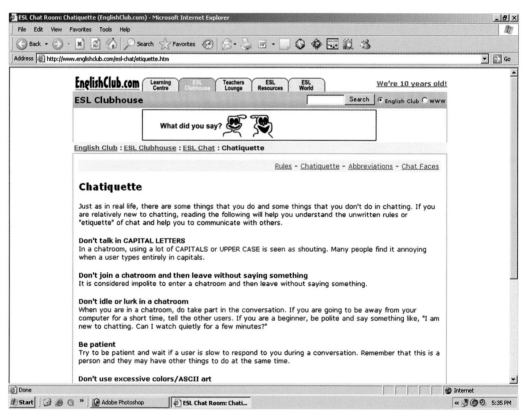

Figure 7.13 Advice on chat etiquette at *EnglishClub.com*.

FINDING GOOD COMMUNICATION ACTIVITIES

Examples in this chapter have illustrated some of the good conversations that learners can engage in for language development. Specific questions that one might consider in developing such communication activities are presented in the table.

What to look for	Focus questions
Learner fit	Does the language fit the learners in terms of level, topics, and activities? Do the tasks create the need to exchange information and collaborate?
Using written language for reflection	Do the written conversations prompt the learners to reflect on both form and meaning?
Using electronic communication for production and interaction	Does the electronic discussion provide opportunities for all learners to produce the language?
Oral interaction with other learners	Does the computer prompt the learners to talk? Does the oral electronic conversation create appropriate linguistic challenges?
Online help and feedback	Do the activities encourage learners to use online help and feedback?
Strategy development	Do the activities help learners understand different types and styles of electronic communication? Do the activities promote good strategies for electronic communication?

CONCLUSION

The examples in this chapter show some of the ways that teachers can use computer technology to help students learn English and learn how to use English online. Many learners come to English class having used these communication tools for many years. Kern (2006) and Thorne and Payne (2005) suggest that students will readily transfer their online communication habits to communication tasks in class. The challenge for English teachers is to help learners expand these habits in two ways. First, students may be accustomed to using only one technology (e.g., text messaging), and they may need to increase their repertoire of communication technologies in order to develop their English further. Second, students use communication technologies outside of class to communicate meanings to each other, but they must learn to use them in ways that will allow them to improve their English during communication tasks in class. Students count on their English teachers to help them develop this new dimension to their use of communication technology.

CHAPTER 8

CONTENT-BASED LANGUAGE

Teaching the particular language that students need for their work and studies is one of the biggest challenges that English teachers face. Specific-purpose language goes beyond the language used in hotels, restaurants, and theaters, which is common to all students, and enters into the specifics of hospitals, offices, laboratories, and so on. The challenge of teaching specific-purpose or content-based language is at least twofold. First, English teachers are seldom knowledgeable about the specific language that is used in the many different areas that their students study or work in because the teachers themselves are not experienced in those areas. Second, although the future doctors, business executives, and research scientists sit side-by-side in English class, they typically have different needs for specific-purpose language. Both of these challenges suggest a need for extensive additional materials and learning activities targeted to specific learner needs. CALL can help meet this need.

Applied linguists claim that language and content are not completely distinct from each other (Mohan, 1986). Instead, language is a means for mapping content to expression. This perspective has been reflected to some extent in the first tip of each chapter of this book, which advises teachers to seek CALL materials with good learner fit. "Learner fit" refers to the level of language difficulty and the level of the content. Appropriate levels for each are needed for students' engagement and learning. In other words, content is one of the important factors in selecting communicative materials.

In this chapter, however, we turn that idea upside down. In content-based teaching, the content is the reason for learning. That is, content-based language instruction for engineers, for example, includes the language that engineers use to map engineering ideas to expression. The engineering content is not there just to keep the learners interested. Instead, the content determines the choice of patterns of vocabulary and grammar that they will learn.

Teachers working to design entire courses for English for special purposes (ESP) in university academic departments in the United States describe the institutional challenges inherent in this endeavor (Swales, Barks, Ostermann, & Simpson, 2001). The reality of ESP teaching is that materials must provide a lot of the necessary individualization. Individualization is reflected in language and content, but content-based learning involves the same types of language skills that have been discussed in the previous chapters. Therefore, the examples of content-based or specific-purpose language in this chapter demonstrate the same language skills. Based on a review of content-based CALL, Arnold (2006) notes that the research is very limited. However, drawing on the few existing studies (in addition to advice from experts in content-based learning), this chapter offers four tips.

TIPS FOR TEACHING CONTENT-BASED LANGUAGE WITH CALL

The four tips described in this chapter are listed below. They are based on the ideas concerning second-language acquisition that we have discussed throughout the previous chapters of this book. The fact is, all communicative language teaching is content-based, because teachers always teach students how to create and interpret meaning. But the difference in this chapter is that it focuses on the particular meanings that learners want to be able to construct and interpret.

TIPS

1. Select CALL materials with appropriate language for students' specific-purpose needs.
2. Choose CALL activities that explicitly teach field-specific language. ⊙
3. Provide learners with opportunities for interaction with the computer and with other English users to practice field-specific language. ⊙
4. Help learners develop their strategies for finding and using field-specific materials online.

Throughout the rest of the chapter, each of these four tips is explained with

- a description of *what it means* for the teacher who is using CALL for content-based language,
- a summary of *what the research says* about the tip, and
- a suggestion of *what teachers can do* in the classroom.

Along with each tip, illustrations of activities from published CALL software and Web sites are provided. In some cases, CALL programs and Web sites are combined to show teachers how they can integrate different CALL resources. The Web addresses are given so that readers can visit the sites to try out the activities.

FEATURE: Examples of how to use two types of content-based language software are on the CD-ROM at the back of this book. They include a demonstration of Tip 2 and a simulation of Tip 3.

 Select CALL materials with appropriate language for students' specific-purpose needs.

Twenty years ago, English teachers wished that they had libraries full of English texts and recordings so that they could select relevant examples when making lessons for their students. Today, that wish has been fulfilled by the Internet, where teachers can search and find libraries and more! The challenge for teachers of content-based language is to select materials that contain the relevant content-based language and that are at the appropriate level for both teachers and learners.

What the research says

The research on content-based learning tends to focus on the language rather than the learning. The journal *English for Specific Purposes* is full of studies investigating particular registers of language use. Registers are defined in terms of the people who are communicating, what they are talking about, and the type of communication event they are participating in (e.g., a phone conversation or e-mail) because these factors determine the language that people use.

The research studies are important for content-based language teaching because they help teachers understand the variety of English that is targeted. Based on an understanding of important registers, teachers can choose materials that target appropriate registers with appropriate levels of language as well. For example, Diaz-Santos (2000) uses the novel *Jurassic Park* in his course on English for science and technology because of its scientific content dealing with paleontology, genetic engineering, computer science, math, physics, and environmental science. The specific language of these fields is used to construct a story, including the people, places, physical descriptions, theories, and research that learners need. The narrative provides learners with access to the language of these fields at a level that both they and their teacher can comprehend.

What the teacher can do

Using *Google* to find reading and listening Web sites that contain materials about specific content areas and that are still accessible to a general audience of English language learners is not easy. And though developers of a few ESL Web sites such as those illustrated in Figures 8.1 and 8.2 on pages 198 and 199 have done some of this time-consuming work, much work still remains for teachers. They must determine the quality of the materials, determine whether the level of the materials is appropriate for their students, consider whether the length of the materials is appropriate for the assignments they have in mind, and consider how to sequence materials coming from different sources.

Material	*Arlyn Freed's ESL/EFL ESP*
Level	Intermediate to Advanced
Description	This Web site lists fields of interest for ESP learners, as shown in Figure 8.1. It provides teachers and students with links to a variety of resources under various headings, such as "Business English" and "Military English." For example, the "Business English" link leads to more links to textbooks, vocabulary exercises, online quizzes, *The Wall Street Journal*, and *Financial Times*. Teachers can use this site as a starting point when looking for online ESP materials.
Web site	http://www.eslhome.com/esl/esp
Notes	This free Web site has many links for business and finance, medicine, and science.

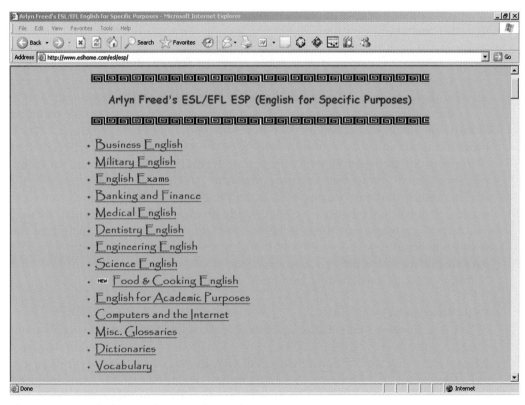

Figure 8.1 ESP links at Arlyn Freed's Web site.

Material	*UsingEnglish.com*
Level	Intermediate to Advanced
Description	The site in Figure 8.2 provides ESP resources for teachers. It categorizes links under headings such as "Medical English," "Military English," "Legal English," and "Writing in Engineering and the Sciences." It is a good place for teachers to get started compiling materials.
Web site	http://www.usingenglish.com/links/English_for_Special_Purposes/index.html site
Notes	Web sites that teachers find from these links could be used in WebQuests (assigned tasks, or quests, in which students search for and combine information from different Web sites).

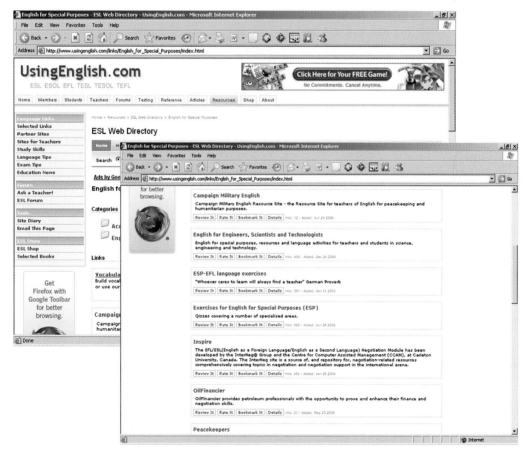

Figure 8.2 Resources on *UsingEnglish.com*.

2 | **Choose CALL activities that explicitly teach field-specific language.**

Texts that cover topics of interest frequently are not already packaged into language lessons. Therefore, teachers must analyze such texts to select and teach field-specific language explicitly. Such explicit instruction can include preteaching the vocabulary, lexical phrases, and grammar found in the specific-purpose texts.

What the research says

Few studies have assessed the effects of field-specific language teaching. One study found that the specific-purpose text types that learners had studied in their reading classes were useful to them later in their university studies (Hyon, 2001). In a study of the use of CALL for teaching business English, Brett (2000a) designed CALL software to draw learners' attention to the specific linguistic characteristics of conducting business in English and assessed learners' use of the software and attitudes toward it (2000b). The findings suggested that learners appreciated the opportunity to study the specific language that they needed, and that the computer (with its video and interactive capabilities) was a good tool for focusing learners' attention on the important aspects of the language event. Unfortunately, CALL materials for areas other than business are not plentiful, and therefore, teachers must take some lessons from projects such as Brett's to help turn specific-purpose language into specific-purpose language lessons.

What the teacher can do

Teachers can look for CALL materials that focus on language used for particular topics. Often this language includes vocabulary, and it may include descriptions of typical situations and the phrases that accompany them. Figure 8.3 shows an example of CALL for medical English, whereas the Web site in Figure 8.4 on page 202 focuses on English for tourism. In both cases, the CALL materials highlight and provide practice with language that is common for that particular purpose. In other words, these sites explicitly teach English (in contrast with the sites in Tip 1, which suggests finding materials to make into lessons).

Material	*englishmed.com*
Level	Intermediate
Description	The Web site in Figure 8.3 provides learners with practice using and listening to medical English. Students can choose from a focus on doctors, nurses, pharmacy, or general staff. Each section begins with an overview of a situation, along with relevant vocabulary (which is linked to an online dictionary). Students then watch and listen to a cartoon depicting the situation. The cartoons are followed by simple exercises that focus on word formation and language use in context.
Web site	http://www.englishmed.com/
Notes	This free Web site uses British English.

For a demonstration of students using this program, see the CD-ROM at the back of this book.

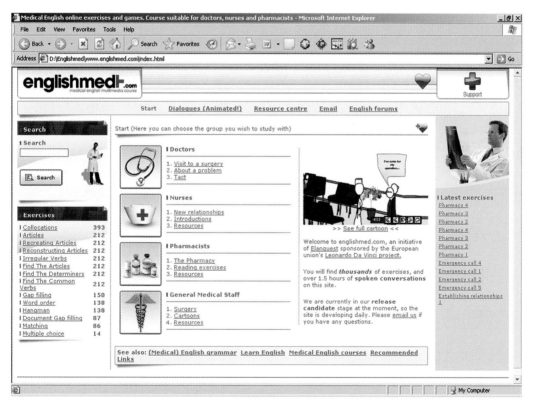

Figure 8.3 Practice with medical English at *englishmed.com.*

Material	*EnglishClub.com*
Level	Intermediate
Description	This Web site provides directed practice for using English for different jobs. In Figure 8.4, an example of English for tour guides is shown. Students read key words, phrases, and questions, and then they practice them in exercises. They compare their own responses with the correct answers. Students could probably work their way through this exercise in an hour or two. Teachers could use the questions and phrases to develop role-play activities that could be conducted in subsequent classes.
Web site	http://www.englishclub.com/english-for-work/tour-guide.htm
Notes	Work topics covered at this free Web site include English for hotel, airline, and food-and-drink staff, as well as medical professionals and police.

Figure 8.4 Tour guide English practiced at *EnglishClub.com*.

Provide learners with opportunities for interaction with the computer and with other English users to practice field-specific language.

Before the Internet, specific-purpose language was taught primarily through written texts, but in fact, specific-purpose language takes place in all forms of communication. Moreover, the language of the various registers differs, and therefore, it is important to give learners opportunities for interactions in various types of communicative situations, including electronic communication with others in the field, face-to-face communication, and interaction with Web pages.

What the research says

Research on language for specific purposes shows the different linguistic choices that language users make when they write a research article, compose an editorial, participate in a conversation, and so on. For example, Ferguson (2001) found important differences when looking at the following language events in medical discourse: research articles, editorials, and doctor-patient conversations. Lemke (2002) points out that a lot of the specific-purpose language that learners need to understand is displayed in the designs of the text and graphics on interactive Web sites. Learners need to interact with the computer by reading and understanding messages, making choices, and interpreting the consequences of their choices. One study reported on an online writing center for professional communication that was characterized as genre specific, context specific, and highly interactive. Intended as a resource that students can use outside of class, the center taught ways to communicate in various business-related genres such as letters and press releases. The initial evaluation was positive and the developers recommend continuation of such online centers that are focused on specific-purpose communication (Jacobs, Opdenacker, & Van Waes, 2005).

What the teacher can do

Teachers can look for CALL materials that engage learners with interesting, meaningful, and communicative exchanges. Some software has been developed specifically for English for special purposes. Figure 8.5 on page 204 shows an example of business English software. These types of programs not only provide language support in areas of vocabulary and grammar, but they also provide students with controlled materials with which they can practice communication skills.

Another way that students can become involved in communicative exchanges within their disciplines is by participating in online forums. One forum that is designated for general science and technology is shown is Figure 8.6 on page 205. Although students may not be ready to participate fully in field-specific professional forums, they can certainly benefit from these more controlled environments while they observe communication in other forums.

Material	*Talking Business* from Pearson Longman, Inc.
Level	Intermediate
Description	This software program provides students with extensive practice in business English. In the example in Figure 8.5, students listen to a conversation between Pierre and Alison in which they discuss Pierre's quarterly sales. The students interact with the computer as they type in the target sales and actual sales for each product and then check the correctness of their answers.
Web site	http://www.pearsonlongman.com/ae/multimedia/programs/TB.htm/
Notes	A different demo unit of this commercial program, *Handling Information*, can be downloaded from the Web site.

⊙ For a simulation that leads you through this program, see the CD-ROM at the back of this book.

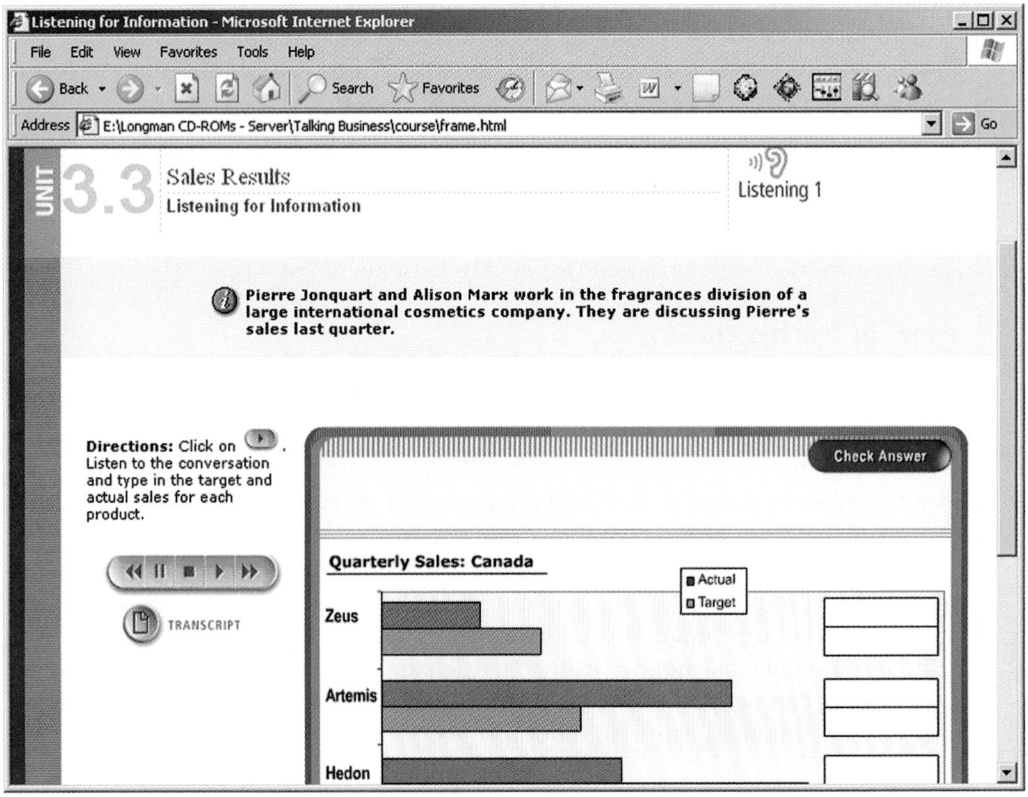

Figure 8.5 Business English practice with *Talking Business.*

Material	*Englishforums.com*
Level	Intermediate to Advanced
Description	This Web site provides forums on a variety of topics such as information technology, legal English, medical English, and business and finance English. Figure 8.6 shows an example of English for general science and technology. Students can post topics or questions, and they can respond to others.
Web site	http://www.englishforums.com/English/EnglishSpecificPurposes/ Group13.htm
Notes	The address above goes to the general ESP page. This Web site also includes forums related to learning English, such as English grammar and word games, basic English, and writing.

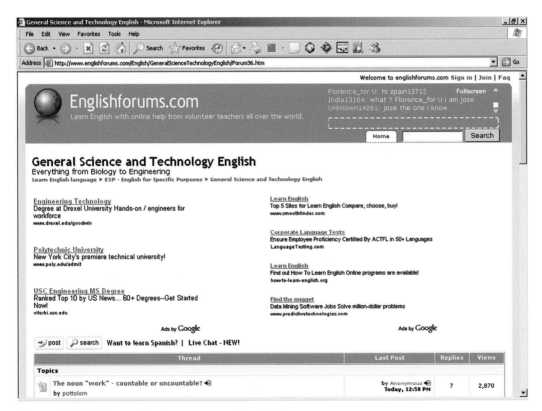

Figure 8.6 Field-specific language at *Englishforums.com*.

Help learners develop their strategies for finding and using field-specific materials online.

More than any other type of language, learners will need field-specific language to be able to develop on their own after they leave their English classes. Therefore, it is important for learners to know how to make the most of the electronic resources on the Web.

What the research says

Researchers have developed courses that teach strategies to help university students learn the language of their disciplines. Yoon and Hirvela (2004) investigated the use of corpora in two academic ESL writing classes with students from fifteen academic fields, most of which were science related. They used the Collins COBUILD Corpus, which is free on the Web. At first, teachers provided guidance for conducting searches, and then they gradually gave students more responsibility for searching the corpus. Over half of the students surveyed indicated that they used the corpus when writing papers for other courses, and almost 100 percent of the students indicated that they would use the corpus for writing papers in English in the future. All learners reported that using the corpus improved their confidence in writing in English. Lee and Swales (2006) also described such a course and the insights and difficulties associated with it. They referred to the course as a methodology for "technology-enhanced rhetorical consciousness-raising" (p. 72). The implication of consciousness raising is that it has long-term effects.

What the teacher can do

Once teachers have found materials that they think are worthwhile, they can show students how to search for interesting field-specific materials by following their methods for searching. An example of using a general list of sources to find one that concentrates on positive and negative business vocabulary is shown in Figure 8.7. Teachers can also introduce their students to the many free courses that are available online. These courses cover a variety of subjects, so students can work with content and topics that are specific to their fields of interest. One such site is shown in Figure 8.8 on page 208. Teachers should encourage students to use online tools such as dictionaries and concordancers while they are working with field-specific content. By considering a word in one text alongside a list of collocations, learners can get a feel for the scope and nuances of meanings.

Material	*Arlyn Freed's ESL/EFL ESP* and *Mike Nelson's Business English Lexis Site*
Level	High Intermediate to Advanced
Description	Teachers can guide students to more autonomous learning by showing them how to use teachers' resources. In Figure 8.7, the list of resources for business English from Figure 8.1 is displayed in the background. Teachers can encourage students to develop field-specific vocabulary by visiting sites like the business English lexis site in the foreground. This site has positive and negative categories for business terms. Teachers can show students how to copy lists into an Excel spreadsheet in order to keep a "book" of specific-purpose vocabulary words and phrases.
Web site	http://www.eslhome.com/esl/esp/#BE/ and http://users.utu.fi/micnel/ business_ english_lexis_site.htm/
Notes	Both of these Web sites are free.

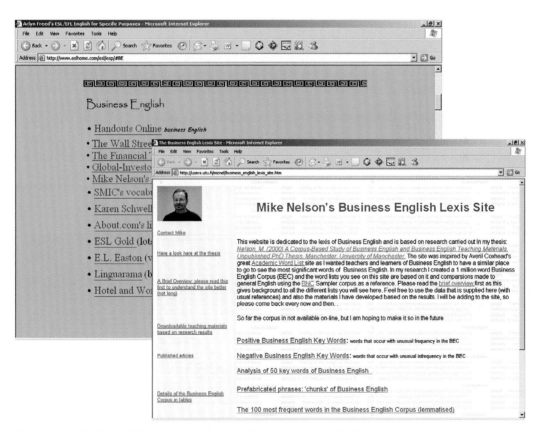

Figure 8.7 Online ESP materials from Arlyn Freed's and Mike Nelson's sites.

Material	Utah State OpenCourseWare and *Cobuild Concordance and Collocations Sampler*
Level	Advanced
Description	The screen shots in Figure 8.8 are from two Web sites that can be used together. On the left is a course on physical acoustics at Utah State University that is made available on the Web through the Open Courseware Consortium. Here, students can direct their own learning by working through course materials. Students are given reading assignments from textbooks, and online they are provided with key terms and ideas, along with animations. While students are reading online, they can work on developing field-specific vocabulary. Using the *Co-build Concordance and Collocations Sampler*, as shown on the right, students can compare the specific and general uses of the term *acoustic*.
Web site	http://www.ocw.usu.edu/ and http://www.collins.co.uk/Corpus/Corpus Search.aspx/
Notes	Both of these Web sites are free. The Open Courseware Consortium has online materials on a wide variety of courses. Click on "Use" at http://www.ocw.consortium.org/index.html to see participating schools (categorized by country) and their course materials.

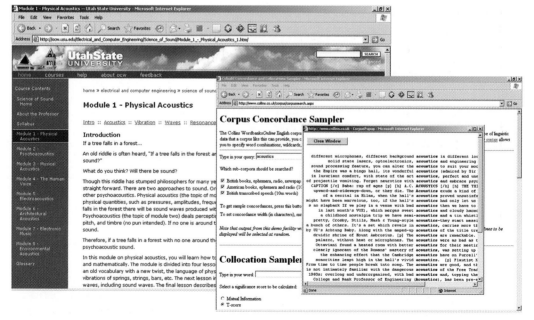

Figure 8.8 Physical acoustics lesson from Utah State University along with the *Cobuild Concordance and Collocations Sampler.*

FINDING AND DEVELOPING GOOD CONTENT-BASED ACTIVITIES

Examples in this chapter have illustrated some of the ways that CALL can help in teaching content-based language. At the same time, teachers and learners must actively seek out materials and, in many cases, transform existing language into language lessons. If learners are expected to apply the language learning benefits of CALL for field-specific language, teachers might consider the points outlined in this chapter when selecting materials. The specific questions that teachers might ask are summarized in the table.

What to look for	Focus questions
Learner fit	Does the specific-purpose language of the activities fit the learners in terms of level, topics, and activities?
Explicit teaching of specific-purpose vocabulary and grammar	Do the activities help learners focus on the particular language used to convey meanings in the content areas?
	Do the activities provide explicit instruction for teaching specific-purpose language?
	Do the programs come with materials to help teachers preteach and develop follow-up activities?
Interaction with the computer and with other people	Do the activities provide opportunities for interaction between the learner and the computer through specific-purpose software?
	Do the activities guide learners to work with classmates and contribute to online discussions through specific-purpose language?
Strategy development	Do the activities provide guidance for learners to develop strategies that will help them identify and analyze specific-purpose language on the Internet outside of class?

CONCLUSION

As Arnold (2006) points out, much more research is needed to strengthen or modify the perspectives on content-based teaching through CALL. It seems clear that the use of CALL in this area is essential because of the opportunities it offers learners for individual instruction with appropriate language content. Moreover, the learning strategies that are discussed throughout this book are essential as learners leave their English classes and become independent, content-based language learners.

AFTER CLASS

Yong Kim studied English with CALL for two of his many years in English classes in Korea. Eventually, he arrived in the United States to attend a university. He saw an announcement on the job board at the Student Services Building for a lab monitor job in one of the computer labs, and he wanted to apply. He had a CV to attach to his e-mail message, but he had to write something in the message. He wanted to write something short, and relatively informal, but it had to be correct. He thought he would not get an interview if his English was not correct. He just wanted to say, "I apply this job. Here is my CV." He knew from English class that he needed to check the verb and its object to see if anything was missing. He went to the *Compleat Lexical Tutor* to check the corpus. He typed "apply" for the main word and "job" for another word and received this sample from the corpus:

that they could apply for this **job** which had higher prestige

This looked good, but it was only one example, so maybe it was a strange phrase. Maybe *apply* was the wrong word for *job*. But, of course, he thought, this is not a corpus with job application letters. The corpus contained a variety of types of texts, not specific-purpose texts. "Apply for" seemed good to him, but he decided to look for some job letters before trying it in his writing. He went to *Google* in search of some more specific examples and typed in "Job Application Letters." The first ten of nearly 50 million entries appeared on the screen, and he began to look at them. The first one looked like this:

Cover Letter Examples

www.business.com Find Sample Cover **Letters**. Your Business Solution Business.com

He was not sure about the meaning of "cover letter," but it said "sample" and that looked good, so he tried that link, only to find another set of lists and then another. He backed out of that list and tried the next link, where he found what he was looking for—a sample letter for a job application.

211

I am writing to apply for the post of Management Trainee, which was advertised on the Student Affairs Office notice board of the Hong Kong Polytechnic University on 30 October 2006.

— elc.polyu.edu.hk/cill/jaleg.htm

He saw "apply for" again. That seemed good, but in this letter they called it a post rather than a job. And, he thought, the example comes from Hong Kong, so it is probably not American English. He was pretty sure that "job" was right, but he tried another link to see if he could find a more American example. He did not want his very brief e-mail to sound strange to Americans because he wanted to get a job interview. He tried the next link and found the following sample:

I am writing to apply for the programmer position advertised in the *Times Union*. As requested, I am enclosing a completed job application, my certification, my resume and three references.

— jobsearch.about.com/od/morejobletters/a/jobappletter.htm

That looked great. He could take some words from those two sentences and have his e-mail completed. He copied the two sentences, and then kept the phrases that he wanted, the ones underlined below:

<u>I am writing to apply for</u> the programmer position <u>advertised</u> in the *Times Union*. As requested, <u>I am</u> enclo<u>sing</u> a completed job application, my certification, <u>my résumé</u> and three references.

His final e-mail looked like this:

I am writing to apply for the lab monitor job advertised at the Student Services Building. I am attaching my résumé.
Thank you,
Yong Kim

Marta Diaz was composing an e-mail to a communication partner in Australia when she got stuck on a word. She was trying to describe the beach she had visited in Ontario over the summer where there were lots of beautiful rocks and trees, the water was clear, and there were no people around. "Canada is a very empty place," she wrote first, and then thought, "What is that word I need?" At that moment she recognized a gap in her language knowledge and consulted an online dictionary. She found that *empty* was often negative, but that *peaceful* was a word associated with a positive meaning of *empty*. She tried *peaceful* and wrote, "Canada is a very peaceful place."

Students who have experienced the CALL activities described in this book while studying English are likely to develop the types of strategies and habits that Yong and Marta demonstrated, which will be valuable to them for the rest of their lives as English users. Such students might read their computer screens with an electronic dictionary open on a window behind their text. They will interrupt their writing to check the corpus. Students who have studied academic writing may have constructed their own small corpus of texts that they can consult to remember how abstracts are written, what words to use to introduce the methods of a research paper, what tense to use in the results section, and when to use first person, for example.

In short, through the use of CALL, students can become autonomous learners with strategies that rely on technology for accessing help with their English. The teacher's choice of CALL activities, along with constant assistance in helping students use technology resources for language study, can make a difference in these language learners' lives.

What did the teacher do to prepare these students? The teacher explicitly taught English by selecting materials at an appropriate level of difficulty and content. She spent time on the Internet and at English teaching conferences finding CALL activities that fit the learners. The time invested paid off well as the materials were interesting to students, and learners felt successful in accomplishing their goals. The teacher selected materials that explicitly taught language and provided interaction between the student and the computer, as well as among the students. When CALL materials did not contain assessments, the teacher developed her own so that the students recognized the importance of what they were studying and received feedback about their successes.

Throughout the course, the teacher taught strategies for learning from electronic resources that students would be able to use after the course was finished. These pedagogical choices that the teacher made in selecting materials served as a kind of hidden curriculum for the students. The students knew they were in class to learn English, but they were also raising their awareness of how to learn and use resources for learning outside of class.

This book highlights the best of CALL for helping students learn, but of course learning takes place in the complex contexts of schools, homes, communities, and the world. Can teachers expect smooth sailing when they use CALL?

Overall, we find that teachers are excited about the opportunities for learning that CALL opens up for students, but there are also some common complaints, worries, and problems. The most frequent complaint heard from teachers is that they think that using the Internet and corpus/concordancer activities for examples of language may increase the problem of plagiarism. After all, if a teacher encourages students to look at the writing of others in order to find out how to put ideas down on paper, why would students not simply take those words, sentences, and paragraphs? Some teachers find that the use of electronic texts provides good opportunities for teaching about plagiarism, through instruction on paraphrasing, quoting, and citing Web sites. We all use words that have been used by others, but we follow rules for creatively combining the previously used words in a way that is unique. In the example earlier, Yong Kim accomplished such a feat as he borrowed the formulaic language of the job application letter without attempting to use the other person's words. He had learned a good strategy in his English class as well as the metalinguistic skills to carry it out.

A worry that teachers have when they introduce learners to activities on the Internet is that they will undoubtedly be sending students into conversations where they will see varied types of Internet English. They may even be inadvertently sending them down a dangerous path of communicating with strangers who may be unkind or even criminal. Teachers can find many opportunities for offering electronic communication in relatively safe environments, such as those created through matching learners within an English class or across different language classes. However, this book advocates connecting learners with the real conversations that take place in professional forums on the Internet, and with that advocacy must come information and warnings about the different kinds of people that learners might encounter in the online world. In a sense, the same warning applies to any form of contact with strangers, but the Internet seems to call for a higher level of caution.

A third issue is technical problems with equipment and software. This potential problem differs dramatically from one school and classroom to another and therefore general advice is difficult to provide. However, it is recommended that teachers who are planning to make use of CALL should gain some basic familiarity with using the computer if they do not already have this knowledge. Most teachers can find short courses, friends, and other sources of guidance on computer use, and this pays off when using the computer in class. However, when significant problems arise, teachers need to know where to turn for help. In very few schools are the English teachers the first or only ones to use computers, which means most schools have a means for getting solutions to technical problems.

Finally, some teachers worry about being in a position where the students know more than they do about the technology. This is a common feeling. There are always students in class who know more about the technology than teachers do. But the technical expertise of these students can be very useful in helping others in the class, as well as teachers. Teachers are, however, more knowledgeable about the content—in other words, what they are doing with the computer. ESL teachers are there to teach English and strategies for learning English through technology. As long as teachers maintain this expertise, students' expertise in information technology should be seen as an asset and not a threat.

All of these are important concerns and are not intended to be minimized by this short discussion. However, they are simply part of the job of English language teaching today. Whether the benefits of technology outweigh the potential problems might be debated, but it will remain an academic debate. The reality is that computer technology is very much a part of students' lives, and therefore, the challenge for teachers is to help them make the best use of the technology as lifelong English language learners.

Abraham, R. (1985). Field independence–dependence and the teaching of grammar. *TESOL Quarterly, 19,* 689–702.

Abraham, R., & Liou, H.-C. (1991). Interaction generated by three computer programs: Analysis of functions of spoken language. In P. Dunkel (Ed.), *Computer-Assisted Language Learning and Testing: Research Issues and Practice* (pp. 85–109). New York: Newbury House.

Adult Reading Activities. Retrieved October 5, 2007, http://www.cdlponline.org/index.cfm.

Alderson, J. C., & Hamp-Lyons, L. (1996). TOEFL preparation courses: A study of washback. *Language Testing, 13*(3), 280–297.

Alessi, S., & Trollip, S. (2001). *Multimedia for Learning.* Boston: Allyn & Bacon.

AMES Click into English. (1998). Version 3.33. Hong Kong: Clarity Language Consultants.

Arnold, N. (2006). Expanding CALL beyond general language classes: The case of courses in language for specific purposes. In L. Ducate & N. Arnold (Eds.), *Calling on CALL: From theory and research to new directions in foreign language teaching* (pp. 269–288). San Marcos, TX: CALICO.

Atkinson, R. C. (1972). Optimizing the learning of a second-language vocabulary. *Journal of Experimental Psychology, 96,* 124–129.

Bejar, I., Douglas, D., Jamieson, J., Nissan, S., & Turner, J. (2000). *TOEFL 2000 listening framework: A working paper.* Monograph Series MS-19. Princeton, NJ: Educational Testing Service.

Belz, J. A. (2001). Institutional and individual dimensions of transatlantic group work in network-based language teaching. *ReCALL, 13*(2), 213–231.

Belz, J. A. (2003). Linguistic perspectives on the development of intercultural competence in telecollaboration. *Language Learning & Technology, 7*(2), 68–117.

Belz, J. A. (2004). Learner corpus analysis and the development of foreign language proficiency. *System 32*(4), 577–591.

Belz, J. A., & Kinginger, C. (2003). Discourse options and the development of pragmatic competence by classroom learners of German: The case of address forms. *Language Learning, 53*(4), 591–648.

Bhatia, V. K. (1993). *Analysing genre: Language use in professional settings.* London: Longman.

Biber, D., Johansson, S., Leech, G., Conrad, S., & Finegan. E. (1999). *The Longman grammar of spoken and written English.* London: Longman.

Blake, R. (2000). Computer-mediated communication: A window on L2 Spanish interlanguage. *Language Learning & Technology, 4*(1), 120–136.

Blake, R. J., & Zyzik, E. C. (2003). Who's helping whom?: Learner/heritage-speakers' networked discussions in Spanish. *Applied Linguistics, 24*(4), 519–544.

Boris, J. *Easy Writer.* Retrieved October 5, 2007, http://www.softwareforstudents.com.

Brett, P. (1997). A comparative study of the effects of the use of multimedia on listening comprehension. *System, 25,* 39–53.

Brett, P. (2000a). Developing cross-cultural competence in business through multimedia courseware. *ReCALL Journal, 12*(2), 196–208.

Brett, P. (2000b). Integrating multimedia into the business English curriculum: A case study. *English for Specific Purposes, 19*(3), 269–290.

Brinton, D. (2001). The use of media in language teaching. In M. Celce-Murcia (Ed.), *Teaching English as a second or foreign language* (3rd ed., pp. 459–476). Boston: Heinle & Heinle.

Brown, G. (1995). Dimensions of difficulty in listening comprehension. In D. Mendelsohn & J. Rubin (Eds.), *A guide for the teaching of second language listening* (pp. 59–73). San Diego, CA: Dominie Press.

Brown, H. D. (2000). *Principles of language learning and teaching.* New York: Longman.

Buck, G. (1995). How to become a good listening teacher. In D. Mendelsohn & J. Rubin (Eds.), *A guide for the teaching of second language listening* (pp. 113–131). San Diego, CA: Dominie Press.

Buck, G. (1997). Testing listening skills. In C. Clapham & D. Corson (Eds.), *Encyclopedia of language and education, Volume 7* (pp 65–74). Boston: Kluwer Academic Publishers.

Buck, G. (2001). *Assessing listening.* New York: Cambridge University Press.

Burston, J. (2001). Exploiting the potential of a computer-based grammar checker in conjunction with self-monitoring strategies with advanced level students of French. *CALICO Journal, 18*(3), 499–515.

Carrell, P. L., & Grabe, W. (2002). Reading. In N. Schmitt (Ed.), *An introduction to applied linguistics* (pp. 233–250). London: Arnold.

Chamot, A., Hartmann, P., & Huizenga, J. (2004). *Shining Star, Level B.* [CD-ROM]. White Plains, NY: Pearson Education.

Chang, K-Y. R., & Smith, W. F. (1991). Cooperative learning and CALL/IVD in beginning Spanish: An experiment. *The Modern Language Journal, 75*, 205–211.

Chapelle, C. (2001). *Computer applications in second language acquisition: Foundations for teaching, testing, and research.* Cambridge, UK: Cambridge University Press.

Chapelle, C. A. (2003). *English language learning and technology: Lectures on applied linguistics in the age of information and communication technology.* Amsterdam: John Benjamins Publishing.

Chen, J., Belkada, S., & Okamoto, T. (2004). How a web-based course facilitates acquisition of English for academic purposes. *Language Learning & Technology, 8*(2), 33–49.

Cheng, L., & Watanabe, Y. (Eds.). (2004). *Washback in language testing: Research contexts and methods.* Mahwah, NJ: Lawrence Erlbaum Associates.

Cheng, W., Warren, M., & Xun-feng, X. (2003). The language learner as language researchers: Putting corpus linguistics on the timetable. *System, 31*, 173–186.

Chenoweth, N. A., & Murday, K. (2003). Measuring student learning in an online French course. *CALICO, 20*(2), 285–314.

Chun, D. M. (1994). Using computer networking to facilitate the acquisition of interactive competence. *System, 22*(1), 17–31.

Chun, D. M. (2001). L2 reading on the Web: Strategies for accessing information in hypermedia. *Computer Assisted Language Learning, 14*(5), 367–403.

Chun, D. M. (2002). *Discourse intonation in L2: From theory to practice.* Amsterdam: John Benjamins Publishing.

Chun, D. M. (2006). CALL technologies for L2 reading. In L. Ducate & N. Arnold (Eds.), *Calling on CALL: From theory and research to new directions in foreign language teaching* (pp. 69–98). San Marcos, TX: CALICO.

Chun, D. M., & Plass, J. L. (1996). Effects of multimedia annotations on vocabulary acquisition. *The Modern Language Journal, 80*, 183–198.

Clarity Language Consultants Ltd. (2004). *Click into English.* Hong Kong: Author.

Coady, J., & Huckin, T. (Eds.). (1997). *Second language vocabulary acquisition.* Cambridge, UK: Cambridge University Press.

Cobb, T., & Stevens, V. (1996). A principled consideration of computers and reading in a second language. In M. Pennington (Ed.), *The power of CALL* (pp. 115–136). Houston, TX: Athelstan.

Colombi, M. C., & Schleppegrell, M. J. (2002). Theory and practice in the development of advanced literacy. In M. J. Schleppegrell & M. C. Colombi (Eds.), *Developing advanced literacy in first and second languages* (pp. 1–19). Mahwah, NJ: Lawrence Erlbaum Associates.

Conrad, S. (2000). Will corpus linguistic revolutionize grammar teaching in the 21st century? *TESOL Quarterly, 34*(3), 548–560.

Coxhead, A. (2000). A new academic word list. *TESOL Quarterly, 34*(2), 213–238.

Crookes, G. (1989). Planning and interlanguage variation. *Studies in Second Language Acquisition, 11*, 367–383.

Crystal, D. (2001). *Language and the Internet.* Cambridge, UK: Cambridge University Press.

Daedalus Group, Inc. *Daedalus Integrated Writing Environment: DIWE 7.* Retrieved October 5, 2007, http://www.daedalus.com.

de Graaff, R. (1997). The Experanto Experiment: Effects of explicit instruction on second language acquisition. *Studies in Second Language Acquisition, 19*, 249–276.

De la Fuente, M. J. (2003). Is SLA interactionist theory relevant to CALL? A study of the effects of computer-mediated interaction in L2 vocabulary acquisition. *Computer Assisted Language Learning, 16*(1), 47–81.

DeKeyser, R. M. (1995). Learning second language grammar rules: An experiment with a miniature linguistic system. *Studies in Second Language Acquisition, 17*, 379–410.

DeKeyser, R. M. (2003). Implicit and explicit learning. In C. J. Doughty & M. H. Long (Eds.), *The handbook of second-language acquisition* (pp. 313-348). Oxford, UK: Blackwell Publishing.

Derwing, T. M., & Munro, M. J. (2005). Second language accent and pronunciation teaching: A research-based approach. *TESOL Quarterly, 39*(3), 379-398.

Derwing, T. M., Munro, M. J., & Wiebe, G. (1998). Evidence in favor of a broad framework for pronunciation instruction. *Language Learning, 48*, 393-410.

Deterding, D. (2005). Listening to estuary English in Singapore. *TESOL Quarterly, 39*(3), 425-440.

Diaz-Santos, G. (2000). Technothrillers and English for science and technology. *English for Specific Purposes, 19*, 221-236.

Doughty, C. (1987). Relating second-language acquisition theory to CALL research and application. In W. F. Smith (Ed.), *Modern media in foreign language education: Theory and implementation* (pp. 133-167). Lincolnwood, IL: National Textbook Company.

Doughty, C. (1991). Second language instruction does make a difference: Evidence from an empirical study of SL relativization. *Studies in Second Language Acquisition, 13*, 431-469.

Doughty, C., & Long, M. (2002). *Optimal psycholinguistic environments for distance foreign language learning.* Paper presented at the Distance Learning of the Less Commonly Taught Languages Conference, Arlington, VA, February 1-3.

Doughty, C., & Williams, J. (Eds.). (1998). *Focus on form in classroom second language acquisition.* Cambridge, UK: Cambridge University Press.

"Dreams of new ways to fly." Learning Resources Site. Retrieved October 5, 2007, http://litera-cynet.org/cnnsf/flydreams/storyweek.html.

Educational Activities Software. *The Real Achievement Reading Solutions.* Retrieved October 5, 2007, http://www.ea-software.com/pdf/reading.pdf.

Educational Testing Service. (2005). *Criterion.* Princeton, NJ: Author.

Egbert, J., & Hanson-Smith, E. (Eds.). (1999). CALL Environments: Research, Practice, and Critical Issues. Alexandria, VA: TESOL.

Ellis, N. C. (2002). Frequency effects in language processing: A review with implications for theories of implicit and explicit language acquisition. *Studies in Second Language Acquisition, 24*, 143-188.

Ellis, R. (1995). Interpretation tasks for grammar teaching. *TESOL Quarterly, 29*(1), 88-106.

Ellis, R. (1998). Teaching and research: Options in grammar teaching. *TESOL Quarterly, 32*(1), 39-60.

Ellis, R. (1999). *Learning a Second Language Through Interaction.* Amsterdam: John Benjamins Publishing.

Eskenazi, M. (1999). Using foreign language speech processing for foreign language pronunciation tutoring: Some issues and a prototype. *Language Learning & Technology, 2*(2), 62-76.

Ferguson, G. (2001). If you pop over there: A corpus-based study of conditionals in medical discourse. *English for Specific Purposes, 20*, 61-82.

Fernández-Garciá, M., & Martínez-Arbelaiz, A. (2002). Negotiation of meaning in nonnative speaker–nonnative speaker synchronous discussions. *CALICO Journal, 19*(2), 279-294.

Fernández-Garciá, M., & Martínez-Arbelaiz, A. (2003). Learners' interactions: A comparison of oral and computer-assisted written conversation. *ReCALL Journal, 15*(1), 113-136.

Ferris, D. (2002). *Treatment of error in second language student writing.* Ann Arbor: University of Michigan Press.

Ferris, D. (2004). The "grammar correction" debate in L2 writing: Where are we, and where do we go from here? (and what do we do in the meantime...?). *Journal of Second Language Writing, 13*, 49-62.

Fiori, M. L. (2005). The development of grammatical competence through synchronous computer-mediated communication. *CALICO Journal, 22*(3), 567-602.

Flege, J. E. (1995). Second language speech learning: Theory, findings, and problems. In W. Strange (Ed.), *Speech perception and linguistic experience: Issues in cross language research* (pp. 233-277). Baltimore, MD: York Press.

Flowerdew, J., & Miller, L. (2005). *Second language listening.* Cambridge, UK: Cambridge University Press.

Folse, K. (2004). *Vocabulary myths.* Ann Arbor: University of Michigan Press.

Gass, S. (1997). *Input, interaction, and the second language learner*. Mahwah, NJ: Lawrence Erlbaum Associates.

Goodfellow, R., & Laurillard, D. (1994). Modeling lexical processes in lexical CALL. *CALICO Journal, 11*(3), 19–46.

Grabe, W., & Kaplan, R. B. (1996). *Theory and practice of writing: An applied linguistic perspective*. New York: Longman.

Gu, P.Y. (2003). Fine brush and freehand: The vocabulary-learning art of two successful Chinese EFL learners. *TESOL Quarterly, 37*(1), 73–104.

Hardison, D. (2004). Generalization of computer-assisted prosody training: Quantitative and qualitative findings. *Language Learning & Technology, 8*(1), 34–52.

Hardison, D. (2005). Contextualized computer-based L2 prosody training: Evaluating the effects of discourse context and video input. *CALICO Journal, 22*(2), 175–190.

Hazenberg, S., & Hulstijn, J.H. (1996). Defining a minimal receptive second language vocabulary for non-native university students: An empirical investigation. *Applied Linguistics, 17*(2), 145–163.

Healy, D., & Johnson, N. *CALL–IS Software List*. Retrieved October 5, 2007, http://oregonstate.edu/dept/eli/softlist/lista.html.

Helgesen, M., & Brown, S. (2007). *Practical English language teaching: Listening*. New York: McGraw Hill.

Herring, S. C. (Ed.) (1996). *Computer-mediated communication: Linguistic, social, and cross-cultural perspectives*. Amsterdam: John Benjamins Publishing.

Hinkel, E., & Fotos, S. (Eds.). (2002). *New perspectives on grammar teaching in second-language classrooms*. Mahwah, NJ: Lawrence Erlbaum Associates.

Hinkel, E., & Fotos, S. (2002). From theory to practice: A teacher's view. In E. Hinkel & S. Fotos (Eds.), *New perspectives on grammar teaching in second-language classrooms* (pp. 1–15). Mahwah, NJ: Lawrence Erlbaum Associates.

Hirata, Y. (2004). Computer-assisted pronunciation training for native English speakers learning Japanese pitch and durational contrasts. *Computer Assisted Language Learning, 17*(3–4), 357–376.

Horst, M., Cobb, T., & Nicolae, I. (2005). Expanding academic vocabulary with an interactive online database. *Language Learning & Technology, 9*(2), 90–110.

Hubbard, P. (2004). Learner training for effective use of CALL. In S. Fotos & C. Browne (Eds.), *New perspectives on CALL for second-language classrooms* (pp. 45–67). Mahwah, NJ: Lawrence Erlbaum Associates.

Hulstijn, J. (2003). Connectionist models of language processing and the training of listening skills with the aid of multimedia software. *Computer Assisted Language Learning, 16*, 413–425.

Hyon, S. (2001). Long-term effects of genre-based instruction: A follow-up study of an EAP reading course. *English for Specific Purposes, 20*, 417–438.

Jacobs, G., Opdenacker, L., & Van Waes, L. (2005). A multilanguage online writing center for professional communication: Development and testing. *Business Communication Quarterly, 68*, 8–22.

Jenkins, J. (2002). A sociolinguistically based, empirically researched pronunciation syllabus for English as an international language. *Applied Linguistics, 23*, 83–103.

Jeon-Ellis, G., Debski, R. & Wigglesworth, G. (2005). Oral interaction around computers in the project-oriented CALL classroom. *Language Learning & Technology, 9*(3), 121–145.

Jepson, K. (2005). Conversations—and negotiated interaction—in text and voice chat rooms. *Language Learning & Technology, 9*(3), 79–98.

Johns, T. (1994). From printout to handout: Grammar and vocabulary teaching in the context of data-driven learning. In T. Odlin (Ed.), *Perspectives on pedagogical grammar* (pp. 293–313). Cambridge, UK: Cambridge University Press.

Jones, L. C. (2006). Effects of collaboration and multimedia annotations on vocabulary learning and listening comprehension. *CALICO Journal, 24*(1), 33–58.

Kern, R. G. (1995). Restructuring classroom interaction with networked computers: Effects on quantity and characteristics of language production. *Modern Language Journal, 79*, 457–476.

Kern, R. G. (2000). *Literacy and language teaching*. Oxford, UK: Oxford University Press.

Kern, R. G. (2006). Perspectives on technology in learning and teaching languages. *TESOL Quarterly, 40*(1), 183-210.

Klingner, J. K., & Vaughn, S. (2000). The helping behaviors of fifth graders while using collaborative strategic reading during ESL content classes. *TESOL Quarterly, 34*(1), 69-98.

Krashen, S. (1982). *Principles and practice in second-language acquisition*. Oxford, UK: Pergamon.

Kress, G. (2004). *Literacy in the new media age*. London: Routledge.

Lam, W. S. E. (2000). Second language literacy and the design of the self: A case study of a teenager writing on the Internet. *TESOL Quarterly, 34*(3), 457-482.

Lamy, M-N., & Goodfellow, R. (1999). Reflective conversation in the virtual language classroom. *Language Learning & Technology, 2*(2): 43-61.

Lee, D., & Swales, J. (2006). A corpus-based EAP course for NNS doctoral students: Moving from available specialized corpora to self-compiled corpora. *English for Specific Purposes, 25* (1), 56-75.

Lee, L. (2001). Online interaction: Negotiation of meaning and strategies used among learners of Spanish. *ReCALL Journal, 13*(2): 232-244.

Lee, L. (2004). Learners' perspectives on networked collaborative interaction with native speakers of Spanish in the US. *Language Learning & Technology, 8*(1), 83-100.

Lemke, J. (2002). Multimedia semiotics: Genres for science education and scientific literacy. In M. J. Schleppegrell & M. C. Colombi (Eds.), *Developing advanced literacy in first and second languages: Meaning with power* (pp. 21-44). Mahwah, NJ: Lawrence Erlbaum Associates.

Lightbown, P., & Spada, N. (1999). *How languages are learned*. New York: Oxford University Press.

Liou, H.-C. (1991). Development of an English grammar checker: A progress report. *CALICO Journal, 9*(1), 57-70.

Liou, H.-C. (1993). Investigation of using text critiquing programs in a process oriented writing class. *CALICO Journal, 10*(4), 17-38.

Loschky, L., & Bley-Vroman, R. (1993). Grammar and task-based methodology. In G. Crookes & S. Gass (Eds.), *Tasks and language learning: Integrating theory and practice* (pp. 123-167). Clevedon, UK: Multilingual Matters, Ltd.

Lynch, T. (1998). Theoretical perspectives on listening. *ARAL, 18*, 3-19.

Lyster, R., & Ranta, L. (1997). Corrective feedback and learner uptake: Negotiation of form in communicative classrooms. *Studies in Second Language Acquisition, 19*, 37-66.

MacDonald, D., Yule, G., & Powers, M. (1994). Attempts to improve English L2 pronunciation: The variable effects of different types of instruction. *Language Learning, 44*, 75-100.

Mendelsohn, D. (1994). *Learning to Listen: A strategy-based approach for the second-language learner*. San Diego, CA: Dominie Press.

Mendelsohn, D. (1995). Applying learning strategies in the second/foreign language listening comprehension lesson. In D. Mendelsohn & J. Rubin (Eds.), *A guide for the teaching of second-language listening* (pp. 132-150). San Diego, CA: Dominie Press.

Merit Software. *Paragraph Punch*. Retrieved October 5, 2007, http://www.paragraph-punch.com.

Mishan, F. (2004). Authenticating corpora for language learning: A problem and its resolution. *ELT Journal, 58*(3), 219-227.

Mohan, B. (1986). *Language and content*. Reading, MA: Addison-Wesley Publishing Company.

Mohan, B. (1992). Models of the role of the computer in second language development. In M. Pennington & V. Stevens (Eds.), *Computers in applied linguistics: An international perspective* (pp. 110-126). Clevedon, UK: Multilingual Matters, Ltd.

Morley, J. (1984). *Listening and language learning in ESL: Developing self-study activities for listening comprehension*. Orlando, FL: Harcourt Brace Jovanovich, Inc.

Morley, J. (1995). Academic listening comprehension instruction: Models, principles, and practices. In D. Mendelsohn & J. Rubin, *A guide for the teaching of second language listening* (pp. 186-221). San Diego, CA: Dominie Press.

Morley, J. (2001). Aural comprehension instruction: Principles and practice. In M. Celce-Murcia (Ed.), *Teaching English as a second or foreign language* (3rd ed., pp. 69–85). Boston: Heinle & Heinle.

Nagata, N. (1993). Intelligent computer feedback for second language instruction. *The Modern Language Journal, 77*(3), 330–339.

Nagata, N. (1998). Input vs. output practice in educational software for second language acquisition. *Language Learning & Technology, 1*(2), 23–40.

Nassaji, H. (2003). L2 vocabulary learning from context: Strategies, knowledge sources, and their relationship with success in L2 lexical inferencing. *TESOL Quarterly, 37*(4), 645–670.

Nation, I. S. P. (2001). *Learning vocabulary in another language*. Cambridge, UK: Cambridge University Press.

Negretti, R. (1999). Web-based activities and SLA: A conversation analysis research approach. *Language Learning & Technology, 3*(1), 75–87.

Nutta, J. (1998). Is computer-based grammar instruction as effective as teacher-directed grammar instruction for teaching L2 structures? *CALICO Journal, 16*(1), 49–62.

O'Brien, M. G. (2006). Teaching pronunciation and intonation with computer technology. In L. Ducate & N. Arnold (Eds.), *Calling on CALL: From theory and research to new directions in foreign language teaching* (pp. 127–148). San Marcos, TX: CALICO.

Oh, S-Y. (2001). Two types of input modification and EFL reading comprehension: Simplification versus elaboration. *TESOL Quarterly, 35*(1), 69–96.

Ohta, A. (2000). Rethinking interaction in SLA: Developmentally appropriate assistance in the zone of proximal development and the acquisition of L2 grammar. In J. Lantolf (Ed.), *Sociocultural theory and second language learning* (pp. 51–78). Oxford, UK: Oxford University Press.

Open Book Learning. (2004). *OpenBook AnyWhere*. Alpharetta, GA: Author.

Oxford, R. (1990). *Language learning strategies*. New York: Newbury House Publishers.

Paltridge, B. (2001). *Genre and the language learning classroom*. Ann Arbor: University of Michigan Press.

Payne, S. & Whitney, P. J. (2002). Developing L2 oral proficiency through synchronous CMC: Output, working memory, and interlanguage development. *CALICO Journal, 20*(1), 7–32.

Pellettieri, J. (2000). Negotiation in cyberspace: The role of *chatting* in the development of grammatical competence in the virtual foreign language classroom. In M. Warschauer & R. Kern (Eds.), *Network-based language teaching: Concepts and practice* (pp. 59–86). Cambridge, UK: Cambridge University Press.

Pen Pals at *Linguistic Funland*. Retrieved October 5, 2007, http://www.tesol.net/penpals/penpal.cgi.

Pennington, M. (1999). Computer-aided pronunciation pedagogy: Promise, limitations, directions. *Computer Assisted Language Learning, 12*(5), 427–440.

Peterson, P. (2001). Skills and strategies for proficient listening. In M. Celce-Murcia (Ed.), *Teaching English as a second or foreign language* (3rd ed., pp. 87–100). Boston: Heinle & Heinle.

Pica, T. (1994) Research on negotiation: What does it reveal about second-language learning conditions, processes, and outcomes? *Language Learning, 44*(3), 493–527.

Piper, A. (1986). Conversation and the computer: A study of the conversational spin-off generated among learners of English as a second language working in groups. *System, 14,* 187–198.

Plass, J. L., Chun, D. M., Mayer, R. E., & Leutner, D. (1998). Supporting visual and verbal learning preferences in a second-language multimedia learning environment. *Journal of Educational Psychology, 90,* 25–36.

Read, J. (2000). *Assessing vocabulary*. Cambridge, UK: Cambridge University Press.

Readers respond. *TOPICS: An On-Line Magazine for Learners of English*. Retrieved October 5, 2007, http://www.topics-mag.com/readers/cheating-forum.htm.

Reading section. ESL Independent Study Lab, Louis and Clark College. Retrieved October 5, 2007, http://www.lclark.edu/~krauss/toppicks/reading.html.

Reading Upgrade. Retrieved October 5, 2007, http://www.readingupgrade.com/test/demo.htm.

Reading Zone. English-Zone.Com. Retrieved October 5, 2007, http://english-zone.com/index.php?ID=6.

Rost, M. (1994). On-line summaries as representations of lecture understanding. In J. Flowerdew (Ed.), *Academic listening: Research perspectives* (pp. 93-127). New York: Cambridge University Press.

Rost, M. (2002). *Teaching and researching listening.* White Plains, NY: Pearson Education.

Rost, M. (2005). L2 listening. In E. Hinkel (Ed.), *Handbook of research in second language teaching and learning* (pp. 503-527). Mahwah, NJ: Lawrence Erlbaum Associates.

Rost, M., & Fuchs, M. (2003). *Longman English Interactive 3.* White Plains, NY: Pearson Education.

Rubin, J. (1995). The contribution of video to the development of listening comprehension. In D. Mendelsohn & J. Rubin (Eds.), *A guide for the teaching of second-language listening* (pp. 151-165). San Diego, CA: Dominie Press.

Sadow, C., & Sather, E. (1998). *On the air! Listening to radio talk.* New York: St. Martin's Press.

Schleppegrell, M. J. (2004). *The language of schooling: A functional linguistics perspective.* Mahwah, NJ: Lawrence Erlbaum Associates.

Schmidt, R. (1992). Awareness and second language acquisition. *Annual Review of Applied Linguistics, 13*, 206-226.

Schmitt, N., & Carter, R. (Eds.). (2004). Formulaic sequences in action: An introduction. In N. Schmitt (Ed.), *Formulaic sequences* (pp. 1-22). Amsterdam: John Benjamins Publishing.

Schmitt, N., & Zimmerman, C. B. (2002). Derivative word forms: What do learners know? *TESOL Quarterly, 36*(2), 145-171.

Sharwood Smith, M. (1993). Input enhancement in instructed SLA: Theoretical bases. *Studies in Second Language Acquisition, 15*, 165-179.

Skehan, P. (1998). *A cognitive approach to language learning.* Oxford, UK: Oxford University Press.

Skimming exercise. University of Victoria. Retrieved October 5, 2007, http://web2.uvcs.uvic.ca/elc/studyzone/570/pulp/hemp1.htm.

Smith, B. (2004). Computer-mediated negotiated interaction and lexical acquisition. *Studies in Second Language Acquisition, 26*, 365-398.

Smoking. (1999). *Issues in English.* Version 1. Hurstbridge, Victoria, Australia: Protea Textware.

Stockwell, G., & Harrington, M. (2003). The incidental development of L2 proficiency in NS-NNS email interactions. *CALICO Journal, 20*(2), 337-359.

Swain, M. (1985). Communicative competence: Some roles of comprehensible input and comprehensible output in its development. In S. M. Gass & C. G. Madden (Eds.), *Input in second-language acquisition* (pp. 235-253). Rowley, MA: Newbury House Publishers.

Swain, M. (1998). Focus on form through conscious reflection. In C. Doughty & J. Williams (Eds.), *Focus on form in classroom second-language acquisition* (pp. 64-81). Cambridge, UK: Cambridge University Press.

Swain, M., & Lapkin, S. (1995). Problems in output and the cognitive processes they generate: A step towards second language learning. *Applied Linguistics, 16*, 371-391.

Swales, J. (1991). *Genre analysis.* Cambridge, UK: Cambridge University Press.

Swales, J. M., Barks, D., Ostermann, A. C., & Simpson, R. C. (2001). Between critique and accommodation: Reflections on an EAP course for masters of architecture students. *English for Specific Purposes, 20*, 439-458.

Sykes, J. M. (2005). Synchronous CMC and pragmatic development: Effects of oral and written chat. *CALICO Journal, 22*(3), 399-431.

Tarone, E. (2005). Speaking in a second language. In E. Hinkel (Ed.), *Handbook of research in second-language teaching and learning* (pp. 485-502). Mahwah, NJ: Lawrence Erlbaum Associates.

Tarone, E., & Yule, G. (1989). *Focus on the language learner.* New York: Oxford University Press.

Thorne, S. L. (2003). Artifacts and cultures-of-use in intercultural communication. *Language Learning, & Technology, 7*(2), 38-67.

Thorne, S. L., & Payne, S. (2005). Evolutionary trajectories, Internet-mediated expression, and language education. *CALICO Journal, 22*(3), 371-398.

TOPICS: An On-Line Magazine for Learners of English. Retrieved October 5, 2007, http://www.topics-mag.com/.

Tozcu, A., & Coady, J. (2004). Successful learning of frequent vocabulary through CALL also benefits reading comprehension and speed. *Computer Assisted Language Learning, 17*(5), 473-495.

Tuomey, E. *WriteFix.* Retrieved October 5, 2007, http://www.writefix.com/argument/.

Tyner, K. (1998). *Literacy in a digital world: Teaching and learning in the age of information.* Mahwah, NJ: Lawrence Erlbaum Associates.

University of Sheffield. *eTandem.* Retrieved October 5, 2007, http://www.shef.ac.uk/mirrors/tandem/etandem/etindex-en.html.

Ur, P. (1984). *Teaching listening comprehension.* Cambridge, UK: Cambridge University Press.

Van Lier, L. (1996). *Interaction in the language curriculum: Awareness, autonomy, and authenticity.* London: Longman.

Vandergrift, L. (1996). The listening comprehension strategies of core French high school students. *Canadian Modern Language Review, 52,* 200-223.

Vandergrift, L. (2003). Orchestrating strategy use: Toward a model of the skilled second language listener. *Language Learning, 53*(3), 463-496.

Vandergrift, L. (2004). Listening to learn or learning to listen? *ARAL, 24,* 3-25.

Vantage Learning. *MY Access!* Retrieved October 5, 2007, http://www.vantagelearning.com/myaccess/.

Wang, J., & Munro, M. J. (2004). Computer-based training for learning English vowel contrasts. *System, 32,* 539-552.

Warschauer, M. (1995/1996) Comparing face-to-face and electronic discussion in the second language classroom. *CALICO Journal, 13*(2-3): 7-25.

Warschauer, M. (1997). Computer-mediated collaborative learning: Theory and practice. *The Modern Language Journal, 81,* 470-481.

Warschauer, M. (2000). The changing global economy and the future of English teaching. *TESOL Quarterly, 34,* 511-535.

White, J. (1998). Getting the learners' attention: A typographical input enhancement study. In C. Doughty & J. Williams (Eds.), *Focus on form in classroom second-language acquisition* (pp. 85-113). Cambridge, UK: Cambridge University Press.

"Wild Children IV Emily Carr." University of Victoria's ESL Study Zone. Retrieved October 5, 2007, http://web2.uvcs.uvic.ca/elc/studyzone/490/wchild/wchild17.htm.

WordQ. Retrieved October 5, 2007, http://www.wordq.com.

Writing Zone. Retrieved October 5, 2007, http://english-zone.com/writing/para-strctr.html.

Yano, Y., Long, M. H., & Ross, S. (1993). The effects of simplified and elaborated texts on foreign language reading comprehension. *Language Learning, 25,* 297-308.

Yoon, H., & Hirvela, A. (2004). ESL students' attitudes toward corpus use in L2 writing. *Journal of Second Language Writing, 13,* 257-283.

Yoshii, M., & Flaitz, J. (2002). Second language incidental vocabulary retention: The effect of text and picture annotation types. *CALICO Journal, 20*(1), 33-58.

NAME INDEX

A

Abraham, R., 41, 50, 76, 184
Alderson, J.C., 83
Alessi, S., 6
Arnold, N., 196, 209
Atkinson, R.C., 17, 21

B

Barks, D., 195
Bejar, I., 125, 127, 135
Belkada, S., 187
Belz, J.A., 173, 178
Bhatia, V.K., 97
Biber, D., 4, 56
Blake, R., 173
Bley-Vroman, R., 51
Brett, P., 139, 200
Brinton, D., 139
Brown, G., 127
Brown, H.D., 2
Brown, S., 131, 135, 142
Buck, G., 127, 135, 142
Burston, J., 106, 187

C

Carrell, P.L., 63
Carter, R., 159
Chapelle, C., 7
Chapelle, C.A., 3, 72
Chen, J., 187
Cheng, L., 4, 115
Cheng, W., 56
Chenoweth, N.A., 43, 53
Chun, D.M., 65, 69, 88, 151, 181
Cobb, T., 32, 35, 72
Cobb, Tom, 35
Colombi, M.C., 2
Conrad, S., 4, 56
Coxhead, A., 13
Crookes, G., 115
Crystal, D., 190

D

De Graaff, R., 41
DeKeyser, R.M., 79
De la Fuente, M.J., 178
Derwing, T.M., 151, 156, 169
Deterding, D., 153
Diaz-Santos, G., 197
Doughty, C., 3, 39, 41, 69, 106
Douglas, D., 125, 127, 135

E

Ellis, N.C., 69
Ellis, R., 5, 39, 56, 72
Eskenazi, M., 152, 153

F

Ferguson, G., 203
Fernández-Garciá, M., 184
Ferris, D., 106
Finegan, E., 4, 56
Fiori, M.L., 51, 173
Flaitz, J., 21, 72
Flege, J.E., 153
Flowerdew, J., 127, 135, 139, 142
Folse, K., 11, 17
Fotos, S., 4, 39

G

Gass, S., 171
Goodfellow, R., 32, 173
Grabe, W., 63, 119
Gu, P.Y., 17

H

Hamp-Lyons, L., 83
Hardison, D., 156, 162
Harrington, M., 178
Hazenberg, S., 13
Helgesen, M., 131, 135, 142
Herring, S.C., 190
Hinkel, E., 4, 39
Hirata, Y., 162
Hirvela, A., 206
Horst, M., 32
Hubbard, P., 72
Hulstijn, J., 125, 131
Hyon, S., 200

J

Jacobs, G., 203
Jamieson, J., 125, 127, 135
Jebski, R., 76, 184
Jenkins, J., 153
Jeon-Ellis, G., 76, 184
Johansson, S., 4, 56
Johns, T., 56
Jones, L.C., 24

K

Kamoto, T., 187
Kaplan, R.B., 119
Kern, R.G., 76, 171, 181, 193

Kinginger, C., 173
Klingner, J.K., 24, 76
Krashen, S., 3, 65
Kress, G., 88

L

Lam, W.S.E., 190
Lamy, M-N., 32, 173
Lapkin, S., 106, 171
Laurillard, D., 32
Lee, D., 206
Leech, G., 4, 56
Lemke, J., 203
Lightbown, P., 5, 7
Liou, H-C., 50, 76, 106, 184, 187
Long, M.H., 65
Loschky, L., 51
Lynch, T., 125, 139
Lyster, R., 53

M

MacDonald, D., 156
Martínez-Arbelaiz, A., 184
Mendelsohn, D., 127, 135, 139, 142
Miller, G., 135
Miller, L., 127, 135, 139, 142
Mohan, B., 76, 184, 195
Morley, J., 125, 135, 139, 142
Munro, M.J., 151, 156, 169
Murday, K., 43, 53

N

Nagata, N., 43, 53
Nassaji, H., 17, 80
Nation, I.S.P., 4, 13
Negretti, R., 190
Nicolae, I., 32
Nissan, S., 125, 127, 135

O

O'Brien, M.G., 162
Oh, S-Y., 65
Ohta, A., 51
Opdenacker, L., 203
Ostermann, A.C., 195
Oxford, R., 145

P

Paltridge, B., 97
Payne, S., 171, 178, 193
Pellettieri, J., 51
Peterson, P., 131, 145
Pica, T., 3, 171
Piper, A., 184
Plass, J.L., 69, 72
Powers, M., 156

R

Read, J., 29
Ross, S., 65

Rost, M., 125, 131, 135, 139, 142, 145
Rubin, J., 139, 142

S

Sadow, C., 127
Sather, E., 127
Schleppegrell, M.J., 2, 6
Schmidt, R., 69
Schmitt, N., 17, 159
Sharwood Smith, M., 69
Simpson, R.C., 195
Skehan, P., 115, 159
Smith, B., 24, 173
Spada, N., 5, 7
Stevens, V., 72
Stockwell, G., 178
Swain, M., 51, 53, 83, 106, 110, 171
Swales, J., 101, 195, 206
Sykes, J.M., 178

T

Tarone, E., 88
Thorne, S.L., 171, 193
Tozcu, A., 17, 21
Trollip, S., 6
Turner, J., 125, 127, 135
Tyner, K., 88

V

Vandergrift, L., 131, 139, 145
Van Lier, L., 65
Van Waes, L., 203
Vaughn, S., 24, 76

W

Wang, J., 156
Warren, M., 56
Warschauer, M., 7, 88, 110, 181
Watanabe, Y., 4, 115
White, J., 69
Whitney, P.J., 178
Wiebe, G., 156, 159
Wigglesworth, G., 76, 184
Williams, J., 3, 69, 106

X

Xun-feng, X., 56

Y

Yano, Y., 65
Yoon, H., 206
Yoshii, M., 21, 72
Yule, G., 88, 156

Z

Zimmerman, C.B., 17

SUBJECT INDEX

A

Academic papers, examples, 101
Academic texts, examination, 49
Accents, impact, 127
Accents (instruction), CALL materials (selection), 152
    research, implication, 153
    teacher action, 153, 155
Activities
    creation, 174
    information-gap types, 174
Adult education topics, inclusion, 66
Adult Learning Activities, 65
Adult Learning Activities (California Distance
    Learning Project), 67
Adult Multicultural Education Service, partnership,
    82, 84, 103
Advertisements, examples, 101
After class work, 211–214
American Accent Program, 158
Analytic skills, necessity, 4
Answers
    accuracy, program determination, 30
    evaluations, inclusion, 29
        research, implication, 29
        teacher action, 29
Argument and Opinion Essay Writing.
        See WriteFix
Argumentative essays, language (usage), 99
Arlyn Freed's ESL/EFL ESP, 198, 207
Asynchronous communication tool, 182
Audience consideration, 119
Audio clips, 130
Audio script/exercises, 137
Auditory learners, impact, 139
Aural language, meaning, 131
Auralog. *See Tell Me More*
Automatic processes, 135
Autonomous learning, 207

B

Background knowledge, activation, 129
BetterAccent Tutor (BetterAccent, LLC), 163
BiblioCite, usage, 111
Blackboard's Vista WebCT, 180
Blog
    creation, 183
    development, 189
    example. *See* Our Class 2006 Blog
Body language, 139
Bottom-up activities, usage. *See* Listening
Bottom-up approach, 132
Bottom-up processes, focus, 131
Brigham Young University. *See VIEW: Variation in*
    English Words and Phrases
Browsealoud, 166
Business English
    forums, 205
    heading, 198
    instruction, CALL (usage), 200
    lexis site, 207
    practice, 204

C

California Distance Learning Project. *See Adult*
    Learning Activities
CALL. *See* Computer-assisted language learning
Cartoons, usage, 201
Celtic words, 180
Chat program, development, 179
Chat tool, 180
Chemnitz Internet Grammar (Chemnitz University
    of Technology), 47–49
    output display options, 49
    research project, 47
Clarity Language Consultants, Ltd. *See Newspaper*
    Editor; Study Skills Success
Classroom
    collaborations, 50
    evaluation, usage, 29
    management system, setup, 181, 183
    strategies, 2
Click into English (Clarity Language Consultants,
    Ltd.), 82, 84, 92, 102–103, 122
    Australian integrated skills program, 84
    integrated-skills CALL program, 92
Cloze activities, usage, 66
Cloze-type activity, 74
CMC, usage, 184
CMC conversations, 178
Cobuild Concordance and Collocations
    Sampler, 208
Collaboration
    development, 184
    process, 119

Collins Cobuild Corpus, usage, 206
Comics, inclusion, 66
Communication
    activities, locating, 193
    focus questions, 193
    instruction, CALL (usage), 172
    learners strategies, instruction. *See* Electronic
        communication
    online help, usage, 172, 187–189
        research, implication, 187
        teacher action, 187
    providing, importance, 173
    research, implication, 173–174
    skills, 171
        practice, 203
    tasks, design, 172–177
    teacher action, 174
    usage. *See* Written electronic communication
Companion software, example, 89
Compleat Lexical Tutor (Lextutor), The, 32. *See also*
        Vocabulary Profiler
    example, 33
    usage, 34
    Web site, 14
Comprehensible output, 110
Comprehension
    checking, 140, 143
    questions, 144
        answering, 134
Comprehension-checking activities, 135
Computer
    feedback, 50
    teaching philosophy, 3–4
    tool, usage, 2
Computer-assisted language learning (CALL),
        definition, 1
    activities, 3, 96
        supplementation, 6
        usage, 5
    activities, video (inclusion), 126, 139–141
        research, implication, 139
        teacher action, 139
    advice, research summary, 12
    CALL-IS Software List, rating, 73
    consideration, 8–9
    development, 3
    dialogues, usage, 165
    learning experiences, creation. *See* Positive CALL
        learning experiences
    limitation. *See* Pronunciation
    materials, 7

advantage, 3
selection. *See* Grammar
value, 63
pedagogical fit, teacher determination, 8–9
program, 102
    development. *See* Multimedia CALL program
    selection, 29
reading materials, 76
selection, 197–199
software
    notetaking/listening, opportunity, 138
    selection, 153
specialness, 6–8
usage. *See* Grammar; Linguistic knowledge/
        strategies; Writing
Web site, grammar (inclusion), 43
Computer interaction, 204
    learner opportunity, 21–23, 45–46, 72–75, 196
        research, implication, 21, 45, 72, 203
        teacher action, 21, 45–46, 72–73, 203
Computer-provided help functions, 24
Concordancer, usage, 33
Concordances, usage. *See* Explicit online vocabulary
        learning
Confusion, clarification, 145
Connected Speech (Protea Textware Pty., Ltd.), 164
Consensus opinion, 76
Content-based language, 195
    finding/developing, 209
    focus questions, 209
    instruction
        CALL, usage, 196
        studies, importance, 197
    practice, 5–6
Controlled processes, 135
Conversation
    computer prompting, 184
    deceleration, 178–180
    reference, 72
Conversational exchanges, creating/
        recording, 160
Core language knowledge, development, 8
Cornell System, The, 138
CorpusSearch, selection, 49
Correctness, feedback. *See* Grammar
Courseware Companion, usage, 52
Cover letter, examples, 211–212
CPR4ESL. *See Gerry's Vocabulary Teacher*
Criterion Online Writing Assessment (Educational
        Testing Service), 116–117
Crossword puzzles, variety, 27

Crossword Puzzles for ESL Students (The Internet TESL Journal), 27

D

Daedalus Integrated Writing Environment (DIWE) (The Daedalus Group, Inc.), 111–112, 120
    functions, 111
Dave's ESL Cafe, 56. *See also Student Discussion Forums*
Definitions, usage, 7
Diagnostic analysis, 116
Diagnostic grammar quiz, 53
Dialects, usage, 155
Dictionaries
    definition, display, 33
    usage, 109. *See usage Explicit online vocabulary learning*
Dilemma (Educational Activities Software), 73
Discourse
    community, access, 101
    complexity, impact, 127
Discriminating sounds exercises, 155
Discussion boards, 182
DIWE. *See Daedalus Integrated Writing Environment*
Doctors, focus, 201
Double quotes, paralinguistic hand signal, 140
DynEd Advanced Listening, 147

E

EASY—English Academic Success for You (EASY, the ESL Series), 20
    skills integration, 20
Easy Writer, 98
eChatBoX, 174–175
Educational Activities Software. *See Dilemma*
Educational Testing Service. *See Criterion Online Writing Assessment*
Edulang. *See Vocabster*
8 in 1 English Dictionary (English Computerized Learning, Inc.), 18
    translations, availability, 18
Electronic communication, learners strategies (instruction), 172, 190–192
    research, implication, 190
    teacher action, 190
Electronic journals, usage, 97
Electronic text, usage, 64
ELLIS Academic-Basic (Pearson Digital Learning), 31
ELLLO: English Language Listening Lab Online, 130

E-mail
    message, production, 110
    posting, rules, 191
    process, 191
    programs, 177
        spell checkers, 188
    sending, 27
    usage, 176
End-of-unit test, results (display), 55
English
    dictionary program, usage, 18
    grammar, study (three-way approach), 47
    grammatical features, usage, 49
    guidance, teacher assistance, 3
    instruction (reading, usage), CALL materials (selection), 64, 79–82
        research, implication, 79–80
        teacher action, 80
    knowledge (expansion), opportunities (creation), 96, 110–114
        research, implication, 110
        teacher action, 110
    learning, learner guidance, 3
    questions, 191
    styles, usage, 3
    vocabulary, 4
    vocabulary (explicit instruction), CALL materials (selection), 17–18
        research, implications, 17
        teacher action, 17
English as a Second Language (ESL)
    classroom, 32
    literacy textbook series, CD-ROM accompaniment, 89
    speakers, communication (necessity), 153
    students, activities, 28
    usage, 1
EnglishClub (Web site), 192, 202
English Computerized Learning, Inc. *See 8 in 1 English Dictionary*
English for special purposes (ESP), 195
English for Specific Purposes (journal), 197
Englishforums (Web site), 205
English Language Center (Monash University), 144
English Language Centre Study Zone (University of Victoria), 77, 90–91
English language learners, target, 118
English language pedagogy, 1–3
    components, 2
    parts, 2
English-medium school, study, 125

englishmed (Web site), 201
English Online. *See Real English*
English-Zone.com, Web site, 101, 104
ESL. *See* English as a Second Language
ESLgold—Grammar (ESLgold), 42
ESL Independent Study Lab (Lewis and Clark
       College), 66
ESLRADIO (Monash University), 144
ESL Reading, 68
ESL WebQuests, 185
ESP. *See* English for special purposes
Essays
   drafting, 109
   language, usage. *See* Argumentative essays
   submittal, 116
   viewing. *See* Model essays
eTandem (University of Sheffield), 114
European Union documents, examination, 49
Evaluations. *See* Answers
Excel spreadsheet, lists (copying), 207
Exercises, copying/pasting, 92
Expedition 360, 134
Explain button, usage, 111, 120
Explanation, request, 171
Explicit evaluation, inclusion, 96, 115–118
   research, implication, 115
   teacher action, 115
Explicit grammar instruction, 82
Explicit instruction
   absence. *See* Pronunciation
   offering, 7
Explicit online learning, strategies (development),
      152, 165–167
   research, implication, 165
   teacher action, 165
Explicit online vocabulary learning (learner
      strategy development), online
      dictionaries/ concordances
      (usage), 32
   research, implication, 32
   teacher action, 32, 34
Explicit practice, usage, 53–59
   research, implication, 56
   teacher action, 56
Explicit teaching
   improvement, 79
   usage, 45
Explicit vocabulary teaching, 37

F
Face-to-face communication, 203
Face-to-face conversation, 171

Facial expressions, 139
Feedback. *See* Computer
   appropriateness, 87
   benefit, 96, 106–109
      research, implication, 106
      teacher action, 106
   impact, 119
   information, 54
   levels, 118
   providing, 37, 83, 152, 162–165. *See also*
      Informative feedback
      research, implication, 162
      teacher action, 162–163
   quality, 106
   receiving, 115
   types, 53
      interpretation, 162
Field-specific language, practice, 203–205
   research, implication, 203
   teacher action, 203
Field-specific language (instruction), CALL activities
      (selection), 196, 200–202
   research, implication, 200
   teacher action, 200
Field-specific materials, online usage, 196, 206–208
   research, implication, 206
   teacher action, 206
Field-specific vocabulary, 208
Finance English, forums, 205
Focus on Grammar 2—Course Companion
      (Pearson Education, Inc.), 52
Folktales, inclusion, 66
Follow-up activity
   construction, 69
   inclusion, 80
Form-focused instruction, 41
Forum, usage, 78
Free study mode, 19
French, learning, 1
Functional topics, range, 141

G
Genre, instruction (CALL selection), 96, 101–105
   research, implication, 101
   teacher action, 101
Genre, reference, 97
Gerry's Vocabulary Teacher (CPR4ESL), 25
Gestures, 139
GMAT, 19
Google, 166
   usage, 56, 59
Grammar, 39

activities, locating, 60
analysis, usage, 45
classroom suggestions, 40
conversation, types, 50
correctness, feedback, 39, 53
discovery, usage, 45
discussion board, 58
errors, assessment, 54
explanations, 42
explicit teaching, usage, 45
focus questions, 60
help, 6
icon, usage, 103
instruction
    CALL, usage, 39–40
    usage, description, 40
learning strategies, development, 53–59
    research, implication, 56
    teacher action, 56
patterns, discovery, 47
production, 45
question, posting, 58
quiz. *See* Diagnostic grammar quiz
    evaluation/feedback, 53
tasks, impact. *See* Learner interaction
test, usage, 54
types, usage, 98
Grammar, teaching
advice, summary, 40
CALL, usage, 40
CALL materials, selection, 41
    research, implication, 41
    teacher action, 41, 43
Grammar HELP! Student Handbook, usage
    (option), 98
Grammar-toons, usage, 46
Grammatical features, usage, 49
Grammatical forms
consciousness, increase, 50
production, 45
Grammatical functional topics, range, 141
Grammatical patterns, search, 56
Grammatical points, 56
Graphic organizers, types, 121
GRE, 19
Greenpeace, usage, 59
Guidance, providing, 4

H
Headphones, usage, 186
Help, usage, 72

Homework, written response, 129
HotPotatoes (University of Victoria), 90

I
Ideas
    organization, 121
    relationships, expression, 147
    review, 72–73
IELTS exam, preparation, 54
IELTS International, 133, 138
Individual learning, effects (focus), 115
Inductive learning, usage, 53–59
    research, implication, 56
    teacher action, 56
Inferences, making, 145
Information
    chunking, 135
    components, 173
    entry, 137
Information technology, usage, 205
Informative feedback, providing, 115
Integrated-skills CALL program. *See Click into*
        English
Interaction
    meanings, 72
    opportunities, 203
Interactive help, benefit, 96, 106–109
    research, implication, 106
    teacher action, 106
Interactive writing tool, 107
InterChange, usage, 111
International Web sites, usage, 110
Internet, usage, 190
Internet English, types, 213–214
Internet TESL Journal. *See Crossword Puzzles*
        for ESL Students
Internet TESL Journal, 27
Intonation, 139
    instruction, 151
    patterns, comparison, 163
Issues in English (Protea Textware), 71

J
JACET 4000 BASIC WORDS, 179
Japanese
    encoding, 179
    learning, 1
Jigsaw activity, 174
    usage, 50
Jigsaw tasks, inclusion, 174

K

Kanto-Gakuin University, 179
Key vocabulary, introduction, 20
Keyword in context (KWIC), usage, 49
Key words, reading, 202
Knowledge, activation, 133. *See also* Background
    knowledge

L

Language
  ability, development, 63, 95
  acquisition, location, 171
  assistance. *See* Text
  CALL materials, selection, 196–199
    research, implication, 197
    teacher action, 197
  development, 6
    reflection, usage, 95
  events, following, 203
  knowledge
    inclusion, 64, 83–87
    research, implication, 83
    teacher action, 83, 86
  learning, 114
    divisions, teacher perspective, 5
  retention, short-term memory, 136
  review, 72–73
  selection, 3
  sounds, nonpermanence, 162
  usage. *See* Argumentative essays
Language Education Chat System (L.E.C.S.)
    (Kanto-Gakuin University), 179
Learner
  ability, development, 41
  assistance, 76
  communication, 187
Learner comprehension, evaluation, 64
  inclusion, 83–87
  research, implication, 83
  teacher action, 83, 86
Learner interaction
  grammar tasks, impact, 50–52
    research, implication, 50
    teacher action, 50
  impact, 28
  research, implication, 24
  teacher action, 24
  text, impact, 64, 76–79
    research, implication, 76
    teacher action, 76

  vocabulary tasks, impact, 24
Learner-learner interaction, 187
Learner performance, evaluation, 152, 162–165
  research, implication, 162
  teacher action, 162–163
Learner response, evaluation, 53
  research, implication, 53
  teacher action, 53
Learning
  activities, structuring, 3
  direction, 208
  efficiency, 145
  process, answer knowledge (importance), 85
Learning Upgrade, LLC. *See Reading Upgrade*
L.E.C.S. See Language Education Chat System
Legal English
  forums, 205
  heading, 199
LEI. *See Longman English Interactive*
Letters, representation, 132
Lewis and Clark College. *See ESL Independent
    Study Lab*
Lexical phrase, examples, 32
Lextutor. *See Compleat Lexical Tutor*
Lingonet, 28
  demo, usage, 28
Lingualnet, 134
Linguistic Funland TESL Pen Pal Center,
    110, 113, 177
Linguistic knowledge, limitation, 63
Linguistic knowledge/strategies (instruction), CALL
    (usage), 96, 101–105
  research, implication, 101
  teacher action, 101
Linguistic levels, impact, 96
Linguistic processing, improvement, 135
Listening, 125
  activities, locating, 148
  affective dimension, 127
  CALL materials, selection, 126–130
    research, implication, 127
    teacher action, 127
  comprehension, testing, 142
  difficulty, cognitive dimensions, 127
  focus questions, 148
  input, 24
  materials, top-down/bottom-up activities (usage),
    126, 131–134
    research, implication, 131
    teacher action, 131
  passages, usage, 129

receptive process, 125
transformative impact, 125
Literacy
abilities, range, 88
tasks, 2
Longman English Interactive (LEI) 3 (Pearson
Education, Inc.), 23, 70, 80–81,
85–86, 146
British/American versions, availability, 70, 80
integrated skills program, 85
Longman English Interactive (LEI) 4 (Pearson
Education, Inc.), 160
Low-stakes tests, positive effects, 83

M

Marzio School and Real English, LLC. *See Real
English Online*
Matching activities, usage, 66
Meaning, inference, 56
Meaning-focused language, production, 106
Medical English
forums, 205
heading, 199
usage/listening, 201
Merit Software. *See Paragraph Punch*
*Michigan Corpus of Academic Spoken English
(MICASE) Concordancer*, 189
Microphone, usage, 186
Microsoft *Outlook*, 187–188
Microsoft *Windows Live Messenger*, 186
Microsoft *Windows Messenger*, 176
Microsoft Word, usage, 167
Mike Nelson's Business English Lexis (Web site), 207
Military English, heading, 198, 199
Model essays, viewing, 99
Model paragraph, usage, 104
Monash University. *See* English Language Center;
ESLRADIO
Monologue, listening, 164
Multimedia, inclusion, 73
Multimedia CALL program, development, 89
Multiple-choice questions, usage, 66
MY Access! (Vantage Learning), 106, 109, 118, 121

N

Native varieties. *See* Speaking
Natural Reader (NaturalSoft Limited), 167
Negotiation, process, 119
News flashes, usage, 51
Newspaper articles, examples, 101

Newspaper Editor (Clarity Language
Consultants, Ltd.), 51
NewsVOAcom (Voice of America), 128
Nicenet, 182
Notice language, 178–180
Nouns
clauses, testing, 55
plurals, usage, 18
Nurses, focus, 201

O

Observation skills, activation, 77
Old English, 180
One-on-one instruction, 156
Online help, usage. *See* Communication
Online listening strategies, development, 145–147
research, implication, 145
teacher action, 145
Online magazine. *See TOPICS*
Online quizzes, 198
Online reading strategies, development (assistance),
64, 88–92
research, implication, 88
teacher action, 88
Online talking, 192
Online texts, comprehension, 88
Online vocabulary
learning, online dictionaries/concordances, usage.
See Explicit online vocabulary learning
support, 21
OpenBook English (OpenBook Learning, Inc.), 106,
108, 157
OpenBook ESL (OpenBook Learning), 74
Open-ended programs, 159
Opinions, examples, 101
Oral interaction, opportunities (providing), 172,
184–187
research, implication, 184
teacher action, 184, 187
Oral interactive communication, 178
Oral language, fluency (development), 159
Oral practice, opportunities (providing), 152
research, implication, 159
teacher action, 159, 162
Our Class 2006 Blog, example, 189
Outlook. *See* Microsoft Outlook

P

Paragraph Punch (Merit Software), 101, 105
Paralinguistic hand signal. *See* Double quotes

Participation opportunities, 181–183
 research, implication, 181
 teacher action, 181, 183
Partnership, facilitation, 114
Pause
 activities, 164
 groups, 164
 rate, 127
Pearson Digital Learning. *See ELLIS Academic-Basic*
Pearson Education, Inc. *See Longman English Interactive 3; Side by Side Interactive; Understanding and Using English Grammar; Focus on Grammar 2; Shining Star*
Pearson Longman, Inc. *See Talking Business*
Pen pals, 113
 request, 177
Performance, summaries, 142–144
 evaluation, 53
 research, implication, 53
 teacher action, 53
 inclusion, 29
 research, implication, 29
 teacher action, 29
 research, implication, 142
 teacher action, 142
Personal characteristics, impact, 181
Pharmacy, focus, 201
Phonetic transcriptions. *See* Vowel sounds
Phonics-based software program, 74
Phonics practice, 157
Phonology, 131
Phrases
 emphasis, search, 64, 69
 research, implication, 69
 teacher action, 69
 reading, 202
Phrases, providing, 105
Pictures, meaning, 132
Planet English, 137, 143
 Australian English, usage, 137, 143
Playback, usage, 158
Play icon, usage, 20, 146
Politeness, conventions, 192
Pop-up box, usage, 84, 103, 120
Positive CALL learning experiences, creation, 174
Postcard language (emphasis), blue font (usage), 102
Posting, rules. *See* E-mail
Post-lesson reinforcement, recommendation, 42
Pre-lesson preparation, recommendation, 42
Prelistening activity, 146

Prelistening exercise, 129, 133
Prereading exercise, usage, 68
Prompts, responses, 182
Pronunciation
 explicit instruction, absence, 156
 instruction, 151
 CALL, limitation, 162
 listening/playback capability, 18
Protea Textware. *See Issues in English*
Protea Textware Pty., Ltd. *See Connected Speech*
Public speeches, examination, 49

Q
Questions
 asking, 147
 reading, 202
 usage, 202
Quillsoft. *See WordQ*
Quizzes
 knowledge, time lag, 86
 usage, 37

R
Radio programs, usage, 128
Randall's ESL Cyber Listening Lab, 129
Reading, 63
 activities
 levels, variation, 90
 locating, 93
 assignments, 208
 focus questions, 94
 input, 24
 passage, 92
 presentation, 82
 program, progress evaluation, 87
 strategies, development, 88
 teaching, CALL (usage), 64
 texts, CALL materials (selection), 64–68
 research, implication, 65
 teacher action, 65
 topics, exercises, 90
 vocabulary/comprehension activities, 67
ReadingEnglish.net. See WebLadder
Reading Upgrade (Learning Upgrade, LLC), 87
Real English (English Online), 141
Real English Online (Marzio School and Real English, LLC), 136
Registers
 formal forms, 56
 grammatical feature, distribution, 46

Repetition
    request, 171
    usage, 69
Responses, evaluation, 142–144
    research, implication, 142
    teacher action, 142
Role play activities, development, 202
Rosetta Stone, 22, 132

S

SAT, 19
Scrambled sentence, practice, 46
Scratch pad
    opening, 138
    providing, 92, 122
Second-language acquisition, text (usage), 65
Second-language knowledge, problems
        (identification), 83
Second-language researchers, 106
Selective listening, opportunities (providing), 135–138
    research, implication, 135
    teacher, action, 135
Sentences
    average length, 179
    exercises, 155
    groups, 47
    words, usage, 25
Shining Star (Pearson Education, Inc.), 89
Short-term instruction, 156
Short-term memory. *See* Language
Side by Side Interactive (Pearson Education), 46
Software. *See* Computer-assisted language learning
    types, 156
Sounds
    exercises. *See* Discriminating sounds exercises
    modeling, 157
    signal, decoding, 131
    types, 151
Sounds (instruction), CALL materials
        (selection), 152
    research, implication, 153
    teacher action, 153, 155
Speaker, attitude, 147
    understanding, 139
Speaking, 151
    activities, 168
        homework, 165
    focus questions, 168
    instruction, CALL (usage), 152
    native varieties, 153

Speaking skills (instruction), CALL materials (usage),
        156–158
    research, implication, 156
    teacher action, 156
Specific-purpose language, 195
Specific-purpose needs, 196–199
    research, implication, 197
    teacher action, 197
Specific-purpose vocabulary words/phrases, 207
Speech, usage, 154
Speechinaction. *See Streaming Speech AC*
Speech recognition plug-in, 107
Speech Works 4, 155
Spell checkers. *See* E-mail
    usage, 187
Spelling errors, usage, 98
Spoken phrases/sentences, vocabulary
        consideration, 159
Spoken texts, 135
Spoken words, written words (relationships,
        establishing), 22
Streaming Speech AC, (Speechinaction), 154
Student compositions, inclusion, 66
Student Discussion Forums (Dave's ESL
        Cafe), 58
Students, grouping, 25
Study Skills Success (Clarity Language Consultants,
        Ltd.), 54, 133, 138
Subtitles, usage, 134
Synchronous communication, written mode, 50
Synonyms, usage, 23
Syntactic complexity, impact, 127
Syntactic structures, focus, 80

T

Talking Business (Pearson Longman, Inc.), 204
Teachers
    classroom suggestion, 12
    resources, usage, 207
*Teacher's Guide for ESL-EFL Students
        (DIWE 7)*, 111
Technology, functions, 6
Television programs, usage, 128
    Tell Me More (Auralog), 161
frames, usage, 161
Tense system, 41
TESOL, master's degree (requirement), 185
    Text
    box, usage, 107
    impact. *See* Learner interaction

language, usage, 65
  selection, 98
Text, language assistance, 72–75
  research, implication, 72
  teacher action, 72–73
Textbooks
  links, 198
  usage, 208
Text-to-speech, inclusion, 107
Text-to-speech application, 167
Text-to-speech program, 166
Text-to-speech software, 165
Thesaurus, inclusion, 109
Three-stage presentation, 155
TOEFL, 19
  test preparation, *WordSmart* (suitability), 15
  vocabulary, selection, 19
Top-down activities, usage. *See* Listening
Top-down focus, 131
Topics
  controversy, 177
  issues/opinion, presentation, 71
TOPICS (online magazine), 78–79, 183
Transcription method, usage, 74
Transcripts, usage, 128
Translater, usage, 109
Translations, reliance, 22
Tri-view method, usage, 134

U

Understanding
  awareness, increase, 142
  blockage, 63
*Understanding and Using English Grammar—
    Interactive* (Pearson Education, Inc.),
    43–44, 55
University of Sheffield. *See eTandem*
University of Victoria. *See English Language Centre
    Study Zone*; HotPotatoes
UsingEnglish.com (Web site), 191, 199
Utah State OpenCourseWare, 208
Utterances, comparison, 163

V

Vantage Learning. *See MY Access!*
Variation in English Words and Phrases (VIEW)
    (Brigham Young University), 56, 57
Verbs, conjugation, 18
Video
  clip, 143
  instruction, 141

listening, 131, 140
  selection, 139
VIEW. *See Variation in English Words and
    Phrases*
Visual display, creation, 185
Visual learners, impact, 139
Vocaboly, 19
  vocabulary program, 19
Vocabster (Edulang), 30
Vocabulary, 11
  acquisition, 11
  activities, locating, 36
  CALL usage
    meaning, description, 12
    research, implications, 13
    teacher action, 13
  computer interaction, 37
  conclusion, 38
  drills, 155
  evaluation types, 37
  exercise, 198
  example, 23
    student performance, tracking, 30
  explicit instruction, 17
    CALL materials, selection. *See* English
  focus, 31, 80
  glosses, 130
  growth, monitoring, 14
  help, 6
    example, 23
  increase, 36
  instruction, inclusion, 20
  introduction, 24
  knowledge, 21
    determination, 14
  learners
    fit, 37
    interaction, 37
  learning
    effectiveness, 69
    focus, 80
    online dictionaries/concordances,
      usage. *See* Explicit online vocabulary
      learning
  level, 13
  pool, user selection, 19
  practice, 24
  presentation, movie usage, 20
  software, purchase (necessity), 15
  strategy development, 37
  tasks, impact. *See* Learner interaction
  teaching. *See* Explicit vocabulary teaching

CALL materials, selection, 13–16
CALL usage, 12
goals, 11
tools, 35
words/phrases. *See* Specific-purpose vocabulary
  words/phrases
Vocabulary Profiler (Compleat Lexical Tutor), 35
Voice
  communication, 184
  recording, 158
Voice of America (VOA). *See NewsVOA.com*
  Special English, 19
Voice of America (VOA) reading program,
  adaptation, 75
Vowel sounds, phonetic transcriptions, 19, 154

W
Web-enchanced language learning (WELL), 8
WebLadder (ReadingEnglish.net), 75
WebQuest. *See also* ESL WebQuests
  illustration, 185
  usage, 199
Web reading, 88
WELL. *See* Web-enchanced language learning
Whiteboard, 180
Word, frequency (usage), 13
Word, usage. *See* Microsoft Word
Word pair drills, 155
Word processing program, usage, 110
WordQ (Quillsoft), 107
Words
  brainstorming, 27
  emphasis, search, 64, 69

research, implication, 69
  teacher action, 69
providing, 105
targeting, 19
usage. *See* Sentences
WordSmart, 15
  online placement test, inclusion, 15
  suitability. *See* TOEFL
Work, division, 4–6
Workplace practice, 155
WriteFix (Argument and Opinion Essay Writing),
  99–100
Writing
  activities, locating, 123
  focus questions, 123
  guide, 122
  instruction, CALL (usage), 95
  strategies, development, 96, 119–122
    research, implication, 119
    teacher action, 119, 121
  strategies, study, 119
  texts, models (selection), 96–100
    research, implication, 97
    teacher action, 97
  tool. *See* Interactive writing tool
Writing Zone, usage, 104
Written communication, usage, 178
Written electronic communication, usage, 172,
  178–183
  research, implication, 178
  teacher action, 178
Written interactive communication, 178
Written synchronous CMC, usage, 18

Chapter 1: Page 14 *Compleat Lexical Tutor*, Vocabulary Test, http://www.er.uqam.ca. Used with permission. http://www.lextutor.ca. **15 and 16** *WordSmart Challenge* screen shots reprinted with permission of WordSmart Corporation. Copyright © 2007 WordSmart Corporation. http://www.word smart.com/wsc_b/index2.php. **18** "8 in 1 English Dictionary" from http://www.englishelearning.com. Copyright © English Computerized Learning Inc. Used with permission. **19** *Vocaboly*, http://www.voca boly.com. Used with permission. **20** *EASY, the ESL Series* CD-ROM, Part 2 Community Essentials, Unit 8 Health Care. http://www.easysol.com. Used with permission. **22** *Rosetta Stone®*, http://www.rosettas tone.com/en. Used with permission. **23** *Longman English Interactive 3* from Pearson Education, Inc., http://www.pearson longman.com/ae/mulitmedia. Used with permission. **25 and 26** *Longman English Interactive 3* from Pearson Education, Inc., http://www.pearson longman.com/ae/mulitmedia. Used with permission. **27** *The Internet TESL Journal*, http://iteslj.com and http://iteslj.org/cw/3/ck-dolch01.html. Used wih permission. **28** *Lingonet*, http://www.lingonet.com/nets.htm. Used with permission. **30** *Vocabster* from Edulang, http://www.vocabster.com. Used with permission. **31** *ELLIS Academic-Basic* from Pearson Digital Learning, http://www.pearsondigital.com/ellis. Used with permission. **33 and 34** *Compleat Lexical Tutor*, "Linked Word Lists," http://www.lextutor.ca/lists_learn. Used with permission. **35** *Vocabulary Profiler* from *The Compleat Lexical Tutor*, http://www.er.uqam.ca. Used with permission. **36** *Vocabulary Profiler* from *The Compleat Lexical Tutor*, http://www.er.uqam.ca. Used with permission.

Chapter 2: 42 *ESLgold—Grammar* at http://eslgold.com. Copyright © ESLgold.net. Used with permission of ESLgold. **43 and 44** *Understanding and Using English Grammar—Interactive* from Pearson Education, Inc. http://www.pearsonlongman.com/ae/multimedia/programs/uuegi.htm. Used with permission. **46** *Side by Side Interactive* from Pearson Education, Inc. http://www.pearsonlongman.com/ae/multimedia/programs/SbS.htm. Used with permission. **47, 48,**

and 49 *Chemnitz Internet Grammar* from the Chemnitz University of Technology, http://www.tu chemnitz.de. Used with permission. **51** *Newspaper Editor* from Clarity Language Consultants, Ltd. http://www.clarity.com. Used with permission. **52** *Focus on Grammar 2—Course Companion* from Pearson Education, Inc. http://www.pearson longman.com/ae/fog_level2/SR/ pdfs/2_07web_sh.pdf. Used with permission. **54** *Study Skills Success* from Clarity Language Consultants, Ltd. http://www.clarity.com. Used with permission. **55** *Understanding and Using English Grammar—Interactive* from Pearson Education, Inc. http://www.pearsonlongman.com/ae/multimedia/programs/uuegi.htm. Used with permission. **57** *VIEW: Variation in English Words and Phrases* from the Brigham Young University Web site, http://corpus.byu.edu/bnc/. Used with permission. **58** *Dave's ESL Cafe's Student Discussion Forums*, http://www.eslcafe.com/forums/student. Copyright © 2007 Dave's ESL Cafe. Used with permission. **59** Google™ Advanced Search is reprinted with permission of Google, Inc. http://www.google.com. GOOGLE is a trademark of Google, Inc. Copyright © 2007 Google. *Greenpeace Canada*: "Greenpeace Canada Privacy Complete," http://www.green peace.org/canada/. Used with permission.

Chapter 3: 66 *ESL Independent Study Lab—Reading* from the Lewis and Clark College Web site, http://www.lclark.edu/~krauss/toppicks/reading.html. Used by permission of Michael Krauss, Lewis & Clark College. **67** *Adult Learning Activities* from the California Distance Learning Project, http://www.cdlponline.org/ index.cfm. Used with permission. **68** *ESL Reading*, "Site Map," http://www.eslreading.org/sitemap/sitemap.html. © 2007 Kieran McGovern. Used by permission. **70** *Longman English Interactive 3* from Pearson Education, Inc. http://www.pearsonlongman.com/ae/multimedia/ programs/lei3_4.htm. Used with permission. **71** *Issues in English* from Protea Textware, http://www.proteatextware.com.au/iie.htm. Used with permission. **73** *Dilemma* from *Educational Activities Software*, "Father Against Son," http://ea-software.com. Copyright © Siboney

Consultants, Ltd. http://www.clarity.com. Used with permission. **134** *Lingualnet*, http://www. lingual.net. Used with permission. **136** *Real English®*, screen shot from dictation exercise "What Time Is It?" http://cla.univ-fcomte.fr/english/ dictations/realenglish/realindex.htm. Copyright © 2007 The Marzio School and Real English L.L.C. Used with permission. **137** *Planet English*, http://www.planetenglish.com. Used with permission. **138** *Study Skills Success* from Clarity Language Consultants, Ltd. http://www.clarity.com. Used with permission. **140** *Longman English Interactive 3* from Pearson Education, Inc. http://www.pearsonlongman.com/ae/multimedia/ programs/lei3_4.htm. Used with permission. **141** *Real English®*, screen shot from video lesson "How Do You Spell Your Name," http://www.real english.com. Copyright © 2007 The Marzio School and Real English L.L.C. Used with permission. **143** *Planet English*, http://www.planetenglish.com. Used with permission. **144** *ESLRADIO.NET* from Monash University, http://www.eslradio.net/ radio.htm. Used by permission of Stephen Lock. **146** *Longman English Interactive 3* from Pearson Education, Inc. http://www.pearsonlongman.com/ ae/multimedia/programs/lei3_4.htm. Used with permission. **147** *DynEd Advanced Listening, DynEd Demo V6-6*, http://www.dyned.com/ products/al/. Copyright © 2007 DynEd International Inc. Used with permission.

Chapter 6: 154 *Streaming Speech AC* from Speechinaction, http://www.speechinaction.com. Used with permission. **155** *Speech Works 4*, main menu, http://www.multilingualbooks.com. Used with permission. **157** *OpenBook ESL* from OpenBook Learning, Inc., http://www.openbook learning.com. Used with permission. **158** *American Accent Program CD-ROM* from Multilingual Books. Copyright © 2007 Internet Language Company. Used with permission of Kenneth Tomkins. **160** *Longman English Interactive 4* from Pearson Education, Inc. http://www.pearsonlongman.com/ ae/multimedia/programs/lei3_4.htm. Used with permission. **161** TELL ME MORE® from Auralog used with permission of Auralog, Inc. http://www.tellme more.com / http://www.auralog.com. **163** "Better Accent Tutor Demo" from *BetterAccent Tutor*, http://www.betteraccent.com. Copyright © 2007 BetterAccent, LLC. Used with permission. **164** *Connected Speech* from Protea Textware Pty., Ltd., http://www.proteatextware.com.au/cs.htm. Used

with permission. **166** *Browsealoud* text-to-speech program used by permission of Texthelp Systems Inc. Google™ Search is reprinted with permission of Google, Inc. http://www.google.com. GOOGLE is a trademark of Google, Inc. Copyright © 2007 Google. **167** *Natural Reader* from NaturalSoft Limited. http://www.naturalreaders.com. Used with permission.

Chapter 7: 175 *eChatBoX*, http://www.echatbox, screen shots used with permission from 24 hours-English for busy people, http://www.24hours.it. **176** Microsoft® *Windows Messenger™* is a trademark of Microsoft Corporation in the United States and/or other countries. Microsoft product screen shot reprinted with permission from Microsoft Corporation. http://get.live.com/messenger/ overview. **177** *Linguistic Funland TESL Pen Pal Center*, http://www.tesol.net/penpals. Used with permission. **179** *L.E.C.S. Language Education Chat System*, home page. http://home.kanto-gakuin.ac.jp/~ taoka/lecs. Used with permission. **180** "Blackboard's Vista WebCT" is the property of Blackboard and is used with the permission of Blackboard Inc. http://www.blackboard.com. **182** *Nicenet*, "Conferencing Topics," http://www.nicenet.org. Copyright © by Nicenet. Used with permission. **183** *TOPICS Online Magazine* "Create Your Own ESL/EFL Web Logs," http://www.topics-mag.com/ call/blogs/ESL_EFL. Copyright © 2007. Used by permission of Sandy and Thomas Peters. **185** *CALL-ESL*, "On the Road Again: A WebQuest for Intermediate to Advanced ESL Students," http://www.call-esl.com/samplewebquests/lesson template2.htm. Used by permission of Paula Emmert. Image from Animation Factory, used by permission of Jupiter Images. **186** Microsoft® *Windows Live™ Messenger* is a trademark of Microsoft Corporation in the United States and/or other countries. Microsoft product screen shot reprinted with permission from Microsoft Corporation. **188** *Microsoft® Outlook™* is a trade-mark of Microsoft Corporation in the United States and/or other countries. Microsoft product screen shot reprinted with permission from Microsoft Corporation. http://office.microsoft.com/en-us/ outlook/ HA100518161033.aspx. **189** "Our Class 2006 Blog," http://ourclass07.blogspot.com. Used by permission of Rosa Ochoa. MICASE search results, http://micase.umdl.umich.edu. Used by permission of Dr. Ute Römer, University of Michigan, English Language Institute. **191** *UsingEnglish.com*, "Ask a